Living With Ava

MEARENE JORDAN

Ava Gardner
M·U·S·E·U·M
SMITHFIELD·NC·USA

Photographs courtesy of Mary Edna Grantham and the Ava Gardner Museum.

CONTENTS

Foreword   v

1   Starting Work   1

2   Getting Over Artie   9

3   Starlet Miss G and Our Friend Clark Gable   14

4   A Touch of Venus and Nudity   21

5   Enter the World's Richest Man and Katharine Hepburn   29

6   To Fall in Love with Frank Sinatra   36

7   Spain and the Flying Dutchman   42

8   Shipwrecked on Lake Tahoe – Jailed in Carson City   46

9   Suicide   54

10   Tears at Sands Hotel   59

11   The Quarrels   65

12   Mogambo and the Pregnancies   72

13   Old Love…and New Love   77

14   Flying Blind With Howard Hughes   86

15   Lovable Papa Hemingway   96

16   Publicity Chief David Hanna and the South American Scandals   100

17   The Sammy Davis Disaster   110

18   The Trouble with Lovers   117

19   Love in Lahore   120

20	Spanish Flamenco!	128
21	A Personal Explosion	137
22	Ending the Furious Fifties	146
23	Ava and the Goya Nude	153
24	On the Beach with the Tennis Champ	158
25	A Matter of Life and Certain Death	164
26	Ships That Pass in the Night	169
27	Puerto Vallarta and Mexico	175
28	The Chacala Bus and Tennessee Williams	183
29	The Delights of Mismaloya	190
30	Miss G and the Beach Boys	195
31	"In the Beginning…"	204
32	Disaster	215
33	The Empress of Austria-Hungary	222
34	Hanging Judge Roy Bean	227
35	The Blue Bird	231
36	Settling Down	238
37	Last of the Laughter	246
	About the Author	253

FOREWORD

Many books have been written about the fascinating public and private life of Ava Gardner, one of the most famous and beautiful film stars of all time—but none can compare to *Living with Miss G,* by Mearene "Rene" Jordan, who was by Gardner's side for most of the last 40 years of her life.

While some biographers had to rely on second-hand knowledge and newspaper and magazine articles that were often unreliable or deliberately inaccurate, Jordan (whose nickname is pronounced "Reenie") was on the scene for countless real-life Gardner episodes that rivaled any fiction.

The underlying dynamic of *Living with Miss G* is that Jordan is black; she was Gardner's maid, and the two had a bond of sisterhood unheard of in the upper echelons of the film industry, and rarely anywhere else.

In an era when the "N" word was used harshly, freely and frequently and movie stars were often treated like property of the studios, the two women protected and comforted each other as sisters, had spats like sisters, and were blessed to have each other to lean on as they traveled the diverse and rocky paths of their lives.

Those paths began nearly 900 miles apart, Jordan's in a poor section of St. Louis, Missouri, and Gardner's in a small farm community near Smithfield, North Carolina, and even the most tuned-in gypsy fortune-teller would have been hard-pressed to predict that their paths would cross.

On the other hand, it appeared that fate had conspired to create their sisterhood from the get-go. The two had a lot in common. Jordan was born near the beginning of 1922, on January 16, and Gardner put an exclamation point on that year by arriving on Christmas Eve. Both had loving and devoted parents who worked hard to support seven children. Jordan's father was employed by the American Car Foundry in St. Louis, and her mother earned money by house-cleaning. Jordan had five sisters and one brother, and Gardner had four sisters and one brother (another brother died as a child).

During the Great Depression years Jordan often went hungry, and at age 11 she knocked on doors in St. Louis and earned 25 to 35 cents by shampooing and ironing or curling women's hair.

Around the same age, Gardner worked in tobacco fields, and her parents learned the local school board could no longer pay them to live in and maintain the boarding house for teachers at the local elementary school. Gardner's mother was the boarding house cook. So the future movie star had to leave her many relatives and friends in her beloved native community and adjust to life in Newport News, Virginia, in a boarding house for shipyard workers.

In 1946 Gardner's true-life Hollywood fairy tale, complete with wicked witches and ogres, was well under way, and just beginning for the brilliant young woman she hired as her maid. Forty-four years later the final chapter closed with Ava's untimely death. Now at age 90 Rene Jordan shares some of that story, pulling no punches. Her book is expertly written, with many heart-warming, heart-rending, amazing, amusing, surprising—and yes, sometimes shocking—stories that are made public for the first time. The book also puts to rest some of the falsehoods and rumors that plagued Ava Gardner until the day she died.

The star once told Thomas J. Lassiter, editor of *The Smithfield Herald,* "I don't care what you write about me, as long as it is the truth."

From her final resting place in Smithfield's Sunset Memorial Park, and beyond, one can imagine that one of the most famous film stars of all time is smiling, and saying in that soft, smoky voice of hers, "Thank you, my beloved sister Rene, for writing the truth."

Doris Rollins Cannon,
author of *Grabtown Girl: Ava Gardner's North Carolina Childhood and Her Enduring Ties to Home*

1 STARTING WORK

It was 1946, I was twenty-four years old, and I sure did need a job. Not any old job would do because when you are that age and black, you can hear Mama's voice from the past ringing loud and clear in your memory. "Now you hear me, Mearene Jordan, when you get a job, it's got to be a real job, understand me? A real job." I understood all right. None of those teetering-on-the-brink of you-know-what jobs. No night club or hat-check girl stuff—a real job.

So good thing for my sister, Tressie. She had arranged for me to get an interview with Ava Gardner, and although I'd left school at sixteen, this was my first try for a real good job. Tressie had been working as a daily in Artie Shaw's Bedford Drive house, and she had seen what went on between Artie and Miss G, and she didn't like it. She said to Miss G when it was plain that they were breaking up, "Now when you get a little place of your own, you will need someone to help you, someone you can trust. You can trust my kid sister, Rene. When you want her, you just ring her up."

At the moment, Tressie and I were living in a rooming house back in East L.A., but she was going back to Chicago where her husband was a bellhop on the Super Chief running between Chicago and L.A. I'd seen Miss G when I visited Tressie while she was working on Bedford Drive, but I'd never spoken to her, and I was nervous to do so. But when the rooming house landlady told me there was a phone call for me, I hurried to take it.

"Rene, this is Ava Gardner. I've just found this cute little apartment; just one bedroom, living room, kitchen and bathroom. Would you like to come and see it, and we'll talk about money and that sort of stuff, and see how we get on?"

I said, "Sure Miss G." I invented the name on the spur of the moment and used it until the day she died. We fixed a meeting for the next evening after she got home from the MGM studios.

It was on very timid feet that I approached the house and pressed the doorbell. Almost on the rebound–boom!–it opened. There stood Miss G–slender as a bamboo pole, but with visible curves, hair caught up in a red bandana, oval

1

face, cleft in chin, green eyes sparkling, and a wonderful, warm smile. "You Rene?" she asked.

"Yes," I responded.

She took my hand and sort of led me in. It sure was no film star's apartment, just an itty-bitty place, but she was proud of it, flipping me around and saying, "Now here's the bedroom, isn't that pretty? And the dining room with this couch which you could sleep on if worse came to worse…and this neat little dining area set back here so we can eat candlelight dinners. What about that, huh?" She laughed with such joy that I had to laugh with her. It was the very first place of her own that Miss G had ever had. "Red Skelton, you know the comedian, owns the whole block, and my business manager thinks it's too expensive. What do you think?" she asked.

I said, "I think it's great." And compared to my rather crummy single room back in a boarding house in East L.A., it certainly was.

I looked around to see where she'd gone. She'd slipped out into the tiny kitchen and reappeared with a tray holding a bottle of gin, another of vermouth, some lemon, a jug containing ice, and two wide-brimmed, thin-stemmed martini glasses. She set the tray down, laughed again, so pleased and happy that anyone would think I was her dearest friend instead of a rather nervous black girl who was applying for the job as maid. Miss G asked if I knew how to make a martini. "Not really - gin and something," I replied.

"Vermouth - a few drops. Just show the bottle to the gin. It's got to be bone dry." She wiped both rims with lemon. She sloshed gin into the jug full of ice, added the few drops, and stirred the mixture around with her fingers. "Never touch it with metal, Rene." She poured two glasses, added a sliver of lemon. We sipped. Miss G asked if I could make those, and I replied that I sure could try.

"Good, you've got the job. I can't pay you much to start with. All I get is forty dollars a week from my business manager. That's twenty for food and living expenses, and twenty for the bits and pieces a girl needs. I'll try and twist his arm and get twenty for you. Will that be all right?"

I remembered what Tressie had said when she first told me of her plan. She said for me to go down there and help that child. She needs a friend. She's breaking her heart over that Artie Shaw, and he isn't worth it; she needs help real quick. At that moment, I couldn't think of any way Miss G needed helping at all, but I said, "Sure."

I liked Miss G from that very first moment. I suppose that when my older sister said for me to go down there and look after that girl, I took that responsibility seriously. For the rest of her life I took it seriously, and she did the same for me.

To begin with I was simply a "daily" who came in early to get her up, give her breakfast, and then clean the apartment. Often I'd go off to baby-sit or do somebody else's chores and get back to Miss G's place before she returned from the studio around six, to get a snack ready for her. In those first few weeks, if need be, my twenty dollars practically all went to paying for the food we ate. Gin was only $2.00 a bottle, and we weren't hard on the vermouth, as we liked the martinis bone dry.

Almost from the start, I became aware of Miss G's shyness and loneliness. She didn't want me to leave and used little excuses to keep me there. "Rene, you can't be in any hurry to get back to that old rooming house in East L.A." she'd say. By this time, Tressie had packed up and gone back to Chicago to be with her husband. "Let's knock back a couple of martinis and split a hamburger," or "Let's have a couple of drinks and I'll drive us down to Olvera and find a jazz club" were often Miss G's way of keeping me with her.

I didn't protest. I was as lonely as she was. Sure she'd had two husbands, and they had run her around a lot, but now she was on her own and bewildered and hurt. I guess to a certain extent, she was drawn to me because she'd relied on black children and black adults all through her growing up years. Bappie, Miss G's oldest sister, told me that when Miss G was three or four years old, she'd often disappear for hours at a time, but they always knew where to find her. They'd track her down to the row of black workers' cottages – one family with six small kids – and there would be Ava, one little white face surrounded by six little black faces, all eating biscuits the size of doorsteps and having a great time.

Sex was a sort of dirty word with Miss G's mama, a woman of strict Baptist principles, who did not, or could not bring herself to explain the facts of life to her daughters. When Miss G had her first period, and believed she was bleeding to death, it was not to her mama she rushed, but to the old, fat, warm-hearted black lady who worked in the Gardner household. She was the one who comforted her and explained exactly what was happening.

Miss G solved our lodging situation when MGM gave her a yearly raise in pay, and we found a larger apartment in Westwood. We had two bedrooms, a lounge, kitchen, and bathroom, and I was installed. We were a team. I've got to state here, having already mentioned the royal "we" and the protective bodyguard status I assumed later, that in these first days of our relationship, the situation was completely reversed. Ava was my bodyguard.

I'll never forget that first jazz joint she took me to in downtown L.A. She was known there and in a lot of other places too because Artie Shaw was rated as a species of saint in those quarters. We slipped in and sat in the back. The décor was a sort of black – you couldn't see much – and I hoped nobody could see me as I knew what would happen. The spotlights were on the band which was belting away so loud that it was like sitting in a tunnel with a train going through. Then the big, tough, tuxedoed waiter spotted me and started to beam in, and I thought, "Uh-oh!" He had one of those don't-tangle-with-me faces that looked as if it had been stomped on by a horse, and he started in with the dialogue. No, when he approached us, he let his eyes talk: "Leave now or get thrown out."

He gave my white side-kick a glance, saw it was female, and hesitated, especially as it was giving him a real hard look with a nasty glint from those green eyes. Then he recognized her as part of the Artie Shaw entourage and realized that he'd made a sizable mistake. "Oh–er–sorry, Miss Gardner." His face creased into an apologetic smile that made it look as if it had been stomped on by two horses.

"We would like two large dry martinis...now," said Miss G, her voice as cold as an ice cube.

"Yes ma'am," he replied, and he was gone.

"Rene, honey," said Miss G in a level voice, "If they throw you out, they're gonna have to throw me out, too, and I have a feeling they don't want to do that." She had made her point. In the future, we were at peril quite a few times, but nobody threw us out. Nobody wanted to throw Miss Ava Gardner out of anywhere.

Two minutes later, Horseface came back with the martinis. He'd worked us all out by now and took great care not to spill my martini down my dress. He said, "How's Mr. Shaw these days? I haven't seen him around for some time." Miss G was now tapping her fingers on the table in time with the rhythm.

"Don't know and don't care," she replied sharply. "Just keep the martinis coming, right?"

"Yes, Ma'am," came his quick reply.

However, I knew Miss G was lying. I knew she was breaking her heart over Artie Shaw. I knew she was looking at the bandleader and seeing instead Artie's tall figure, the handsome sunburned face, the dark, sleeked-back hair, broad smile, clarinet poised to swing into the next number, and the crowd applauding and beginning to chant: "Artie–Begin The Beguine...Begin The Beguine"–the enchanting melody that Artie had made his own and taken to the top of the charts. I knew what would happen when we got home.

I suppose we left that jazz joint when it closed at around 1:00 a.m. If you were in the movie business you went to bed pretty early...unless you were Miss G.

When we got home, as usual Miss G said, "Rene, honey, why don't we have one for the road?" I'd fix the drinks and start watching her very carefully because I could read her almost like a thermometer and would know which way she was going to go.

So often the tears would start to pour down her cheeks, and her head would fall, and she'd sob and sob. I would sit next to her and cradle her head in my arms, and she would weep out, what to her was a never ending disaster. She was no good, useless as a wife–nobody wanted her. Two marriages had failed. Why, why, why? I knew that at that time, she was really only talking about Artie Shaw.

Why had he thrown her out? She had tried so hard to please him. She'd read all the books he gave her, she had learned about music, she'd taken extension courses at the University of California, Los Angles (UCLA), and made good grades in literature and economics. She had even taken up chess, taught by a Russian master Artie had found for her, and she had beaten Artie in the only game they ever played. That was probably a mistake as Artie hated losing. Oh, God, she had tried so hard to become an intellectual and make Artie and his friends like her. Why didn't she have a real home and a real husband? Why wasn't she happy like her mother and father had been?

I was born in St. Louis, Missouri in January of 1922, and it was cold and miserable. Miss G was born in Grabtown, just a small collection of houses, about eight miles from Smithfield, North Carolina, on Christmas Eve, 1922. Smithfield was only a little town then (still is), and it was snowing. Miss G didn't mind the snow, but she was furious about Christmas Eve, saying "It meant I only got one present instead of two. I can still see those smiling auntie's faces. 'We put them both together dear.'" However, Miss G and I both had happy childhoods because we both had good solid mamas and papas who took the business of raising a family seriously.

But I knew her father had died when she was fifteen, and her mother when she was twenty, and I knew that in those first few months of our acquaintanceship, her depression led to her almost becoming suicidal. I was so worried that when she was out, I'd search the place for hidden sleeping pills and even razor blades.

It was a strange thing though. I'd get her to sleep, and in the morning she'd wake up looking beautiful. No hangover, never mentioning the despair of those midnight hours, and she'd roar off towards the studio with a smile on her face and the car radio blaring.

One evening, Miss G got home from the studio and was having dinner. As usual, she was going through her steak and baked potato as if she had just discovered food. We were flush with funds at the start of the month. She caught my amused look, paused with her fork on the way to her mouth, and said, "Rene, from the time I was a kid and Mama started us off with a breakfast of bacon, eggs, grits and toast, and all the goodies, I've eaten like a horse." I replied that I knew her Mama was one hell of a cook, and that no matter what Miss G ate, she never put on any weight. Miss G completed the journey with the fork and went on, "Yep, Mama was one of the great cooks of the district. Get yourself the right parents and you have a lifetime without indigestion. What did you eat when you were a kid, Rene?"

"Nothing," I answered.

Miss G frowned and said, "Come on, Rene."

I replied, "Very often, nothing." Miss G put down her fork and looked at me very hard, and I knew we were at the start of one of our heart-to-heart talks about the past, because we both did have lots of things in our pasts.

"Nothing?" repeated Miss G. "And you were one of six sisters?"

"That's right. You want to hear the story?"

Miss G giggled, "You know nothing is going to stop you."

"My Pa was a steel riveter working for the American Car Foundry in St. Louis. He was a big guy, a bit proud and standoffish. The depression was on. He was in his late thirties, and no one messed with James Mack Jordan. We lived in one of the poorest parts of the city, a row of little apartments; rabbit hutches really with two rooms, one behind, one in front."

"But six girls," protested Miss G forcibly, "How did you sleep?"

"We had two mattresses in our room with three girls to each mattress, head to toe."

Miss G screwed up her forehead in disbelief and asked about lavatories and that sort of thing. I replied that they were in the alleyway behind the apartments and called "thunder boxes." I explained that in the twenties and thirties, it was normal living in the black quarters of St. Louis.

Miss G put her knife and fork carefully together. She had finished eating.

"Did you have bad feelings about the whites?"

"Not at all. As a child growing up in a black neighborhood, you didn't even think that way. The whites belonged to a different sort of world. St. Louis has always been a black city - black schools, black churches, black everything. We went to a park, Forest Park, where we played, but we knew there were certain areas that were off limits and that only white folks could go there. It never bothered us and we had plenty of room," I explained.

"You had a happy childhood?" asked Miss G, her voice filled with disbelief.

"Sure, I had a happy childhood even when Pa was only working a day here and a day there. During the depression, you took it all for granted. When he wasn't working, we weren't eating.

He was a family man with his own set of values. No smoking or drinking in the family, and no dirty words."

Miss G pushed her plate away and hooted with laughter. "It was just the same as my family. My Pa was sort of quiet, introspective, withdrawn, but Mama never stopped talking, never stopped 'doing.' She had her own big garden behind the house growing all sorts of veggies. There were chickens, a cow, and my father kept his mule which he used to work the tobacco fields." As an afterthought, she said, "Did your Mama cook very much?"

"Ma wasn't a great cook. Pa did most of the cooking. If we had a decent meal, he cooked it."

"What would you call a decent meal?" asked Miss G.

"Something that wasn't burned half up. Mostly it was oatmeal or rice before going to school. We didn't come home for lunch because there wasn't any. Whatever you did you did on a bowl of oatmeal. We drank coffee because Ma was addicted to coffee. Ma didn't waste money on milk. You went from the breast to the coffee pot. The only milk we had was canned Pet milk. She would buy a can of Pet milk and thin it with water. The last one to get oatmeal would get more water than milk, but she'd put more sugar in that. I can tell you, Miss G, the real advantage of being poor is that you don't get that cholesterol stuff, and you don't have heart attacks because there ain't anything to attack." Miss G roared with laughter and then asked if I went to school.

I explained that we went early at eight o'clock. It was an all-black school, and I started at six years old. When you went to school at six, you already knew your alphabet, could count to a hundred, and could read Coca-Cola off the billboards. You got a good head start from your parents. Now they send kids to school early for a Head Start! We finished school at 3:30 and went home. Food depended on what sort of day Pa had. When he didn't work at the Car Foundry, he'd go around to the Coal Depot. He couldn't get hired there, but they let him pick up the coal that fell off the trucks. He would get a basket and then go sell it. Maybe he would have fifty cents or a dollar and sometimes as much as 75 cents, and that paid for food.

The store across from the Foundry where he was employed would give him credit so that he could run up a little account there - maybe three or four dollars a week. They knew exactly how much he was going to make, so I guess that store was probably owned by the American Car Foundry. I do remember he used to come home about once a week with a brown paper bag with peanut butter, sometimes apple butter, maybe peas and beans and bread. When he managed to get work on a Friday, then there was a real treat. He would bring us goodies like American cheese, bologna, and a little jar of mayonnaise. We would all be jumping up and down singing, "Here comes Papa. Here comes Papa!" Food sure was important and sometimes we didn't get it. Sometimes we wouldn't have any food at all. Maybe we would run out of food the night before, and then the next day we would know it. Our parents didn't talk in front of us, but Mama would just say, "You all stay in bed today. You don't get up till I tell you." Then we'd know that food was pretty scarce or was gone, and she didn't want us out playing or working up an appetite.

Miss G had stopped laughing, and was just listening. She put her hand out and laid it over mine and said, "Rene, we have to feed you up."

I said, "Miss G, that was a long time ago."

Ava Lavinia Gardner, hometown girl from North Carolina in 1941, became the deadly
Kitty Collins in The Killers (1946). This was the role that propelled her to stardom.

2 GETTING OVER ARTIE

One Sunday we were driving to Malibu along Sunset Boulevard on a bright blue sunlit California day. "Let's go out and have lunch at the pier," said Miss G. "Might even take a swim and join the crowd."

We were always doing that sort of thing, spur of the moment stuff, going places. Get behind the wheel, point the car somewhere, press the accelerator. Somewhere here we come!

I've always loved Sunset Boulevard. Just the name to start with, and because it has a real sunset at the end. Bang, right there at the junction lights there's Santa Monica to the south, then north to Malibu, where in the evening time the sun falls over the rim of the world.

It's where the cowboys got off their horses saying, "I guess that's it fellas."

Miss G was wearing her usual casual, day-to-day outfit; a bandana tied around her hair in a flamboyant bow, a bright yellow blouse, balloon green skirt, bobby socks and saddle shoes. She was still growing up. She had been dressed the same way one day previously when I returned home from shopping and found her fuming.

"Rene, why do I look so young?" she demanded. "I stay up all night boozing or dancing and I get insulted every minute of the day."

"Insulted? Who's going to insult you for looking the way you do?" I asked.

"The bank," she snorted.

"You're overdrawn?" I asked seriously.

"No!" she screamed. "I'm not overdrawn. I'm in credit."

"So what's the problem?"

"I pushed my check under the grill, and the teller picked it up as if it were a bit of lavatory paper," she said. "Then he says, 'And you're supposed to be Ava Gardner?' By this time, I'm getting indignant and snap, 'Sure am.' Do I get my money? No I do not. 'Just a minute,' he says and walked away towards the back of the bank. He stopped for a moment to talk to some old geezer who gave me a long distance accusing look. Then he disappeared. In a few minutes he came back and said, 'I had to check the signature.' I'm now boiling. 'Why?' I demanded. He's still hostile. 'Because you don't look like Ava Gardner,' he said."

9

Miss G was still annoyed. I was gurgling with laughter. "He was dead right!," I said. "Miss G, you look like one of the kids swinging out of high school. You sure don't look like that sexy babe who was giving George Raft come-on signs in *Whistle Stop*. It's playing at every movie house around here. I bet the poor guy saw it last night; that scene with you in the silk nightie climbing the stairs; you with your mascaraed eyes and scarlet mouth. He probably stayed awake all night thinking you were the sexiest girl he had ever seen."

Miss G began to laugh too and said, "Maybe next time I'll go in covered in my movie makeup and he'll drop dead."

In those days, Sunset Boulevard was a narrow, twisting, up-and-down highway, hard against the mountains, and there was not a lot of traffic on it. If you started driving west at, let's say Crescent Heights, you'd find the Garden of Allah, a maze of small apartments and cottages which housed young writers and directors hoping to make a name for themselves in the film industry. It disappeared long ago.

Up on the right is the Chateau Marmont, a hotel modeled on some fanciful French chateau. It is still standing. Proceed along Sunset Strip, and you come to La Cienega falling away down its steep hill. Soon after, you arrive at the grassy strip that separates two smooth highways. On either side, there are posh mansions, and farther along on the right is one of Hollywood's landmarks, the Beverly Hills Hotel.

Continue going along Sunset Boulevard until you get to the Bel Air Hotel. Miss G certainly had a funny story to tell about that place, and she told it often.

"I lived there for a few weeks in 1943," she explained. "I'd just divorced Mickey Rooney. For the very first time, I was out on my own. On my starlet salary of around a hundred dollars a week, with most of it gobbled up by my business manager and agent, I was pretty broke. The Bel Air Hotel was cheap. I had also just met Howard Hughes, the richest man in the world, so people said. He'd met me through a girlfriend of mine who was also a starlet. The first few times he took me out, I got him mixed up with Howard Hawkes, the famous film producer. I wondered what the hell Howard Hawkes wanted me for. Then I found I'd got Howard Hughes, and I knew what his intentions were straight away. Not that he had any hope. He was tall, sweet, liked staying out late, and knew all the posh places, but he wasn't what I was looking for. So as long as he stayed at arm's length, that was okay.

"I'd found this room in the Bel Air Hotel, which had originally been a stable. There were only six or eight rooms. It didn't even have a restaurant. Being an ex-stable, it sure did have a whole colony of rats. Having been born and bred in North Carolina farm country, I was well acquainted with the species.

"Anyway, I hadn't known Howard Hughes for many weeks, but I did know that when he sent you flowers, he sure did send you flowers. He didn't send one rose, or a dozen, but a hundred! This time he had sent me orchids. Not one orchid--a hundred orchids--and they filled the bedroom.

"I'm asleep that night and what do I hear? I hear a munching noise. A bloody rat is eating my orchids! I'm furious! I leap out of bed and grab my nearest weapon, my tennis racket, and start swiping away trying to knock the hell out of the rat, or at least get him out of the room. Swish! I missed him and that's about fifteen of Howards's orchids mowed down. Swish again – a fine backhand – and that's another twenty or so on the hit list. By the time I'd finished, Howard's hundred orchids were a shambles, but I'd beaten the rat and he had vanished.

"That was a shame really, because I would have allowed him a few courses. I never minded rats all that much. As I said, as a farm girl, I got to know rats pretty well. I quite liked their poor little hairless pink babies. How did they know they were going to be dragged into the world and called 'Rats?' They probably thought they would grow up as pretty little bunnies."

Onward past UCLA, Miss G is in the outside lane and passing everything in sight.

"Tell me more about Artie," I said.

She turned her head and gave me one of her big smiles. "You know, Rene, until I met Artie Shaw, I had a happy mind, a perfectly contented mind. Possibly, it wasn't very brainy, but after all it was my mind. It did what I wanted and I got along very well with it."

"You mean to tell me that Artie blew it?" I said.

"Sure did," Miss G answered. "Not all in one go, and I don't think he did it intentionally. He sure did do the Svengali thing; the Professor Higgins in Shaw's Pygmalian thing. Quite a few husbands act like that. Don't kid yourself that men just think they own women, they know they do! For about the last ten million years, they've been proving that. Nowadays, of course, they use the excuse they just want to improve us little darlings for our own good, which really means for their own good."

"But you loved him from the time you first met?" I asked.

"Totally," said Miss G. "The chemistry was right. He was twelve years older than me. He was tall and dark, sardonic and handsome. You know, the romantic novelist's crap. He was a famous band leader. That exerted big leverage. Remember Rene, we were out of our minds with adoration for the big bands – Duke Ellington, Glenn Miller, Tommy Dorsey. I grew up on those sounds."

"But you didn't start an affair straight away?" I asked.

"No. Artie wasn't a hustler," explained Miss G. "The quick jump into bed, that's just for the common people. Oh boy, what a line he had! Every night we talked and talked. When I think about it, I wasn't doing the talking. Artie was. It was all Artie's intellectual stream of consciousness. I just sat there wide-eyed and listened.

"After about eight months with Artie softening me up with his brainy bulldozing, he decided we'd better get on with the common thing and go to bed together. We went back to his big Jacobean style house on Bedford Drive and got into bed. That worked terribly well. So we got married in October of 1945.

"Gee, when I think about it, it's not so long ago. We spent our honeymoon in his house. We didn't go anywhere or do anything. I traveled around with him doing his one night stands and I enjoyed it. I sat backstage and drank bourbon and loved it all and had a great time going to Chicago and New York. He played all the big ballrooms, but mainly it was one-nighters around California."

"When did it all start going wrong?" I asked.

"It started to go wrong when we got married!" said Miss G. "It was bliss before that. You know, Rene, at that period in my life I really did want to settle down and have a child. Artie shook his head very profoundly saying, 'You are too young.' You know, when I think back, I think really all he had in his mind was that our marriage was never going to work. And he was so stingy – no, let me rephrase that remark – he was so <u>mean</u> that he was looking for a cheap way out as soon as we were married.

"Lana Turner and I have had a lot of discussions about lovers and husbands, usually when we were in the ladies room powdering our noses. We both agreed that Artie was the meanest man we had ever met. We also agreed that we were absolutely madly in love with him, but he treated all his women the same way, about as generously as Scrooge."

"Miss G, you're still upset about the whole Artie thing?" I asked. "My sister Tressie always said he was always putting you down something terrible."

"That's right," said Miss G. "But that was when Artie was through with me, tired of me, and he could be very cruel when he wanted to get rid of someone. He had all sorts of egg-head friends, mainly left wing guys who knew all the answers to the world's problems and who had written books about them-- musicians, writers, professors. I'd try and put in a line occasionally, and there would be a little titter from under the beards, and Artie would say, 'Now Ava, you know nothing about that subject. So why don't you go and get the maid to serve the coffee.' I'd run off like a little serving mat on wheels."

"You put up with all that?" I asked in an unbelieving tone.

"I loved him, Rene," Miss G insisted. "I loved him so desperately that I could stand all the jabs. I thought it was all my fault. I was dim. I was uneducated. There was no hope of me even staying in the same room as those up-market professors. I even went to see a psychiatrist to get my IQ tested. He said that was ridiculous, that I didn't need a test. I said, 'I <u>want</u> an IQ test.' And I got one. Apparently, I've got quite a high IQ."

"So……," I said.

"I've never believed a high IQ made me any smarter," Miss G said.

I was to hear this talk from Miss G for the rest of her life. To the very end, she was lamenting her lack of a college education, a college degree. There she was, one of the greatest beauties of this century, and one who could more than hold her own in any company, with absolutely anyone. She had a great gift for comedy, a warm, richly earthy woman full of love for her friends, children and animals; and a shrewd nose for the phony and dishonest. And she thought a college degree mattered!

We drove up the hills and around the curves and I asked, "Artie made a lot of money?"

"Artie always made a lot of money," she said. "The Bedford Drive house was worth a fortune. He sold the house because he thought if we got divorced – and as I've said, I don't think Artie ever intended to stay married to anyone for too long – I might get a piece of it. We moved to a little ratty house, out in the valley. It was when I was doing *The Killers*. It was good for me because I was only five minutes from the studio."

"Didn't you have a say in all of this?" I asked.

"No. Artie ran the show completely," Miss G said. "I was not really a wife as wives should be. I had no say in anything. There was a say between my mother and father. They agreed between themselves their course of action. But with Artie – no. He went through wives like cold drinks. I was wife number five. Lana Turner was number three. Artie was searching for film experience with Lana and I think with me too. His wives sort of matched what he was doing at the moment. I think I ended his interest in film, at least temporarily."

We reached the ocean at Pacific Palisades. There were white tops on the waves, and they were running in fast onto the beach. Kids in bathing suits festooned the seawall. The sun still shone, dazzling and hot.

"Miss G, do you mean to tell me Artie never bought you <u>anything</u>?"

"He never bought me a stitch of clothing, a skirt, a dress, a sweater, or lingerie," she said. ."He did give me a small pair of gold earrings, which I promptly lost. He never gave me anything after that, but a wedding ring, and that's about it."

For the rest of her life she was going to insist that Artie Shaw was one of the great loves of her life. Probably he was, but it was a very painful experience.

We cruised along the coast road, passing the bits where the cliffs are always falling onto the road, and reached the small white wooden fishing pier that sticks out into the sea at Malibu. We always loved the unpretentious little restaurant which occupied the landward end. We got a table looking down at the sand and surf, ordered a bottle of icy cold white wine and touched glasses before ordering food.

Miss G said, "I'm going out with Howard Duff tonight, Rene, and I might be home late, or I might not be home at all."

"Okay, Miss G," I said.

"Well, what are we going to eat?" she asked.

"Shrimp," I said. It was a very pleasant meal.

Miss G didn't come home that night and didn't come home a lot of other nights afterwards. Artie Shaw gradually faded from her mind. Tressie's medicine—my companionship and encouraging her to date again—had worked.

3 STARLET MISS G AND OUR FRIEND CLARK GABLE

The first time in those late months of 1946 that I mentioned to Miss G that she was a film star her laughter almost cracked the martini glasses.

"Film star! Rene, you must be joking!" she said. "I arrived in Hollywood, when – around four years ago. I was supposed to be earning a salary of fifty dollars a week, but for the first year all they doled out was thirty-five because there was a little clause in the contract giving MGM the right to stop payment for twelve-week lay-off periods. "If Bappie hadn't come to Hollywood with me – because of Mama's insistence that I had to have my older sister look after me – and she hadn't gone downtown and got a job at I. Magnum's we'd have starved to death! As it was, we lived in one crummy room with a pull-down bed, a gas ring, and a kitchen-cum-bathroom as big as a closet. Film star! More like slave laborer. I don't think you sat around just looking pretty at MGM; they worked you hard eight until five."

Miss G had just arrived home from MGM. I could always tell what sort of day she'd had by the look on her face, the smile or no smile, the slight abruptness or the loud, "Christ, where are the martinis?"

I served them. She sat on the settee, sipped hers and said, "Where's yours?" Miss G always made that point, unless she saw the glass clasped in my hand. I never drank a martini with Miss G unless invited.

"I've got it here," I said. I sat and waited. She smiled, "Got called into Mr. Mayer's office today." I sat still and waited. Miss G liked to take her time over her daily recounts. "Told you the first time I got that invitation that his face looked as if it had skied down a steep hill and run into a brick wall. He'd heard that Mickey Rooney was planning to marry me. Marriage would ruin the Andy Hardy series. Mr. Mayer suddenly might find his top box office star too old for the job. Disasterville."

"So this time?" I questioned.

"Arrived at his office…"

"A big office?" I interrupted."

"His office was about the size of a tennis court. Mr. Mayer sat at the far end at a big desk. Paintings and photos of the famous race horses he owns were all along the walls. You feel you might have to break into a gallop to get to his desk. This time he is smiling and waves me to a chair. "Make yourself comfortable, Ava. You're looking very pretty today."

"Thank you, Mr. Mayer."

"I think you did very well in *Whistle Stop*."

"Thank you, Mr. Mayer;' I said. "I didn't mention the fact that as MGM had rented me out to United Artists for several thousand dollars, MGM had done very well too."

"'I wasn't quite so taken with *The Killers*,' Mr. Mayer went on. 'Bit savage I thought. A whole film about two hired killers who set out to murder a man who's betrayed another set of crooks. Not much of a happy ending was it, Ava?'"

"No, Mr. Mayer."

Miss G said she didn't mention the fact that, for the second time in succession, MGM had hired her out for a nice fat fee to Universal Studios.

"'I thought *Whistle Stop* a more suitable vehicle. Got along okay with George Raft?'" Mr. Mayer asked.

"Sure did, Mr. Mayer."

Miss G gave me one of her sly grins. "As I've told you, Rene, I got on great with George. He was a lovely man. He was sweet as a pussy cat and married. He was solid Catholic, but thought a little roll in the hay was a legitimate perk from time to time. As soon as he knew I hadn't the time, we became great friends."

She continued, "So Mr. Mayer cleared his throat for the shock announcement. "'I just wanted to tell you, Ava, that we've just bought the film rights to Frederic Wakeman's best seller, *The Hucksters*. Hard hitting stuff about the radio industry's advertizing tricks. We're casting Clark Gable in the lead, bringing over a young English actress, Deborah Kerr, to play opposite him, and you will play the part of Clark Gable's girlfriend.'"

Miss G's face was lit up. I'd never seen her so happy. I said, "Great!"

The doorbell rang. I put my glass down and said, "Now who the hell can that be?" and made my way towards the door with Miss G saying, "If it's anybody we don't like, just say I'm not in."

I opened the door and fainted. Well metaphorically, I fainted. There he stood, towering over me—the dark hair, the crinkled eyes, the wide smile.

"Hi. Is Ava in?" Clark Gable!

For years even before we even knew each other, Miss G and I, plus another hundred million or so women had seen *Gone With the Wind* and fallen in love with Rhett Butler. Now he was standing outside our door! I managed to make my tongue move and my voice speak.

"Y – yes, she is. I'll tell her you are here. Please come in." I darted away in front of him, my face creased up, and my mouth trying to fashion the name.

"Who?" said Ava, puzzled.

15

Before she could say any more, Mr. Gable had accepted my invitation and with about three strides was in our bijou apartment. "Hi, Ava," he said. "I hope you don't mind me dropping in unannounced like this. You've heard about *The Hucksters?*"

"Yes, only about an hour ago," Miss G replied. "Please sit down. Can we get you a drink? We're on martinis."

"Celebrating, I hope," Gable said.

"Well sort of," said Miss G.

"Got any Scotch?" Gable asked.

By the grace of God we had. And I began to learn that Mr. Gable liked his Scotch mahogany-colored. That is big whiskies!

Gable was so sweet. He wanted Ava to talk about her part, to want to do it, but as Miss G had said to me a thousand times, "For goodness sake, I don't choose my parts. When MGM says I'm playing this part, I'm playing that part."

Gable knew that, but he wanted to set her at ease, encourage her, and give her confidence. Mr. Clark Gable was a great guy. Later I said, "Clark Gable comes to talk to you and you insist you are not a star, huh?"

As much as I was always insisting on this status for her, Miss G never had an easy time accepting it. In my mind, though, she'd been a star from the very start – just maybe not a film star. At age nineteen and after only six months in Hollywood, she'd married Mickey Rooney, reputedly the highest paid actor in the business. She was on the glamour bandwagon. Their divorce after just over a year of marriage made headlines all over the globe. Nice young married couples didn't do that.

Then apparently she was the girlfriend of one of the richest men in the world—Howard Hughes—and she's also dating Howard Duff, who gossip has it desperately wants to marry her. She's photographed with other wealthy, good-looking guys in various restaurants and night clubs, and she's totally beautiful. So the magazines and gossip columnists love this stuff, and her reputation as a sexpot starts to form.

However, at heart, she is still a pretty little milkmaid waiting for Mr. Right (we've talked about Artie Shaw, and he doesn't count). And she is working bloody hard at MGM. In 1942 alone, the first year of her indoctrination, she made five appearances in films.

"Rene, love," said Miss G explaining her activities during her introductory year in the business. "Mainly they used me for publicity stills which were distributed all over the country, you know, 'girlie' bathing suit stuff to help the war effort or at least give the boys a bathing suit treat."

"But didn't you appear in five films that year?" I reminded her.

"I was wallpaper, Rene, wallpaper! A face in a crowd of teenagers, a dancer swirling on a crowded floor, someone walking down a street. MGM had scores of 'starlets' like me. Fifty bucks a week, and the option to fire you after the first three months or any three months after that if they didn't like you. It was a constant turn-over. It was cheap labor; okay, it was a job. They trained you and nobody twisted your arm to sign the contract."

In her very last picture of 1942, Miss G finally got out of the crowd scene, got a tiny part all to herself, about thirteen seconds worth of individual attention. The movie was *Kid Glove Killer*, and she was a car-hop glimpsed at a hotdog drive-in. At least she met a young actor named Van Heflin, also in the cast, and his wife Frances, and that started a long friendship.

The director was Fred Zinnemann, starting his rise to the very top, and who later would give Frank Sinatra his great opportunity when he was down on his luck, in *From Here to Eternity*.

The year 1943 had continued with short appearances in all manner of quickie films, including *Pilot No. 5* and a cast that included Franchot Tone, Marsha Hunt, Gene Kelly and Van Johnson. Miss G was "Girl."

Some others in those early years were: *Young Ideas, The Lost Angel, Swing Fever*, all in 1943; *Three Men in White, Maisie Goes To Reno*, and *She Went To The Races*. They were all quickie films to meet the boom-times of wartime Hollywood.

But another film was made that year which gave Ava Gardner a very tiny part, but at least a name – Katy Chotnik, and almost certainly influenced her career in a near incredible manner. The producer was one of the young and trusting refugees from Nazi-dominated Europe employed by MGM. His name was Seymour Nebenzal. The picture was *Hitler's Madman*, another quickie rushed out on a small budget and an inadequate production—a film that received scant critical or public attention, a film which left no discernable mark in movie history. But its horrific subject would survive forever in world history. It concerned the true story of two young Czech parachutists trained in Britain and dropped near Prague in the spring of 1942. Their mission was to assassinate Reinhard Heydrich, Gauleiter of Czechoslovakia, Hitler's evil subordinate who had formulated the policy of The Final Solution – the slaughter of all European Jews. Heydrich was assassinated.

The ensuing manhunt did not discover who had carried out Heydrich's killing, or where they might be hiding. To the Nazi powers who now gripped all Europe in an iron fist, this was an outrage. An example must be made which the whole world would understand. Hundreds of Prague citizens were murdered in concentration camps, but that was not enough. Some more draconian measure must be taken. Lidice, a small mining village about twenty miles outside Prague – which had absolutely nothing whatsoever to do with the assassination or protecting its perpetrators – was the target chosen for annihilation. At dawn on June 10, 1942, it was surrounded by S.S. troops with artillery and tanks.

All the men and teenage boys were shot, one-hundred and ninety in all. The women and children were shunted into trucks to be taken mainly to Ravensbruck concentration camp; practically all were never to be seen again.

In the line of young and attractive girls lined up for that transportation was Katy Chotnick, the part Ava Gardner played in that film. In that film, the camera panned slowly across those girls who knew that were destined for intolerable horror or death. It paused only for a second on Ava's figure in shapeless peasant dress, dark hair fluffed around her face, and on Ava's fierce expression – a glowering intensity of sheer hatred.

To the movie audience, Ava Gardner was unknown. They forgot the scene as soon as they left their seats. But Seymour Nebenzal did not forget it.

Mr. Mayer might have kept Miss G playing in cardboard cut-out-of-peaches-and-cream parts yearning to play opposite Lassie, until she was too old to matter. Strange really that L.B. Mayer, who was a very astute film maker, did not sense that potential in Miss G. Plainly, Mayer was more interested in good honest family films with happy endings, and nothing was wrong with that. Mayer also liked owning beautiful racehorses, so it was strange that he did not discern he had quite an exceptional young actress filly cantering around in his own film stables.

It was noticeable later in MGM's *The Hucksters*, the film she appeared in with Mr. Gable, that Miss G was wearing one of the most skin-fitting, bosom-revealing, hung-on-by-flimsy-bows-on-the-shoulders, black dresses in the history of movies. Mayer had obviously caught on by then.

But that was still a year or so down the road, and for the moment, Seymour Nebenzal was well ahead of Mayer. He'd been alerted to Ava Gardner's potential by *Hitler's Madman*, and as its producer he had the opportunity to study her during the production. She was beautiful. She had been married twice to famous men. She must, therefore, be a female with intense attraction. Perhaps she could be blended into that role which so few actresses can play convincingly; the lovely wanton, good-time girl for whom anything goes.

Seymour Nebenzal wanted Miss G with a passion that could only be assuaged by money. Indeed he had to wait three years while Miss G played in seven more dumb MGM films as a complete nonentity until he could get his hands on her again. And by this time, he was working for United Artists. He offered MGM five thousand dollars – Miss G's salary for a whole year – to loan her out for a limited number of days. With alacrity, L.B. Mayer agreed.

Whistle Stop was not a good picture. Its plot was ridiculous. Miss G's role as the slightly shop-soiled babe who has been hanging around Chicago's hot spots for the last two years, and returned to her home town to rescue her ex-lover from a never-do-well existence, was daft. The fact that her lover was George Raft, at that moment fifty years old while Miss G was a flawless twenty-three, was daft. The fact that her main endeavor was to fix George in gainful employment in a nightclub was not only ludicrous but beyond comprehension. All his life, George Raft had been playing nightclub roles. He looked as if he had been born in a nightclub. He got the job.

The relevant word was nightclub. At last Seymour Nebenzal had got Ava out of the concentration camp line-up and into the dim-lit world of movie nightclubs. She could stand next to the shiny black piano in a slinky black, sequined dress, alabaster white limbs shining in the spotlight, totally sexy, totally gorgeous, the girl every man in the whole wide world wanted to go to bed with.

The first clever pair of movie producer's eyes to focus on Miss G after that *Whistle Stop* revelation was that of Mark Hellinger. He was a smart operator out of New York City, well-cut dark suit, sharp profile, and inevitable white tie. He had a lot of friends. He was "in" with the Algonquin-round-table-Dorothy Parker clique. He was a buddy of Artie Shaw, who may have helped steer him in

Miss G's direction.

He also had a famous friend named Ernest Hemingway, who had granted him the movie rights to adapt one of his short stories, *The Killers*. Universal Films agreed to collaborate. Hellinger set up the package. First was the loan of Miss Ava Gardner from MGM for seven weeks at $1,000 a week, so in three short months Miss G had already repaid MGM more than twice her yearly salary.

Then he hired Robert Siodmak. Like Seymour Nebenzal, he was also an expert in the shadowy, harsh black-and-white of "film noir" so fashionable in that period. The screenwriters were two guys who were to earn reputations as among the best in the business—Anthony Veiller and John Huston. This was the first time Huston became aware of Miss G's existence. At that time, Huston was a major in an Army film unit, and as the Army did not care for officers moonlighting in Hollywood pictures, the major did not receive a credit but grabbed the cash.

Miss G made two hundred dollars a month. Our share was forty dollars for Miss G and twenty dollars for me. Our total income was sixty dollars a month. I was always mystified about where the rest of Miss G's salary went.

I said to Miss G, "What happens to the other hundred and forty?"

Miss G smiled and patiently explained the facts of life to her dumbbell maid. "Rene, in the film business, you have to have a business manager, someone who looks after your funds. You know—taxes, insurances, agent's fees, investments. My business manager knows what he's doing."

Apparently, Artie Shaw had recommended him, and as Artie was the stingiest man Miss G had ever met, she expected this guy to be the same sort. He was.

Miss G went on about her business manager quite a bit. He had a pretty young wife, two lovely kids, a great house on the beach, and he gave great parties. He knew all the right people, and handled lots of big names, such as Doris Day and Van Heflin.

A little later, Miss G said, "Rene, my business manager's wife asked me if you could do a little housework for them occasionally, and do a bit of babysitting when they stay out late at parties and dinners. There's an extra bedroom where you can sleep. They won't wake you when they come in, and they'll pay the usual rate."

I said sure. So that's how I discovered what an expensive lifestyle they had, whereas Miss G and I scrimped along on bits and pieces. For her business manager and his wife, every night it was roast beef, filet mignon, or salmon steaks, and wines to match. I discovered a lot more too.

When I babysat, I'd put the kids to bed, and then hop into my own. Every night when they came home late, their voices carried loud and clear to my bedroom. The wife was often grumbling about money, but the husband was as cheerful as a guy who's just made a year's salary at a race track.

"Don't worry about money, darling," I heard him say. "It's rolling in. Those dumb actors don't know what's happening to their investments. Up and down, up and down, but it's always down for them. My plans are going great. In three years' time, we will be millionaires."

I could not quite believe what I was hearing. As I babysat for them and they came home late, he was always a bit drunk and boasting about the way he was hiding these vast amounts of money in phony investments. At first I thought, Rene, it's none of your business, and what do you know about investments anyway? Then I began to think about that one hundred and forty dollars a month he ripped off from us. It was my business because my business was the welfare of Miss G. After the first martini one night, I blurted out what I had discovered.

"Miss G, I think that your business manager is a crook."

Miss G blinked and put down her martini. "Rene, you must be crazy."

"A real con-man crook," I repeated for emphasis.

Miss G looked thoughtful. I think she remained thoughtful for a couple of days, as she knew that neither she nor I were ever likely to get a banker's job on Wall Street.

Then she told Bappie about what I'd reported. Bappie blew up. Bappie always thought that Miss G's money was her own money, and she could not afford to let her waste it. Bappie had a good nose for crooks. We left Miss G's business manager very quickly.

4 A TOUCH OF VENUS AND NUDITY

I was cooking the spaghetti sauce when Miss G came home to heave her usual sigh of relief, reach for the first martini, and tell me what had happened between her and Clark Gable and Deborah Kerr on the set that day.

We were in the middle of *The Hucksters* and in the future lay six more movies, some comic, some pure rubbish, and one quite tragic.

Miss G went into her first sequence of angst as soon as she came through the door. "God Almighty Rene, do you know what those bastards are telling me to do now?"

I added the tomato puree, the first ladles of finely chopped onions and celery, and stirred gently. I was really much more attached to the aroma than Miss G's dilemma. "I can't guess," I said.

"Universal has just called Arthur Hornblower," she said. I knew that Arthur Hornblower was producing *The Hucksters*. "What for?" I asked.

"Because they want to rent me to play in their movie *Singapore*. They've already started shooting, but their leading lady's dropped dead or got a cold or something, and they've got to find someone to fill in for her."

"Well, Universal loved you in *The Killers*," I said. "They know a good thing when they see one. They'll just have to wait for you to finish *The Hucksters*."

"Rene, that's the whole point. They want me to do both pictures at the same time!"

"But that's ridiculous! Can't you complain?"

"I can complain until I'm blue in the face," said Miss G. "I can refuse and MGM will suspend me – so we don't eat, and that sauce smells great. So in the mornings I'm playing Jean Ogilvie, who's loving and losing Clark Gable in *The Hucksters*, and then scooting across in a hired car to Universal Studios in the afternoons to play Linda Graham, who loses her memory, but gets it back again just in time to live happily ever after with Fred MacMurray."

Hollywood was booming. Studios that had been making a movie a week during the prewar years were still averaging one every two, three or four weeks.

MGM was doing great loaning out Miss G without a bonus and at the same time working her on their own productions.

"Well, that's something!" I said, stirring the sauce and adding a nice dollop of red wine to tickle up the flavor. "I like Fred MacMurray. I think he's great."

"I'll give you my opinion when I get to know him," said Miss G.

"Come and taste the sauce," I urged. "The martinis are chilled and you are going to feel better."

Miss G did as she was bid. I said, "I know where Singapore is, but what the hell has that got to do with a movie?"

Miss G explained, "Ever since Ingrid Bergman and Humphrey Bogart made a smash hit in Casablanca, every studio has been trying to cash in on the act. Pick a foreign-sounding town. Add bobbies, spies, baddies, and boy-meets-girl and off you go. I've got the dreadful script. You'll have to read in for Fred MacMurray."

I read it that night. Fred's character is a pearl smuggler, and Miss G is his girlfriend. Villains are after the pearls, and they kidnap Miss G because they think she might know where Fred has hidden them. Everywhere Japanese planes are swooping and firing machine guns. It was very exciting. Miss G gets knocked on her head and is laid out. When she wakes up, she has lost her memory and forgotten Fred, who thinks she's dead and has gone off to war. Miss G meets a man played by sweet little English actor Roland Culver and marries him.

One critic I notice from our cuttings made this observant remark: "Mr. Culver had also been rushed into the film at a moment's notice, so Ava Gardner and he had considerable difficulty giving a degree of conviction to their scenes as man and wife."

No so with Miss G and Fred MacMurray, because Miss G was getting to know him better every day, and I don't mean on the set.

In the movie, Fred's character comes home to collect his pearls and hand them over to their proper owners. Miss G gets another of those convenient knocks on the head, and lo, her memory returns, and with it her deep love for Fred. Ronnie Culver's character, being a decent English gent, realizes any girl can make a mistake and agrees to an annulment.

Fred and Miss G, avoiding the sunset which is full of Japanese Zero fighter planes, walk happily towards the bedroom – movie bedroom.

It didn't take much more than a week after filming had begun before Miss G slid into the apartment with a smile on her face which I knew meant only one thing. I said, "Fred?"

"Yes."

"But where?"

"Dressing room; locked, of course."

"Just rehearsing for your film love affair?" I asked. Miss G began to sputter with laughter. "You could say that," she said.

The affair didn't last long. Maybe a few weeks longer than the movie took to make. Fred's code name was Mr. Norton. When Miss G rang me and Mr. Norton might be coming around that evening, I took my book to bed knowing I could get a good night's sleep.

Miss G liked Fred. Then she discovered he had a sick wife. I guess by now her sense of morality was getting a bit twisted. She didn't object to secret adultery, but when a guy was two-timing a sick wife, she objected to that – strongly.

Our next film, *One Touch of Venus*, was supposed to be a light-hearted comedy, but for both of us, it held a share of tragedy. Miss G played in four movies during this period, and three out of that four were produced by Universal.

In this case they were quick to recognize Miss G's potential as a comedienne. Anyone who knew her recognized that she had a great sense of humor, a quick wit, followed by a noisy, joyful stream of laughter, and most importantly when needed, a wonderful wide-eyed air of innocence.

One Touch of Venus started light and achieved success as a bright and decorative musical, but as very often happens, it never really came to life as a rather contrived, hard-worked-for comedy. The basic idea was that a marble statue of a beautiful young Greek goddess has been borrowed to aid the sales of a store in a shopping mall. The young store manager, played by Robert Walker, after a few drinks, stops to donate a kiss to the marble lips.

Oh, dear me! Through the tricks of expert cinematography, the statue becomes human, falls in love with the manager, and then pursues him with fiery love aided by magic endowed her by the ancient Greek gods from whom she came.

Naturally, Greek statues looking exactly like Miss G were hard to come by, so sculptor Joseph Nicolosi was commissioned to execute such a work. Miss G was instructed to pose for him in his studio every day until it was completed.

Little difficulties arose. To start with, it was winter and it was cold, and Miss G returned to our apartment after the first sitting with the breathless reaction, "Jesus Christ, Rene, his studio's freezing, and I'm supposed to pose in a pair of shorts and a bra, and he's not very happy with that."

"With what?" I asked.

"Joe is sculpting a bare-breasted Greek maiden. They didn't wear bras back in those golden Greek days," Miss G explained.

"Well, you're very well-proportioned in that respect," I said.

"Mama would turn in her grave if she thought I was being sculptured half nude," Miss G said.

I countered, "Mama's not here, and actresses have to suffer for their art. She'd have much more of a fright if she knew what you and Fred were getting up to in that dressing room."

Miss G had one of the most beautiful figures ever given to a woman. She was, I know, quite shy about exhibiting it. This time common sense prevailed. The topless figure, dress draped artistically over one shoulder, was completed and dispatched to the studio.

Someone had made a mistake! Producers came in, looked, and took annual leave. Executives were spellbound. Assistant directors, when their blood pressure had found refuge in their ankles, screamed that this crazy sculptor had

23

been commissioned to sculpt a clothed figure – not a half-naked one!

The Hollywood Movie Censorship Board, called the Hays Office, would raze Universal Studios to the ground. No one shouldered the blame. The statue was shipped back to poor Joseph Nicolosi with the command that he produce another statute with breasts covered.

At least by now the weather was warmer. That was the funny part.

The tragic part was Miss G's co-star, Robert Walker. He was in his late twenties and fast becoming an alcoholic, helped by several so-called buddies who were also heavy drinkers. The reason for his heavy and consistent boozing was that he was deeply in love with his wife, beautiful actress Jennifer Jones, and now the marriage had fallen apart.

David O. Selznick, famous producer of *Gone With the Wind*, carried a lot of weight in Hollywood in that period. He had become infatuated with Jennifer Jones, and Jennifer had moved across. Robert Walker was heart-broken, and his plight was driven home to Miss G and me in extremely poignant fashion.

Miss G was very fond of Walker. There was no question of any affair between them. She felt motherly towards the poor lad, and on occasions, knowing that he was likely to be picked up by his drunken friends and arrive at the studio next morning with a hangover that rendered him almost unfit for work, would join him for dinner, and try and talk him out of his troubles.

One night in question, Walker got so drunk that he became unfit to drive anywhere, so Miss G piled him into her car and brought him back to the apartment. We had three beds, a double in Miss G's room and two singles in mine. Miss G moved in with me and slept like a log.

Walker tumbled into the double, and I heard him moving around in the bathroom before he made it into bed. For hours he kept me awake because the walls were pretty thin, and his crying and pitiful imploring of Jennifer to come back to him were heard easily. I knew I could do nothing to help him, but I felt so terribly sorry for him.

Next morning I got up with the light just breaking and went into the bathroom to get the bits and pieces I needed to start the day. I opened the cupboard where we kept the brooms and cleaning materials, and wondered what on earth was hanging there. Then I worked it out. It was a sort of leather harness that Robert Walker wore under his loosely cut clothes to fill him out as a muscular figure. I did not touch it.

After he had been to the bathroom, Miss G and I tried to force coffee down him, and off they drove to Universal for the day's shooting.

I did not tell Miss G what I had discovered until she came back that evening with Walker. We felt quite powerless to help. The movies had made him famous and given him what amounted to a false physique, and his skill and charm as an actor had introduced him to the lovely Jennifer Jones. Then it had all crumbled and he had inherited this burden of tragic and overwhelming grief.

He never really recovered. He died in his early thirties.

After two failed marriages, an affair with Howard Duff, and what can really only be described as a roll in the hay with Fred MacMurray, I knew very well that Miss G was not happy with her situation. It was the same old thing.

She wanted to be married. She needed to be married.

That state had been implanted in her mind from the moment she had been born. The Mama and Papa syndrome was as much a part of the North Carolina landscape as the winters and summers and the plants that grew.

Marriage was a woman's destiny. Marriage fulfilled her, gave her children, a role in life and happiness. Her mother and father, despite much hardship, proved that to her. Her sisters were married. Her own two marriages and two quick divorces rankled in her mind as a deep sense of failure. Oh sure, we could laugh and joke about it all, but the feeling wouldn't go away.

Then into our lives after *One Touch of Venus* came another MGM potboiler, *The Bribe*, with Robert Taylor, Charles Laughton, Vincent Price, and John Hodiak. Robert Taylor was very handsome, very experienced, very famous, and very married to Barbara Stanwyck

He had a roving eye, which fastened upon Miss G. And this time, Miss G took it very seriously.

Taylor had first zoomed to movie fame when he played Greta Garbo's lover in *Camille*. The scene between the dying Greta as Camille and Taylor's character at her bedside remains to this day as a gem of cinema history. Trouble was Taylor was now labeled as the swooning lover in the Rudolph Valentino mold, a near gigolo type.

Taylor hated that image. He was in truth very macho–the ranching, riding, hunting, shooting, fishing male—but Hollywood type-casting had fixed him eternally. He hated his part in *The Bribe*.

Filmed on the back lot at MGM against scenery and back projection slides suggesting some vague Latin American background, Miss G played the unhappy wife of the villainous character played by John Hodiak. The wife is rescued from her martyrdom by handsome Federal Agent Taylor. Hodiak is popped into jail, and Taylor gets Miss G as his just reward.

During the weeks it took to make *The Bribe*, I was beginning to wonder if Miss G was going to make a habit of going to bed with her leading men. In our heart-to-heart talks, I began to see that she was dwelling seriously on the possibilities of marriage to Robert Taylor.

Frankly, I couldn't stand the sight of him. He didn't like me either, and he had not the slightest idea that I knew all about his affair with Miss G. If he had, he would have rocketed sky-high, because his opinion of "colored" people hadn't shifted much since the slave trade was banned.

On rare occasions, he did skip back to our apartment to share Miss G's bed, but I crouched like a mouse in my room without his even suspecting my presence. Oh yes, he talked to Miss G about how unhappy he was in his marriage and how hard it was to get a divorce. The lengths he went to keep their romance a total secret were hard to believe.

He was a good pilot and on several occasions flew her out to lonely farmhouses owned by his friends. And Miss G, quickly realizing where she stood, said, "Rene, I'm sometimes surprised he doesn't wear a black beard when we're off on a trip."

It couldn't last. It was far too fugitive and sneaky for Miss G. She liked him enormously but was female enough to know it couldn't last. Taylor had no intention at that time of changing his lifestyle for Miss G or anybody else. He was quite content with his public image as a happily married man with a beautiful film star wife.

I was pleased when her mischievous sense of humor returned and she surprised me with a statement that I thought meant she had got another lover.

"God Almighty, Rene, do you know what that old man is trying to do to me?"

"What old man's doing what to you?" I asked.

"Charles Laughton!"

I remembered that great British film where Laughton, as Henry VIII, was guzzling greasy chicken legs and throwing the bones over his shoulders to the dogs, then leering sexily at the cleavages of his sequence of wives before chopping their heads off. Generally, he was behaving like a dirty old King. I shuddered to think what he was proposing to do with Miss G.

I said, "You mean he's......?" I couldn't imagine what he could be doing. I should have known from that innocent gleam in Miss G's eyeballs.

"Every time we get an hour or so break, he takes me aside."

"And...?" I urged an answer.

"He reads me passages from the Bible," Miss G explained.

Well, I'd heard all about these sexy clergymen! "You mean he's a religious nut, and that he... ?" I sputtered.

By now Miss G was making a choking noise in her throat like a crow cawing, and I knew I'd been had.

"No! Rene, sweetie, Charles Laughton is a famous and brilliant Shakespearean actor, and he insists that I have talent. He insists on improving my diction so I can hit the boards from Broadway to London. Isn't he a dear? He really means it. He reads me passages from the Bible and from Shakespeare and I have to read them back under his instruction."

If she lost out on her romance with Robert Taylor, she certainly made up for it with her great friendship with the wonderful Charles Laughton.

When she started her next star-studded MGM production, *The Great Sinner*, she played the aristocratic beauty, Countess Pauline Ostrovski, and she said, "There you are, Rene! Charles Laughton will be proud of me!"

The other stars were Gregory Peck, Melvyn Douglas, Walter Huston, Ethel Barrymore, Frank Morgan and Agnes Moorehead.

In *The Great Sinner*, it was Gregory Peck who gained Miss G's eternal devotion. She would come back to the dressing room whispering her admiration. "Do you know what he does, Rene? I sneaked a look at his script and margin of each page are tiny notes about his part – voice changes, emphasis, mannerisms – little touches about every scene he plays. I've never see anyone so thorough in my life."

Miss G, as I have already mentioned, had gone to bed with two out of three of her last leading men, but Gregory Peck who, as he admitted, certainly noticed this luminous creature who was playing opposite him, had no intention of joining the sequence.

He had played against dozens of lovely ladies before, and Hollywood was awash with them. Miss G and Peck hit it off from the moment they met and became best of friends. Their friendship was renewed years later when he and his lovely wife Veronique were on location in Australia making *On the Beach*.

With his observant eyes, Gregory Peck also noticed how Miss G's stunning beauty could affect any movie set. The rest of the cast, highly professional and internationally famous, would be acting their heads off while Miss G was standing around without a line of dialogue, but it was apparent that every eye would be focused on her. The same interest occurred when the film reached its cinema audiences.

Like Charles Laughton, Gregory Peck also recognized Miss G's immense potential and tried to encourage her to believe in her talent and work at it. She never did. She lacked that ambition and lacked that confidence. She made her mark because she was always playing herself, her natural self.

At the start of *The Great Sinner*, everything seemed set for a very good movie, maybe a great movie. L.B. Mayer might have written the publicity blurb himself, starting with "MGM sets new standards with this magnificent historical drama."

Based upon Dostoevsky's classic novel, *The Gambler*, and with a wonderful cast, Christopher Isherwood as one of the screenwriters, and with director Robert Siodmak, who had been so successful in the film-noir treatment of *The Killers*, it should have been memorable.

What happened? Like so many movies based upon historical fact or fancy, it never came alive. It was turgid. Despite the talented cast, it did not grip the imagination. You did not believe in it. Despite the costly sets, Sydney Guileroff's wonderful hairstyles and the magnificent costumes, there was only one word for it – boring! As far as I was concerned, the only line in the film I really enjoyed was when Miss G, on her knees beside Gregory Peck, stared up at him with dewy eyes, and whispered in a tremulous voice, "You've won me at roulette. Now what are you going to do with me?"

You need strength of character to answer that.

My own small moment of drama was not quite of the same stature. Miss G and a rather noisy selection of our friends from cast and crew were crowded into our apartment for a small party. All had a lot to drink. It got very late and I got very tired, so – as was my usual habit – I slid away to bed.

Who was in my bed, grinning at me and beckoning that I should join him? Director Robert Siodmak! I screamed. He held up his hand to quiet me, putting his finger to his lips so I would quiet down and recognize the importance of his desires.

I screamed louder. Next door, they were making a lot of noise, so maybe nobody heard me. I yelled, "Out! Out!" and opened my mouth for the third piercing shriek. That convinced him. He threw back the covers, grabbed his shoes and bolted through the door. I suppose Siodmak could have passed it off as one of those casting couch incidents, "Just checking if she was right for the part."

To this day, I'm not sure if anyone had noticed what he was up to. As I've said, it was a pretty noisy party. I only told Miss G. She screamed with laughter, and said, "You should have kicked him in the ass on his way out!"

Maybe it was just a coincidence, or maybe someone knew more about Robert Taylor's romance with Miss G than Taylor thought possible. It did seem a bit odd that Mrs. Robert Taylor – Barbara Stanwyck – should be playing the lead in Miss G's next picture, *East Side, West Side*. Miss Stanwyck played the beautiful East Side hostess married to James Mason, and Miss G played the West Side floozy who was the light of his life.

Barbara Stanwyck was a beautiful woman and a talented actress with a string of successful movies behind her. The fact was that her marriage to Robert Taylor, if not on the rocks, was certainly bouncing around in rough seas. As the older and senior actress, outside her dialogue in the film, Miss Stanwyck scarcely spoke a word to Miss G and treated her with the disdain she used in her film characterization. Maybe some friend of hers had whispered something in her ear. Hollywood gossip spread around like flu germs.

Certainly in the very first opening shot of the film, the camera identified Miss G in the sexiest pose of her entire film career. She was standing silhouetted in a film booth against a lit background. She was wearing a dress that was skin-tight, and molded to every contour of her body. The camera started at the top of her head, and slowly, very slowly, moved downwards to her feet. We could see at once why James Mason's character had forgotten that he sat at an office desk and had a decent golf handicap, and why Miss Stanwyck's character was cross with him.

The scene made Miss G the definitive symbol of sexual desire. She used to say demurely, "I think my audiences have always confused my film characters with my private life."

I could have added "Hurrah!" It certainly got us places and made us many friends. If Miss Stanwyck had anything to do with it, she certainly did us a good turn.

5 ENTER THE WORLD'S RICHEST MAN AND KATHARINE HEPBURN

No big surprise, but the ubiquitous Howard Hughes popped backed into our lives around that time for another go at Miss G. From the day I met Miss G, she was always mixed up with Howard Hughes. He was one of the richest and most powerful men in the United States, and he was a serious factor in both Miss G's life and mine for the seventeen years we knew him.

To begin with, his wealth was inherited. His father, in the early years of oil exploration, had invented a new oil drill bit, the cutting edge at the end of the pipe that bores downwards through the earth. It revolutionized the industry.

Howard, however, was more interested in aviation than oil. He was an exceptional aeronautical designer and a superb pilot. His pioneering non-stop flight around the globe, not long before the Second World War started, in his own plane, with his own crew, gave him world fame. His wheeling and dealing in a variety of enterprises gave him vast government contracts.

One of the major reasons for his success was his determination never to take no for an answer. Failure to achieve an objective could not be tolerated in the Howard Hughes philosophy; and when that determination was backed by billions of dollars, he rarely failed at all. He also followed this principle in his pursuit and conquest of beautiful women – certainly with Katharine Hepburn and later Ava Gardner.

Miss G had been acquainted with him off and on for a bit and she liked him well enough, but I have to say that my first contact with this wealthy super power was not a happy one. Miss G had appointed me as the lady who answers the telephone. I screened the calls, repeating the caller's name loudly enough to give Miss G time to smile and reach for the receiver or look anguished and shake her head.

That particular morning, a sharp voice demanded, "Ava Gardner there?" In my best modulated accent I said, "Who's calling please?" In a loud and irritated accent the voice said, "Why?"

Still maintaining my ladylike accent, I said, "Because if you don't give your name, you ain't gonna know if Miss G is here or not." The phone banged down in my ear. Over the next two or three days, the phone was regularly slammed down in my ear. The caller obviously thought he might catch Miss G herself answering the phone. Eventually, Hughes, who was reputed to hate Jews and blacks, decided to come to terms with reality and grudgingly conceded my existence with a laconic, "Rene, this is Howard Hughes."

Sometimes Miss G was in and sometimes she was out. I remember the time when she came back to the apartment looking very thoughtful. She had been out to dinner with Hughes. His car had been parked outside, with Miss G in it for quite a while. I could imagine what had happened. She laid her handbag on the table, kicked off her shoes and accepted the martini.

She said, "Howard's asked me to marry him again."

"So?" I said, "What did you say this time?"

It was what Hughes said that mattered: "Ava, I know you don't love me, but maybe in time you could learn to do that."

"He sounded so sad and resigned," Miss G said. "I felt real sorry for him. But there's no way...."

We both sipped our martinis reflectively, and Miss G went on. "I said, 'Howard, maybe I will learn to love you, but I can't give you any guarantee. For the time being can't we just keep on being good friends?'"

I said, "Miss G, that is the oldest Hollywood script writer's line of all time."

Miss G sighed and said, "As if I don't know it, but how do you say 'no' politely? Rene, you know as well as I do it's great to have a guy like Howard around to smooth out life's little difficulties. You want to go somewhere in a hurry, you want to get a car to the airport, you want to talk to someone in the know, Howard arranges it. You want a plane ride to romantic places; Howard has half of TWA waiting, but getting married to him...." Miss G pulled a face and left the sentence unfinished.

I said, "If you'd listened to Bappie and she'd had any influence on you, you would have been to the altar with him long ago."

"My eldest sister just can't understand how anyone in their right mind can turn down the richest man in the world," said Miss G with her usual eloquent simplicity.

"Dead right," I said, and as Miss G looked at me suspiciously, I hurried on, "and ninety percent of the women in the world would think so too."

Miss G said, "That weekend he took me up to San Francisco and I refused his treasure trove of jewels, burned scars on Bappie's heart. She's also never forgiven me for nearly knocking his head off when I threw the bronze bell at him in Palm Springs." Miss G often recalled those times when we were in need of a laugh. The San Francisco saga had occurred in the early days of Miss G and Howard Hughes' relationship. Hughes had decided to pull the "rich man and pretty little actress" ploy—deluge her with presents and her heart's desires, and then she would fall into bed with him.

Usually he didn't have to try so hard with women. The mere idea of

Howard Hughes' patronage was enough to make most girls quake at the knees. Let's face it. Miss G was a bit dumb and trusting at the time. "How about going up to San Francisco for a glorious weekend of fun and games?" he had said. Since, so far in their relationship, Hughes had behaved like the perfect Texan gentleman, Miss G had agreed.

They went by train, first class on the Super Chef, chilled champagne and all the goodies. The best hotel in San Francisco on the top of Nob Hill, with a suite, lounge, and bedroom, and Mr. Hughes in a small bedroom, not necessarily to be used, next door. More chilled champagne waiting in the ice bucket in the suite. There was a super dinner with wine, and Hughes presented her with a glorious gold ring set with diamonds, and there was a visit to the best store in town, where Hughes left her to purchase anything she desired. But Miss G did not buy anything. There was dancing at a ritzy nightclub into the small hours, and then back to the hotel in a haze of champagne and giggles with the stage set for the moment supreme. Hughes had more surprises for her stored in a cardboard box in that small bedroom.

Miss G had surprises of a different sort. Beside the elevator door, she spotted the piles of Sunday newspapers ready for delivery and flicked out one of the comic sections. In the elevator, she began to read and continue to giggle. She was still giggling when they reached the suite, and Miss G settled in an armchair to go on reading. The pop of another bottle of iced Dom Perignon did not disturb her, and when Howard came across to give her a glass, she waved him away, saying that she had had enough.

Miss G was always convulsed with laughter when she recalled the episode. "God Almighty, Rene, can you imagine what a dumb little broad I was? Here's Howard, he's given this little moron the time of her life—luxury, jewels, champagne, dancing, a night on the town—and now he expects his little chick to fly into his arms. And what's she doing—reading the comics! What does Howard do? He blows his top. He brings his hand down and smashes the paper out of my hands. What do I do? I'm shocked and outraged. I bolt into the bedroom, lock the door, and shove a heavy chair under the door handle. I'm not talking to that brute again, ever! Now I'm stuck in this bedroom. Fortunately, the place is so full of bottles of chilled champagne that there's half a bottle still left on the dressing table. I drink that, leap into bed, pull the covers over my head and sleep.

"I'm awakened at dawn. Dawn! Can you imagine? And there's a voice at the door saying, 'It's Bappie; open up!' Where the hell has she come from? How did she get here? Howard has rung her in L.A., laid on a car to take her to the airport, laid on a special plane, and another car at San Francisco airport to speed her to the hotel. She must intervene on his behalf. He's sorry. He's full of apologies. He has all this jewelry he was going to give me as tokens of his true love. Bappie's even carrying a piece of the bloody stuff, some diamond and emerald encrusted necklace. There was a lot more like this back in Howard's bedroom. Bappie can't believe that I'm not interested. I think she would have given her left and right arms for the stuff. I send her back telling her to tell him he can stick it all where the monkey stuffs his nuts, and as he'd brought Bappie up on a private plane, he could bloody well make another one available to take me back to L.A. now!"

I often wondered about Howard Hughes. How could a man of such intelligence and courage and inventiveness, a man so worldly, put up with Miss G? The answer was simple – he was besotted with her. Maybe the fact that unlike all the other women in his life who after due courting and pursuit had surrendered, this little Tar Heel from North Carolina refused all his enticements, all his offers.

He had said, "Ava, you have the perfect body and the perfect beauty. You are flawless, and therefore you must have perfect things to complete that flawlessness." One offer was a huge new yacht. He had already owned one huge, sleek, shining vessel named the *Southern Cross*, where he had courted and captured Katharine Hepburn. He would purchase another, and he and Miss G would sail the world together. She could choose her own films, her own leading men and directors and scriptwriters. He would heap upon her furs, jewels, and wonderful places to live. Not even Robin Hood or the Sultan of Brunei could have offered more.

Miss G was not appreciative. She was inclined to add, "Rene, I don't think he cared if I had perfect brains or a scrap of intelligence, or the ability to argue with him. Who wants to be flawless? A plaster saint? Hell, you miss all the fun."

There were other things about Howard Hughes that Miss G found hard to tolerate, including his proprietary claims. Once Hughes had paid the price, he was inclined to think he had dominant rights. After Mickey Rooney and Miss G got divorced after just over a year of fulminating marriage, there was a short cooling period, and then they renewed their friendship. They were both sexy youngsters full of springtime urges, and on several occasions an invitation to dinner culminated in a night in bed. Miss G found this great fun and who did it offend? They had been married, hadn't they?

It sure offended Howard Hughes, however. He had spies who reported to him. They related their suspicions. After all, Miss G was, well almost, his fiancée, and he had his rights.

Between pictures, Miss G had been taking a short holiday with Bappie and her boyfriend, Charlie Guest, an employee of Howard Hughes, in a rented house in Palm Springs. Hughes relayed a message to Charlie from his high-level meeting with Air Force brass in Washington, saying he was arriving in Palm Springs by aircraft that night and he would like Miss G to meet him at the airport.

Miss G was never keen on that sort of arrangement. She said no and went to bed early. She was awakened as Hughes strode into her bedroom. She said, "As soon as I woke and saw him there with that cross look on his face, I knew, and he knew, that he had made a fool of himself. He had expected to find his flawless babe in bed with her ex-husband! I couldn't help smiling, and that made him even more furious. I hate being spied on like that, so I said ever so sweetly. 'Why, Howard, fancy seeing you. If you just wait downstairs, I'll slip into a robe and come down.'"

Miss G could be a real nasty female when she wanted to. She thought she had seen the last of him after the San Francisco fiasco, and now he was playing this sort of game with her. Of course, one of the things you don't do is make a laughing stock out of Howard Hughes. He was waiting for her in the bar, angry because she hadn't been considerate enough to come out to the airfield. It was only a field in Palm Springs in those days, and at night cars would line up in the grass and turn on their headlights to light it up for him to land. Miss G shrugged, and the quarrel started. He hit her hard across the face, giving her a black eye.

Bappie made her opinion quite clear to me and anybody else who cared to listen. Why didn't that "stupid kid sister of mine," a favorite line of hers, grab Howard Hughes with both hands and start spending his money? Bappie was always a realist. If only that stupid kid sister realized what Hughes could do for her film career to start with. Didn't she know that he owned RKO, that as a powerful producer, he had already made two smash hits, *Hell's Angels*, the movie about the fighter pilots of the First World War? What about the western, *The Outlaw*, starring Jane Russell? She's heard he'd even designed the bra that contained Jane's beautiful frontage. Why couldn't that silly young sister of hers wake up?

Anyone wishing to know more about Howard Hughes' specific peculiarities should read Katharine Hepburn's entrancing autobiography, *Me*, which to me was an eye-opener. Both Miss G and I were aware that Howard Hughes had known Hepburn long before our time, in the thirties, but we had no idea of the extent of her involvement with Hughes. In particular, we certainly had not known about one aspect of his personality—his morphine addiction—although we were very close when that aspect became part of his life.

Katharine Hepburn arrived in Hollywood in 1932. Miss G was ten years old at the time, so their respective romances with Hughes were far apart. Katharine first met Hughes on a golf course. He landed his plane not much more than a short nine iron shot from where she was playing. She was not impressed. She was playing with Cary Grant at the time, and Grant was a close friend of Hughes. An exception was made, and he was invited to dinner. Katharine disliked this tall, handsome and gangly Texan. She refused to meet his gaze. Hughes was stricken. He couldn't take his eyes off Hepburn, and pursuit was immediate.

At that time, Hepburn was a new young star rising to fame in American theater. She went on tours across the nation. She played in Boston. Surprise. Hughes happened to be in Boston, and why didn't they have dinner together? Hepburn continued her tours – Detroit, Cleveland, Chicago—and in every city Hughes was ensconced in a suite on the same floor as hers.

Hepburn was at first only amused, then intrigued, and finally fascinated by this extremely original and talented male. She began to like him. There were more dinners and flowers. He taught her to fly. They played very good golf together. They landed his seaplane on sunlit seas and swam off the wings. They had fun and champagne and laughter on his super white yacht, *The Southern Cross*. They were in love!

Although they became lovers, they did not choose to marry. That did not seem necessary to endorse their mutual happiness. They did share Hughes'

California house which backed onto the acres of the Wilshire Country Club, so whenever they felt the urge they could slip through the hedge and hit balls. Hepburn explained that through those years they both fell madly in love but couldn't really understand why. And why she decided to go back east to continue her career while Hughes stayed in the west, they couldn't really understand that either. It happened, and they drifted apart.

In the thirties, Hughes had founded TWA and Hughes Aircraft Company, and his exploits as a pilot were well known and considered at times bizarre. Miss G knew that in the past he had survived two serious crashes. In wartime Hughes Aircraft played an important role, and Miss G, from Howard's conversations, learned he would personally test fly his specialist fighter planes.

I was bemused by this information. "He test flies his own planes?"

"Sure does," Miss G said.

"With all that dough, he can't afford a fleet of test pilots?"

"Rene," said Miss G reprovingly, "you've got to understand Howard Hughes. He designs and builds the plane. It's his baby. He is not trusting his baby to anyone else. First time it climbs into the skies, Howard is at the controls."

Then one day that chilling phone call arrived. Howard Hughes had crashed and was not expected to live. Glen Odekirk, Howard's private pilot, whom we both knew well, spelled it out for us. At first the doctors gave him little chance. Then they raised the odds to fifty-fifty, but it was going to be a close call. It was days before Miss G was allowed in to see him. She reported back at martini time.

"He's still half dead, but the half of him that's still alive is being regularly injected with morphine, and that makes him bright, and if not logical, cheerful. Miss G explained the crash: "The way he tells it, he got the plane off the ground like a swallow rising, and was soon doing four hundred miles an hour. Everything was okay, except that apparently Howard could only steer the plane to the right. Now Rene, if you want to land an aircraft, you've either got to be able to go straight or turn to the left!"

I could see that Miss G was about as good an aeronautical engineer as I was. "Sure thing," I said, "And I guess Mr. Hughes didn't have a lot of time to experiment?"

"Seconds," said Miss G. "If you're flying over L.A. at four hundred miles an hour, and you can only turn right, and you've got to find a place to land...."

She paused for breath, and I ended the sentence for her, "You'd better reach for your prayer book."

Miss G nodded but then continued, "Then out of the corner of his eye, Howard spotted the Los Angeles Country Club golf course."

"Wide fairways, soft bunkers to land in?"

"Rene," said Miss G severely, "he's not a golf ball. He managed to get his landing gear down but it was too late. There was a suburb down below him – rows of houses. He bounced off the roof of one house, hit a telephone pole that sliced off a wing, and then crash! He cascaded into Number 808 Whittier Drive. The plane exploded and caught fire, and he didn't have time to feel grateful that nobody was at home."

Miss G paused for breath. I said incredulously, "He survived all that?"

"The Marines rushed to his rescue," said Miss G.

"Miss G," I protested, "This can't be funny."

Miss G said soothingly, "Rene, we can laugh about it now because Howard is sitting up in bed making jokes, but it's absolutely true. Not a company of Marines, but just one of them, Sergeant William Lloyd, was walking along Wittier Drive when the plane screamed over his head, smashed into the house, and caught fire. In went the Marine Sergeant and by the grace of God managed to haul him out. Of course, by this time everybody in Whittier Drive was ringing for police, fire brigade and ambulances which arrived shortly. Trust Howard to choose a rather posh neighborhood."

"How much was left of him?" I asked.

Miss G said, "All his ribs were broken. One had pierced a lung which was full of blood. He had broken bones all over his body, serious head injuries, and serious burns. The doctors said that it was only his fantastic will to live that saved him. That and all the morphine they pumped into him and are still pumping into him, because he can't move a muscle without pain."

Later, we learned that it was Glen Odekirk who did something immensely ingenious to alleviate that pain. He raced to Hughes Aircraft, gathered some of the top technicians together, and within twenty four hours they had put together a special bed consisting of dozens and dozens of soft interlocking pads. When the body moved, the bed moved with it.

Later we also learned that although the doctors had given instructions that morphine injections were to be eased off, Howard Hughes with his immense authority had grown to appreciate the peace it brought and with a little judicious pressure in the right quarters managed to keep the injections going.

It was weeks later when Miss G reported, "Oh, yes, Howard told me the story. The doctors noticed his dilated eyeballs and said, 'That's it. Morphine stops now!' He's totally off it and back to normal."

Both Miss G and I believed that version forever afterwards until Hepburn wrote her autobiography. She had proof. Her doctor was also Hughes' doctor, and he knew that Howard had not discontinued the drug and was indeed a morphine addict. Almost fifty years after this event, I was shocked at this revelation, because Hughes figured very largely in our lives for many years after that. Miss G and I remained blissfully ignorant of what was happening. Only now, looking back and thinking of those newspaper pictures of Howard Hughes just before his death—hidden away for decades, a haggard skeleton of a man with shaggy white hair, staring eyes, hollow cheeks, finger nails like talons— this knowledge makes sense of the strange events that occurred in the years ahead between Miss G, Howard Hughes, and me.

6 TO FALL IN LOVE WITH FRANK SINATRA

The locality of our Red Skelton apartment block was the happy working ground of a bunch of young writers, actors, songwriters and assorted hopefuls, all trying to make the grade. That was why we were present at the birth of a song that likely will live forever. Mel Torme and Bob Wells, two young songwriters on their way up, arrived at our apartment. They strummed their guitars and sang and said, "Well? What do you think?"

Miss G laughed and repeated, "'Chestnuts roasting on open fire. Jack Frost nipping at your nose....' Great lines!"

I said, "I like it."

Miss G thought we were the greatest at picking the best songs, and most girls loved those dreamy dance tunes. I don't think the boys really needed our judgment, but Miss G was an actress, and she knew people like Artie Shaw, so maybe she had leverage. And we were buddies with Mel and Bob.

"Sing it again," said Miss G. "Give us an encore." They did. By the time we got to the closing bars, we'd picked up the melody, and the harmonizing was superb.

"Great!" we said. "Can't miss!" We really believed what we said.

"Got to get it off the ground though," Mel said. "Got to get it plugged on the radio by a great singer. Any ideas?"

"Bing Crosby." I suggested.

Mel dismissed him: "Too big, too busy, too pricey."

Miss G pointed across at the Sunset Towers. "Frank Sinatra lives there," she said. "Axel Stordahl and Sammy Cahn and all the songwriters live there. Frank and his buddies are always shouting across invitations to join them for a beer."

Mel pursed his lips. He was still not impressed. But Miss G knew her man. "Come on now," she said. "You've got ideas of your own?"

Mel ran his fingers across his guitar strings. "We were thinking of trying this guy who's up and coming on the radio these days. Name's Nat King Cole."

"He's black," I said.

Mel responded, "Sure he's black, and he has a great voice and he's going to be top of the heap."

Well, everyone knows what followed that discussion. "The Christmas Song," written by Mel Torme and Robert Wells and first recorded by Nat King Cole, is still heard and sung around the world. Mel got some money from it and rose to great fame as a singer as well as a songwriter. And though he was never directly involved with the song, Miss G got Frank Sinatra.

At this moment in history, Miss G—after two marriages and love affairs with Howard Duff, Fred MacMurray and Robert Taylor, and with Howard Hughes hovering in the background believing he had proprietary rights even though he did not have bedroom privileges—was lonely. She wanted a man she could marry. She had hopes about Robert Taylor, but it soon became clear that he was the usual devious married man playing around in secret, inevitably sheltered from responsibility behind a seemingly virtuous marriage.

Miss G had met Frank Sinatra before his shouted invitations across from Sunset Towers had begun. During her year of marriage to Mickey Rooney, they were in a nightclub when Frank arrived and moved across to their table for Mickey to introduce his new bride. Frank grinned down at her and made his smart remark. "If Mickey hadn't met you first, I would have married you myself."

Now living next door to each other, it was certain they would meet. Only natural that Miss G would say to me, "We bumped into each other at the entrance to Sunset Towers. Frank wants to take me to dinner."

"Great, when?" I asked.

"Tonight. I know he's still married to Nancy, but that's broken up a long time ago," she said.

"He's still dating Lana." I said.

"Who isn't?" she replied.

She came home very late. As usual, she woke for her coffee, fresh as a springtime daffodil. Her eyes were mischievous as she smiled across the top of the coffee cup. "Rene, nothing happened, and I bet you're disappointed," she said, and laughed at my expression.

"No, I am not disappointed," I said self-righteously. "Was the dinner any good?"

"We had a lot to drink," said Miss G.

"Figures," I said.

I learned that after dinner, they had gone to a shooting gallery and spent their time shooting pellets at dummy animals. Then he took her back to some apartment, not the one in the Sunset Towers. She never did remember where it was, but I guess Frank was expert in that sort of thing.

"Something was wrong with the whole situation," said Miss G. "We'd had a lot to drink and we kissed and clutched. Then I thought, this is not good and I'm leaving. If I'd taken any clothes off, I put them on again and left."

"Didn't Frank yell?" I asked.

"He didn't have time to," said Miss G. "I was out of the door, down the elevator and into my car and on my way home before he knew what hit him.

Thank God, we had taken my car."

That certainly wasn't the end of the story. They'd lit the fuse, and although it was smoldering for a long time there was no doubt in my mind that the rocket would fire.

The stormy years that followed, from 1949 to 1953, reinforced the old saying about the course of true love never running smoothly. Those words were never more clearly illustrated than in the love affair, marriage and divorce between Francis Albert Sinatra and Ava Lavinia Gardner.

Both Miss G and Sinatra loved Palm Springs. Frank, in his affluent years had bought a house out there. It wasn't all that fancy, but Frank loved it and was often in residence. Miss G also adored the clean, desert atmosphere and the high circling mountains. Occasionally she rented a house there too.

Once when she was there with Bappie, Miss G met Sinatra, and he took her home. One story constructed by an enterprising lady biographer was totally untrue. The story alleged the two were driving around shooting out street lights. It also alleged they slightly wounded a passerby with a stray bullet and that both Miss G and Sinatra were arrested and held in the sheriff's office. Sinatra contacted his manager in Hollywood, who rushed up with thousands of dollars to cover up the story. The entire story was total invention!

Sinatra and Miss G grew accustomed to that sort of manufactured rubbish. They were prime targets. Somewhere in the human psyche, envy is endemic. No one grieved for them. Rubbishing and sneering at all the misfortunes of the famous is a favorite media pastime.

Frank Sinatra's history stems from the time in the middle thirties when he came to the public's attention on the Major Bowes weekly radio amateur talent show. He sang with three other guys, and they were known as The Hoboken Four. Then Sinatra moved on in the forties to be featured vocalist with two of the great American band leaders – Harry James and Tommy Dorsey. By the end of the Second World War, his songs were selling a million copies a year and he was the darling of Columbia Records.

In 1946, MGM was turning out one big feature film a week. Sinatra signed a five-year contract allowing him numerous spin-off rights that guaranteed him more than a quarter million dollars a year. He was one of the hottest properties in the movie and radio business at the time.

As a married man, his success had not been so spectacular. In 1939, he had married Nancy Barbato, a local Hoboken girl, and together they produced a son and two daughters. By October 1946, he had walked out on Nancy, and a divorce seemed inevitable.

For the next three years, a sort of uneasy peace existed between him and his family. In Hollywood, Nancy turned a blind eye to movie magazine gossip that Frank was spending time in bed with Lana Turner and Marilyn Maxwell. Even when Miss G entered the scene, long after the marriage was nothing more than a hollow sham, Nancy still clung to the illusion that with public opinion, marshaled by a self-righteous press on her side and the backing of the Catholic Church, her husband would always come home. Nancy had good reason for holding on to that opinion.

Even in those early months of meetings between Miss G and Sinatra, Miss G was aware that his relationship with Lana Turner had been long, erotic and close to ending with wedding bells. In those first days, Miss G knew this and was cautious.

"I like Lana," Miss G said. "She's a good friend of mine. If Frank's going to leave his wife and marry Lana – great!"

Great meant she would accept the situation and probably have her heart broken in the same way Artie Shaw had done. Miss G kept her scars very private. Then she met Lana in the ladies room at a party and Lana told her the story of what had happened, thereby releasing Miss G from all sense of responsibility to her friend.

As Miss G put it, "Lana just couldn't believe it. Here she had been head over heels in love with Frank and thought that he was going to marry her. She thought that at last she had found someone really worthwhile. She thought that Frank felt the same way. One morning, she woke up and there was the headline on the front page of the Los Angeles Times proclaiming that he had gone home to Nancy!"

Nancy Sinatra had won that one. Now, she no doubt thought that Frank would soon tire of his infatuation for that wicked woman, Ava Gardner. She was a wicked, scarlet woman. Everyone could see that from her films.

Nancy was wrong. Sinatra was obsessed, enchanted and mesmerized by Miss G. Not only that, he was terrified by the thought that she might leave him. That was proven over and over again during the next two months as the drama intensified.

After Miss G finished *One Touch of Venus*, her financial situation began to improve considerably. She had a new agent, Charles Feldman, who pressed MGM with gentle firmness that they had a star on their hands with only two more years of her contract left. If Louis B. Mayer didn't want to lose this considerable asset, he'd better raise the ante pretty quickly.

Miss G moved from $750 to $1,000 a week. Now I was making $100 a week. I had a place to live and general outings with Miss G. When Miss G had money, she scarcely bothered to bank it.

"It's there to spend, isn't it?" she said. Clothes, drinks and travel became her curriculum vitae. She also bought a new car, a Cadillac convertible, favored by all the stars. Sinatra had one. It would do 110 miles an hour, and Miss G favored that speed. God help us!

She also decided that our place was a bit small, so she bought a house up in the hills in Nichols Canyon. By that time we had gone from the Red Skelton apartment to another apartment in Westwood. Some of the Westwood residents saw me going in the front door wearing shorts (instead of a maid's uniform) and raised hell, so Miss G decided it best to move out after only a few months. We lived briefly on Olympic Boulevard before moving to the small house in Nichols Canyon. Let me emphasize "small," not posh—no swimming pool, no big garden, just three bedrooms. It came in very handy when Frank and Miss G decided to cohabitate. It was very snug. In between the rows, they were very happy.

To a certain degree, they could keep their relationship secret. That was important because the whole climate surrounding the movie, radio, recording and the fledgling television industries demanded purity. No scandals, no hopping into bed with chorus girls, no homosexuality, just decency, happy endings, villains getting the chop and Mom's apple pie stretched as far as Louis B. Mayer's eye could see.

Sinatra, urged on by a militant Miss G, demanded that Nancy give him a divorce, which she refused to do. This, of course, was the fuel that ignited several incidents. The first was the Shamrock Hotel disaster in January of 1950. The Shamrock Hotel had just been built by a millionaire in Houston, Texas. It was opening with fireworks, champagne and Sinatra singing in the night club. A gig that was to last a week.

It was said that a few days before he was due to appear, George Evans, who had been his agent, mentor and a greatly needed father figure, had dropped dead of a heart attack. In Frank's depressed condition, it was a bitter blow. Even though George and Frank had been quarreling violently—George insisting that Frank abandon Miss G and behave like a good husband and father by returning to his wife and children, an action that Frank adamantly refused to take—Frank was nevertheless devastated by his death. By phone he made this clear to Miss G, and she came up with a big, bright idea.

"Rene, why don't I fly down to Houston and surprise Frank and cheer him up?"

My gentle cough signified disapproval. I knew that only bad publicity would follow such an action. We were tucked away hiding in the trees high in Nichols Canyon. Not a single sightseeing coach loaded with eager tourists, the guide pointing out the houses of the famous stars, passed our door. Once the press caught onto the notion that Ava Gardner and Frank Sinatra were live-in friends, the coaches would be passing every twenty minutes.

I had no time to argue. Miss G was already on the phone to Dick Jones seeking support for her rescue flight. Dick was a friend, an excellent pianist, and a nice guy who composed and conducted for Frank. He reinforced what I thought. He said, "Ava, I don't think that is a wise thing for you to do."

"Of course it is, Dick. We will just be two old friends wishing him luck."

Off Dick and Ava flew to Houston, where, with compulsive idiocy, considering they were trying to duck the press circuit, Miss G booked them at the Shamrock where Frank was already in residence. Frank greeted with unrestrained delight, never giving a thought to the fact that every chambermaid in the hotel was now busy ringing up the *Houston Post* with a gossip tip that Frank and Miss G were now sharing a bedroom.

"I was a dumb schmuck," Miss G admitted sadly on her return. "Frank had been told about this great Italian restaurant and off we went to dinner, just the two of us. There we were just tangling with the spaghetti, when this photographer slides up and points his lens. Rene, you know Frank's explosive fuse is about a hair's breadth wide, and he explodes as if the guy had pushed an 88-millimeter cannon into his ear. He stands up, throws his napkin down into his spaghetti and starts out to tear the photographer limb from limb. Up rushes the manager with nine waiters to help. They had all been quite happy for the good publicity of a visit from Frank Sinatra and Ava Gardner. With the prospect of the place being torn apart, they were very unhappy. Everything got sorted out, and we left without finishing our spaghetti."

She looked at me with sad eyes. "You've seen the papers?"

This dialogue took place naturally a couple of days after her return. By that time, the newspapers from every corner of the known world were reveling in the sensational new love scandal. Frank Sinatra and Ava Gardner were hidden away in a love nest with poor little wife weeping at home.

She got a lot of very nasty letters. Most of them were unsigned. In one respect, the scandal rebounded in her favor. Nancy hired a lawyer and in spectacular manner announced that she had locked Frank out, which was really a bit like locking the cage after the songbird had flown. She added that she had been humiliated by the newspaper reports of Frank's infidelity and would be divorcing him for the sake of the children.

Nancy did not reveal one important bit of news about the divorce—how soon? Three months later, that question had still not been answered. Vague announcements were still leaking out suggesting that the attorneys were working on it.

7 SPAIN AND THE FLYING DUTCHMAN

Pandora and the Flying Dutchman was the brainchild of Albert Lewin, one of MGM's veteran and most respected producers. Miss G was penciled in to play Pandora.

One could say this movie, followed by *Showboat*, *Snows of Kilimanjaro*, and *Mogambo*, established Miss G firmly in the upper echelons of the film star galaxy. Even mediocre movies like *Lone Star*, *Ride Vaquero,* and *Band Wagon* all had her working opposite famous leading men such as Clark Gable, Robert Taylor, and Fred Astaire and, therefore, did her reputation no harm at all. The fact that most of them showed her as the pretty floozy, or good-time girl, did her no harm either. At least, in the minds of the movie public it didn't. Beautiful, naughty ladies are a real box-office attraction.

The costs of filming in Spain, where *Pandora and the Flying Dutchman* was to be made, were about a hundred percent cheaper than in any other country in the world. The Costa Brava, which stretches from the border of southern France to within fifty miles of Barcelona, was chosen as the location. The scenery was spectacular—high green mountains looking across wooded hills of pine and cork trees to a coastline and golden beaches. Tiny, historic towns and a blue, unpolluted Mediterranean were all bathed in brilliant sunshine, making the territory a holiday paradise. The package tour industry was soon to discover its beauty.

Bappie decided it was her turn to take a holiday as chaperone to her "dumb kid sister." Off they went to join James Mason and other talented British actors.

I stayed at home looking after Frank. He was finishing his last film for MGM, *Meet Danny Wilson*. Co-starring with him was Shelley Winters. Frank didn't like the picture, and Shelley didn't like it either. Shelley also didn't like Frank, and Frank didn't like Shelley. The movie was based upon a scenario so similar to the real life story of Frank Sinatra that the critics didn't like it either. As Shelley herself observed, as an experience it was best forgotten. As soon as it was finished, Frank set off to take a holiday with Miss G, who was now busy casting her spells amongst the poor mortals around Tossa de Mar, an exquisite little town near the beach in a fabled setting. True, Pandora was a legendary Greek goddess. Mind you, although the scenario was fascinating and scarcely believable, the story behind the cameras was equally fascinating and totally believable. It was, however, a bit complicated.

Even before she caught the plane, Miss G and I had done our homework because we had never heard of Pandora and her magic box. Zeus, the legendary god whom the Romans named Jupiter, was worshipped as the Supreme Being – "in charge of all mortal things that live and move on earth." Zeus was angry. One of his subordinates, Prometheus, had stolen fire and passed it down for use by those common creatures on Planet Earth. Something had to be done. They had to be taught a lesson. He commanded power. He ordered Hephaestus, the god who ran the workshop in that legendary homeland up in the clouds, to design a beautiful young female to descend to earth and give a hard time to those cheating mortals, especially those guys who lived around the Greek Islands.

He designed a beautiful girl with a glorious voice and the ability to entice, flatter and seduce the opposite sex. She was also endowed with a box, which held all the evils or blessings known to mankind since the world began. Of course, being female and nosy, Pandora opened the box to see what was inside, whereupon all the virtues and evils escaped, flying out like a cloud of smoke. As the story goes, they still torment or comfort us today. This was quite a part for Miss G to handle, but with voice-over narration explaining all the difficult bits, she got along.

Unfortunately, Albert had not been satisfied with simply using the Greek legends. He had to have a male lead to match Pandora, so he introduced an old ship-faring story, the legend of the Flying Dutchman, with James Mason playing the role. The captain of The Flying Dutchman had returned home from a long voyage to find his wife in the arms of a lover. In a mad rage, he killed her. To expiate his crime, he was sentenced to sail the oceans of the world forever. Any unlucky sailor sighting the phantom ship was doomed and probably his ship and shipmates with him. The only hope of redemption given him was that if he could find in these endless journeys a woman who could love him enough to die for him. Then he could rest in a quiet Christian grave. Lo and behold there was our Pandora ready for that very purpose before she slipped back up to tell Papa Zeus what a lot of fun she had.

This was rather a large canvas to cover in a film running around two and a half hours. I could imagine Mr. Louis B. Mayer glancing through the scenario, sighing and saying, "Well Albert, do your best."

To give Pandora the chance to get up to her naughty tricks, a row of suitable young men had to be featured so that she could knock them off, which she did very plausibly. First, there is Nigel Patrick, an unfortunate racing driver; then playboy Marius Goring, who commits suicide because she won't marry him; then along comes the dramatic bullfighter Mario Cabre, who also falls in love with her while she in turn with a slight of hand gets him impaled on a bull's horns.

Finally, there is the Flying Dutchman who does not arrive on his great, white-winged sailing ship but on a super yacht which he anchors at Costa Brava. Pandora swims out to it, and romance blossoms.

It is really very difficult to think of a decent finale for a film of this sort, but Albert Lewin worked one out. After the usual plots and counter plots, an enormous storm breaks loose with flashes of lightning matching the volume of sound from a symphony orchestra. The yacht turns turtle, and the two lovers disappear under the waves. I think James Mason summed it up when he said many years later, "The only good things I can remember about the film are the wonderful photography of Jack Cardiff and the great natural beauty of Ava Gardner."

Miss G adored everything about that journey—the enchanted, unspoiled coastline, the endless wine and booze, the age-old flamenco dancing with feet stamping and heels banging, voices echoing in raucous guitar-inspired melodies, late nights in the dark and in smoky taverns. She had never dreamed such places existed, and it opened a wonderful new playground for her.

She also enjoyed her role in the film. Pandora had to cloak her goddess stature under the disguise of an ordinary mortal in order to succeed in her dirty work of teaching males a lesson. She became Pandora Reynolds, a nightclub singer. She even got to sing (with no one else's voice dubbed over, for a change) a soapy love song entitled, "How Am I To Know?"

She also met for the very first time a bullfighter. Admittedly, an ex-bullfighter, but nevertheless handsome, dramatic and after one look at Miss G determined to die for her, not only in the film, but in real life if need be. He was also a poet. Holy Moses, what more could she ask for – a handsome, poetical bullfighter.

Of course, he did not speak much English, and Miss G did not understand much Spanish poetry, though love does not bother about such elementary differences. Miss G threw herself into the gaiety of Spanish holiday life with the abandon of a high diver who has forgotten there is no water in the pool.

Foolishly, after one long night with a lot of champagne and red wine and heavy foot stamping and heavier breathing, she woke up the next morning to find that Mario Cabre had been her bedfellow for the night. There she was, totally and obsessively in love with Francis Albert Sinatra, in bed with another man, and plainly "it" had occurred. One of those evils she had released from her box must have gotten its targets mixed up.

Frank was coming across after his adventures in *Meet Danny Wilson* and would be arriving in a week or so. "Rene," she confessed in one of our subterranean-sounding telephone calls from six thousand miles away, "what the hell am I going to do now?"

"Miss G," I screamed so she would hear, "you say, 'Mario...who? Never heard of him.' And when they say, 'You know the one who's in the film with you,' you say, 'Oh, him.' And excuse yourself as if it's martini time." I never did get her reaction to that piece of Pandora double-talk since the phone connection was unintelligible.

Mario, his great love now consummated, couldn't talk about anything else. Being a Spanish gentleman, he did not actually say that the deed had been done, but he was pretty explicit that Signora Ava reciprocated his affections. He was now pouring out poetry to his beloved with speed. Lots of reporters were eager to listen, especially the ones who spoke Spanish. What a good story: beautiful, sexy Ava Gardner falls for handsome Spanish bullfighter.

By now, Miss G's common sense had shown her Mario was far more concerned with his own macho image and in the personal publicity that he adored. He appeared to think he had scored similar to the soccer player whose goal wins the World Cup. Of course, he knew all about the American crooner Frank Sinatra. If Mr. Sinatra thought he could win back Mario's beloved—a mere singer confronting a gallant (albeit retired) bullfighter—then it should be a duel to the death. The European press thought this was a great idea. An old-fashioned confrontation with Miss G standing on the sidelines, one hand clutched to her breast like a Victorian heroine.

However, there was no hope of seeing these two gladiators in the bullring. Arriving in London on his way to Spain, Frank's reaction to the press was, "Never heard of the guy." As Frank was noted for taking a swing at people who offended him, he had to be believed.

The thought that Mario might skewer Frank on a bullfighter's sword did worry Miss G considerably. If Albert could get a story like *Pandora and the Flying Dutchman* onto the screen and get away with it he must be able to solve such a simple dilemma. And Albert did. He calmed her down.

"How long was Frank going to spend on the Costa Brava?" he asked.

"No more than three or four days," Miss G told him. He had to speed back to London to appear in the Royal Command performances at the Palladium Theatre.

"No problem," said Albert. There was lots of location work that needed Mario's presence, so he could be safely confined in front of a camera lens. Mario enjoyed nothing more, remaining a safe distance from Tossa de Mar.

Frank arrived, possibly a little more perturbed than he had been in London because of the persistent rumors, but Miss G, with a three-day holiday granted by Albert, took Frank away to a secluded hide-away where they enjoyed a blissful time together. They made arrangements for another romantic interlude in London while Miss G was doing interiors for *Pandora* and Frank was singing at the Palladium. It was then that Miss G received a special gift, a Welsh Corgi, which she named Rags.

Much later Frank, just as suspicious as Miss G, tried to wheedle out of her if there had been any truth in those rumors about Mario. At first she managed to duck the question, but Frank with the natural cunning of the curious and persistent male, and using the old ploy, "Gee honey, it's long ago now. Who cares? We all make little mistakes when we've had a few drinks," pried it out of her.

I said, "You should have kept that revelation in that Pandora's box of yours. Every woman needs one."

Miss G answered sadly, "Dead right. You know, Rene honey, he never forgave me – ever!"

8 SHIPWRECKED ON LAKE TAHOE – JAILED IN CARSON CITY

I had just finished cleaning up in the kitchen and returned to the living room to have a go at cleaning, only to find Miss G ending a conversation on the telephone. She was saying, "Yes, darling. I'll drive like hell. Yes, darling, I know I drive like hell normally, but this time I'll drive like hell cautiously."

I often thought it was the Irish half of Miss G that made her frame statements like that. She put down the receiver and looked up at me. "That was Frank," she explained, as if I didn't know. "He's speeding things up."

"You're driving?" I asked with a touch of alarm.

Miss G pursed her lips and blew a ladylike raspberry. "No, Rene, honey, the main thing, the divorce."

As events now dictated, the divorce was going to be a long, drawn-out affair which was not going to help the tempers of Frank and Miss G. And I anticipated storms ahead. Frank had decided to get his own divorce in Reno, Nevada. He needed six weeks' residence, and then he could file papers. He had already managed to get two singing engagements there at the Riverside Inn in Reno and the Desert Inn in Las Vegas.

He had phoned to say he had rented a house on the hillside above Lake Tahoe and the sooner we got there the better. I thought, Rene, fasten your parachute harness.

In the early fifties America was not dissected by wide interstate highways. The road up to Lake Tahoe and Reno pushed over high mountains and was fringed with forests and precipitous drops on one side. It was about a nine hour drive. In her Cadillac convertible, screeching around bends with gravel flying like buckshot and getting up to ninety miles per hour on the straight bits, it appeared we might do the trip in an hour and a half. Rags sat in my lap. He was probably thinking he needed a parachute harness too.

"Miss G," I said after the first hour, "if you keep going at this rate, we shall arrive dead."

"Can't waste time," said Miss G, ignoring me. "And besides, there is nothing on the road."

We sped closer to Carson City, which was close to our destination, and I began to have hope that we might arrive only half dead from fright. Then, as it grew darker, a deer jumped out from the trees. We hit something. I think it was a rock or a branch, but not the deer. The windshield shattered, and Rags and I were covered in crystal fragments. Rags looked up at me with sad eyes as I brushed him clean. Miss G, afraid that she had hit the deer, leapt out of the car and ran to look up the mountainside. She came back saying, "He's okay. He's going up the mountainside like a rocket."

"We're not." I said. I had not inspected the damage. We had hit a rock, and the offside wheel looked as if it might never function again. Miss G made several attempts to provoke movement. "I think we've bent something serious," she admitted, adding, "I think it's time for a drink." I uncorked the bottle of brandy we always carried for emergencies – this was definitely an emergency.

I then made the original statement, "This must be a main road from somewhere to somewhere, so a car must come along sometime." Two hours later it did, and we squeezed in. They gave us a lift to Carson City where we rang the house at Lake Tahoe. Frank's companion and gofer Hank Sanicola came to pick us up and to arrange with a garage to rescue, repair and return our car.

At the house, Hank stared at me with wide eyes and an idiot grin on his face. "Why, Rene, what's up? You've gone WHITE!" Hank laughed his head off. I said primly, "Mr. Sanicola, you should try driving with Miss G through the mountains when she's in a hurry."

Hank went on laughing. He had been in our lives since we first met Frank. Hank and I spent a lot of time trying to anticipate the occurring permutations of the volcanic eruptions between Frank and Miss G. That way, we could get a little sleep at night. An angry voice from upstairs would send our eyebrows up. The sound of a door slammed or a smashing of crockery would have us on our feet ready for action. I learned about Hank from Miss G. Hank was a nice guy with a nice wife and two kids.

"Frank was in his teens and living in Hoboken," said Miss G, explaining the circumstances of how Frank and Hank met. "Dying to sing; not in the bath, but on the stage, on the radio, on the street, if necessary, but especially with a big band. That was his main ambition."

Frank couldn't read music, and he couldn't play the piano, so in order to learn a song he'd go into a shop where they sold sheet music. Hank was the piano player there. He was hired by the shop to play for the customers who bought the sheet music. Frank got to know Hank as a buddy, and he'd go into the shop to learn all the popular new melodies as Hank played them on the piano.

When Frank started to rise to stardom, he took Hank with him and gave him an assortment of jobs. Hank could more or less pick his own titles – piano player, gofer, manager, etc. Hank was Italian. He was a big, easy-going guy who laughed easily and loved Frank even though at times Frank didn't treat him all that well. Hank and I were co-conspirators on many occasions when the fur was flying. He was the helmsman, in fact, on a never-to-be-forgotten shipwreck episode.

Lake Tahoe must be one of the most beautiful lakes in the world, sitting as it does in a bowl in the Sierra Madre Mountains. Its colors are transparent green, deep amber and sapphire blue, and it is so deep that locals reckon it has no bottom. Indian legend says the coffins of their ancestors lie down in its depths – Gee!

On this particular fine day, Miss G, Frank, Hank and I were going to have a picnic on the far side of the lake in a splendid launch that Frank had hired. The picnic consisted mainly of two or three cases of French champagne which would help us along with our sea shanties. Hank was appointed helmsman. My job, as able sea woman, was to prevent Rags from falling overboard and to assist Miss G with the champagne – a seagoing duty mainly consisting of drinking it.

We were cruising along the pretty shore when the row between Miss G and Frank started. First, there were a few side remarks, then bickering, and then an eruption into a full-scale shouting match. Thanks be to God, they never hit each other—ever—but the verbal cannon balls were of battle intensity. Even though Miss G's language would have been admired by the foulest mouthed bosun in the U.S. clipper fleet, she was quite happy and serene hurling filthy remarks at Frank, who was getting very angry.

Hank looked at me and tossed back what was left of his champagne and raised his eyes to heaven, held his glass out for a refill when there was a bang—crash. The enemy hadn't opened fire, but we had run aground onto a bit of cliff sticking out into the lake. Water poured through a big hole in the bottom of the boat. We were sinking. Frank was in the bow end of the boat and not really a Johnny Weissmuller type and certainly no swimmer. He leapt ashore first. Rags, a real coward at heart, hopped overboard and raced away along the shoreline as if he were competing in the greyhound derby. As deckhand, I felt it my duty to race after him. As Hank told me later, we had no distress rockets to fire. There was only one realistic thing to do. We did it. We abandoned ship. We trudged along in opposite directions to find a telephone and summon help.

Miss G, sloshed to the eyebrows, decided to take over the captaincy of the ship. As she was a superb swimmer, she decided to stay with the sinking ship to the very end. On shore, Frank was growing frantic yelling that if she didn't get off the ship, she'd drown. Miss G, who had spotted a more than adequate supply of toilet paper rolls in the lavatory retaliated by throwing them at him. When her ammunition ran out, she decided to gather up a couple of bottles of champagne, go ashore and surrender to the enemy. When we all collected together again, I think they were both ready to erect a wigwam and live there forever.

Later, we laughed our heads off over our adventure, but the episode we were about to face was far more disturbing. We got the Cadillac back, repaired and resplendent, but the atmosphere in the house was depressing. Miss G and I had attended Frank's nightly stints at the Desert Inn and at Reno, and it was after one of these performances that a row started. You could hear them all over the house.

I heard the front door slam behind her as Miss G abandoned the fight and fled out into the night – the late, dark, dangerous night. Miss G, in tears and distraught, was fast as a gazelle, but had no sense of direction. I set off in a chase when I saw her heading down a steep forested slope which grew steeper as it plunged downward to the lake. This habit of sudden flight could have gotten her into life-threatening trouble on many occasions. As I raced down the slope after Miss G, I had a terrible feeling that if I didn't catch up with her quickly, I would be attending a real post-mortem with a real coroner.

I glimpsed a flash of her white clothing ahead of me, accelerated and grabbed her around the waist. She didn't struggle, just collapsed into my arms and sobbed. At moments like this, she was defenseless, vulnerable, totally defeated. We sat down on the ground, close together. She sniffled a bit, clutched my hand and stopped crying. I thought, this is ridiculous, sitting out here in the darkness. Here they were, two of the luckiest people in the world, the gorgeous Ava Gardner and Frank Sinatra, the greatest popular singer ever. How could they be torn apart by depression and despair?

I couldn't blame Frank. He'd been king of his profession for so long he really had taken it for granted. Professionally he was now locked in a battle against defeat and depression that threatened to destroy him. Every night in the Desert Inn he faced an audience that was tepid about his performance, even though Miss G beat her hands together in applause until they almost fell off. I knew Miss G was his only anchor, but that she herself on these occasions was as vulnerable as he was. It was plain that these constant fights were solving nothing and doing immense damage to their relationship. It was better that they parted for a bit and took stock, thought things through.

"Miss G," I said, "Let's go home."

She nodded, sniffed, stood up and pulled me up beside her. "Let's go home," she repeated. We stumbled back up the slope, went into the house to collect our bags and Rags, didn't see or say goodbye to Frank or Hank. We got into Miss G's convertible and vroommm…. We scorched off as if we were leading in the Indianapolis 500. The trees on either side were shooting past zip-zip-zip, and I knew she was trying to drain out the bitterness left by her quarrel with Frank. But for God's sake, she was going to kill us in the process. Probably for the first time in our driving history, I literally screamed at her.

"For Christ's sake, Miss G, slow down – slow down!" She did, but not by much. Maybe five minutes later a gust of wind took my spectacles off my nose. I'd only just started wearing the things. I shouted, "My glasses have blown off!"

She heard me. "Where?"

I shouted, "God knows, maybe a mile or so back."

For some reason, instead of turning the car around – admittedly, the road wasn't all that wide – Miss G decided to reverse. I'm kneeling on the seat looking in the reverse direction trying to see the glint of my spectacles while Miss G is reversing at about eighty miles an hour. God help us—He certainly did that night. About three miles back I caught the gleam, and there were my spectacles sitting in the middle of the road. We stopped, and I picked them up. I thought, what the hell am I doing wearing spectacles when I can see them at eighty miles an hour going backwards?

I said, "Hey, Miss G, there's a stream here running along the side of the road. Let's take a break and cool our feet." She agreed, so we took our shoes off and sat on the bank. We were trying to get life back into perspective. It was quiet. The water was warm and gurgled through our toes.

Miss G said, "I think we should have a drink." We had a drink from the usual reserve bottle of brandy. Then we had another drink. Stowing alcohol into various compartments of our lives was a part of my life work. We passed the bottle between us–nothing as ladylike as a glass–just swigging from the bottle. After two or three swigs the eternal pain of life seemed to have eased, and we got back into the car and sped off again. After a few brandies the eighty miles an hour speed did not seem so relevant.

We were probably on the outskirts of Carson City when it became relevant again. A young motorcycle cop pulled us over. By this time I had stuffed the brandy bottle under the seat, and I was praying that the brandy fumes had blown away with the wind. The policeman was young, good-looking, but very stern. He did everything very slowly. He spoke very slowly.

"Miss, you were doing eighty miles an hour."

"So what?" says Miss G, belligerently, and I could see that this was not going to turn out very nicely.

"Miss, you were exceeding the speed limit."

"Listen," said Miss G, "there is nothing on the road; it's early in the morning, and it seems you must have got out of bed on the wrong side this morning."

I was now trying to sink myself into the pattern that matched the seat covers. I'm black. In that part of the world in the 1950s, no civil rights supporters had marched on my behalf. No laws had been passed giving black girls the right to exist at all. Policemen were just as likely to hit you on the head with a night stick and then say your head had somehow gotten in the way of them doing their lawful duty. I cringed.

Miss G was really being very rude to the young policeman. His face got very somber.

"I think, Miss," he said with a flash in his eye, which meant trouble, "you had better follow me down to the station. I'll lead the way."

If Miss G thought there was anything ominous about this request, she didn't show it. At a funeral pace, we drove to the police station and followed the officer inside. We went into the front office. In the back, through the open door, we could see a row of barred cells. They were full of prisoners. Another police officer popped his head around from another door, looked at us, yawned and closed the door again. The young policeman sat at a desk and looked at us. Was it my imagination, or did a tiny glint of recognition appear in his eyes? I thought, please Miss G, please be nice to him, because I knew that Miss G could be very nice when she chose to be. Despite all the tears, all the dramas of last night, despite the eighty miles an hour, Miss G looked gorgeous. Tarred and feathered, I'm sure Miss G would have looked gorgeous.

The young officer stared more closely at her. Then he said, "Aren't you an actress? Aren't you Ava Gardner?"

Now, Miss G was no fool. Thank God she realized that compromise was now the name of the game.

"Why officer," she said sweetly. "How did you know?"

"Well...er...I've seen your movies."

"I do hope you liked them," said Miss G, giving him her little girl smile.

"Sure did." There was almost enthusiasm in the young man's voice. I hoped Miss G was not going to blow it. She didn't.

"Well, next time you're in Hollywood, officer, you might like to come on the set and see how a film's made."

His eyes brightened. "I sure would."

Now he had backed himself into a problem. We were on police premises. Official jurisdiction in Carson City must follow the correct procedure. Once, generations of wagon trains had rolled through there. Men were men and shot anyone they didn't like. There were good niggers and bad niggers. I was determined to be a good nigger. However, we had a track record–speeding, using insulting language to a police officer, but at least, we hadn't resisted arrest...yet!

The young policeman looked at Miss G again, tapped his pencil on his desk, cleared his throat and said, "Miss Gardner, a speeding offence in Carson City means that a fine must be paid." He paused, and then added, "In this case, we've got quite a few prisoners in there," he nodded his head indicating the cells through the open door.

"So I see," said Miss G politely.

"As they're always short of cigarettes, if you felt you'd like to dole out a pack of cigarettes a piece, they sure would appreciate that gesture."

"Why of course, "said Miss G. "Rene, honey, pop in there and count how many guys there are."

I thought, can she mean this? She did. So, who was I to spoil this humanitarian gesture? I walked through the door. The scent inside was certainly not Christian Dior or Chanel. The faces were, well, challenging—whiskery, tough, gnarled and silent. A few mouths were open in blank astonishment at the sight of a small black girl walking into their den, pointing a finger and counting them. I may have smiled nervously. I can't remember if my knees were knocking. I returned with the count—between twelve and fifteen. I didn't think a recount was necessary.

Miss G and the young policeman were now engaged in cheerful chatter. Miss G was also fiddling in her bag and extracting dollar notes. For a horrific second, I thought she was going to try and bribe the young man, but no.

"Rene, honey," she said, handing me the money. "This young officer tells me there is a supermarket right next door. Can you pop along and buy us a few cartons of cigarettes?"

I popped along and returned laden with boxes of cigarettes. Miss G followed me into the cell block. There, with a radiant smile, like a welfare worker handing out loaves of bread to the hungry, Miss G pushed the cartons through the bars. It seemed to me that the recipients were far happier with cigarettes than they would have been with freedom. There followed a delighted uproar.

Miss G and I decided that Carson City certainly possessed an enlightened system of justice. We shook the young policeman's hand warmly and drove away. Outside the Carson City limits, Miss G got straight back up to eighty again.

"Rene," she asked, "do you feel tired?"

"Half dead," I said. "What about you?"

"Me too. Nudge me if I start to fall asleep."

The sun was bright over the sea when we finally pulled into the drive at Nichols Canyon. Miss G headed at speed for the bathroom. The phone began to ring. I picked it up. It was Hank Sanicola, sounding as if he'd just had a heart attack and was about to have another.

"For Christ's sake, where've you been?" he croaked. "I've been ringing you for hours."

Of all the fool questions I'd ever heard, that was it. "Where've we been," I started to shout in fury. But he croaked on.

"Frank's taken an overdose. The doctor's here. I'm not certain if he's going to live. Come at once!"

Come at once. The idea of a drive back blew my mind. I screamed, "Miss G, Miss G!"

She came racing out of the bathroom. "What's up? What is the matter?"

I thrust the phone at her. She took it and stood there, her face going white, her voice falling to a whisper.

"Yes, we'll come back. We'll drive back right away." She banged the phone down.

"Rene, an overdose! We've got to drive back now!"

I said loudly, "Miss G, we can't drive back over that terrible road. You'll kill us both."

"Rene, for God's sake, we've got to do something. An overdose. If he's taken too much, he's dead. Hank said he's got the doctor there, but the doctor's not sure he can do anything. Rene, we've got to drive back."

"Miss G, we'll never make it back. Ring up the airlines. We can get a taxi to the airport. That's the quickest way. The most sensible."

We did and arrived by taxi at the Lake Tahoe house. Hank let us in, saying, "The doctor's still here."

The doctor smiled and said quietly, "It's all right. He's sleeping. Yes, you can go in and see him."

Miss G came out ten minutes later and took me aside.

"Rene, I could have punched him on the nose. For the first time in our lives, I could have hit him. He's lying there, and he's sleeping very happily. He wakes up on cue and says in this sad, little voice, 'Oh, God, I thought you were gone.' I could have killed him. He's the only one who's had any sleep. You can be sure he counted exactly how many sleeping pills he took. Hank's had no sleep; the doctor's had no sleep; you and I have had no sleep; even poor little Rags hasn't managed to catch a wink. There he is, rested and fine, with a good appetite. I could have kicked the crap out of him. I really could have." But, of course, she didn't.

9 SUICIDE

Frank's other attempts at suicide, real or faked, during this period were more than simply frightening. I thought they might be lethal, not only to him but to other people. They were induced by two main causes—his deep depression and his constant fear that Miss G would abandon him.

I remember her words, "I'm the goat. I'm the only one available for Frank to take out his frustrations on. Nobody else cares whether he blows his brains out or takes an overdose. I care. He knows that it would blow me apart and that I will always protect him. Hell, it's destroying me too."

Professionally and financially, Frank was at rock bottom. MGM had terminated his contract, and no one in that business seemed to have a part for him—ever. His contract with Columbia Records was still secure because his good friend Mannie Sacks still headed it. In 1946 Frank's records had been selling at the rate of ten million a year, but now their sales had fallen sharply. The Tin Pan Alley gossip confirmed that days of singers like Frank were never going to reach the same peak again.

When Frank had first been locked out of the house by Nancy on the instructions of her lawyers, it was plainly a legalistic device, for Frank knew that his marriage to Nancy was over. He lived in his office in L.A. where Hank Sanicola helped out. I also have to say that it seemed to me that Miss G's jealousy of most of Frank's movements had intensified.

As anticipated, tempers were flaring, nerve-endings stretched and battles between Miss G and Frank always likely to occur, especially when they went out to enjoy a quiet dinner together. Some girl sitting a few yards away would be slightly startled to find she had Frank Sinatra sitting only a few yards away and would throw a few admiring glances in his direction. Often, Frank intercepted the glances and might smile back or nod. What else could he do? Scowl? Put his tongue out? Hide his head in a paper bag? Occasionally some cutie in a low neckline with goo-goo eyes would arrive at the table murmuring something about an autograph. The look in her eyes suggested she and Frank might once have spent time together or that she was prepared to do that now. As Frank in the past had indeed indulged in such affairs, his defenses were not all that secure.

Inevitably, on such occasions Miss G would not say a word, but her face would register an Easter Island stone statue reaction. She might wait for the homeward journey or even until they reached home before firing off the first angry accusations. Sometimes she simply grabbed her bag, left the table and headed for the exit, leaving poor Frank saying, "Now Ava, Ava honey...wait."

Following such an exit on one occasion when they were staying at the Hampshire House Hotel in New York prior to Frank opening at the Copacabana, one of the most spectacular and widely publicized rows took place. When Miss G was telling me her side of the story, she couldn't even remember what the row had been about. Out of the restaurant she stormed to catch a taxi back to the Hampshire House Hotel.

Having another drink in her room and fuming, she was lonely and unhappy. Wasn't there anybody she could turn to for help and advice? Yes, there was somebody—Artie Shaw. She had heard that he was in New York and staying in his apartment. They were divorced but still friends, and Artie was great at solving problems. She knew that Frank hated him, but what did that matter?

It was now close to midnight, but Miss G had never been fussy about ringing her friends or enemies at any time of day or night. She fished her loose-leaf notebook out of her bag and got Artie's number. He was still up.

"Why hallo, Ava. How are you? Advice? At this time of night? Sure. I've got a friend here, but you're not far away. Why don't you grab a taxi and come across for a nightcap? Good, see you in ten minutes." Miss G picked up her bag and was ready to go.

Now comes the funny bit. Miss G left her loose-leaf notebook open at the page where Artie's name and number were written beside the phone. Carelessness? Forgetfulness? In a hurry because of her recent row with Frank? I looked Miss G straight in the eye when she reached this point in her story, and she gave the whole game away with her innocent smile. How else could a lady promote another fight?

Miss G arrived at Artie's flat and found that the "friend" was a girlfriend, and that both she and Artie were wearing their dressing gowns and had either just gotten out of bed or were about to get into it. Artie provided drinks, and they chattered away for about an hour before the front doorbell rang. Artie's slight frown signified, "Who could be calling at this time of night?" as he went to answer. Miss G was not totally surprised when she heard him say, "Why hallo Frank. Hallo Hank. Come on in and have a drink."

She was surprised that he had brought Hank with him. Who better to handle this little matter than the sophisticated and urbane Artie. What was more innocent than this little family group chatting together over a drink? Frank had made a fool of himself. He was humiliated.

The two of them came in. They looked like gangsters out of a B-movie: two hoodlums, raincoats, and ark trilbies, hands deep in their pockets as if they were clutching revolvers. No smiles. Determined chins. A real Jimmy Cagney scenario. Now Miss G realized she had overplayed her hand. She was a little scared. They looked around, observed the girl in her dressing gown, also Artie in his. Both men were slightly embarrassed realizing they'd bombed. Hank raised his eyes to heaven.

Artie tried to diffuse the situation. "Now take your coats off boys, and I'll fix you a drink."

Conversation had leaked away. They stood near the open door. They exchanged glances. Hank raised his eyes to heaven again and received no help. Their only way out was through the door, and they took it. Artie blew out his breath and said, "In that case, let us have another drink." He made no further comment on what had happened. His sweet little girlfriend was bemused and wondered what the hell was going on. Miss G got a taxi back to the Hampshire House and went back to their suite. It consisted of two large bedrooms divided by a large sitting room. Ostensibly Miss G and Bappie were sharing one, and Frank was alone in the other. Very cozy.

Strangely enough, on that notorious night practically the whole of Hollywood seemed to be sharing the Hampshire House Hotel with our loving couple. All of them seemed to have been awakened by that sobering single revolver shot. David Selznick, producer of *Gone With The Wind* and plainly no friend of Frank's, allegedly heard two shots and remarked maliciously, "I hope the bastard shot himself."

Kirk Douglas states in his autobiography that he was in bed asleep but had been awakened earlier by a beautiful woman sitting on the edge of his bed—a woman he recognized as Ava Gardner. Gallantly, sensing she was in trouble, he led her back to his doorway and gently ushered her out. Miss G was absolutely certain she had never been in a bedroom with Kirk—ever!

Other actors sleeping in the Hampshire House had other versions. None were very logical.

The truth of the matter was that Miss G returned home and found Bappie snoring politely in the other single bed. She hadn't been there for more than a minute or two when the telephone rang and it was Frank. In an anguished voice he said, "I can't stand it anymore. I'm going to kill myself."

A second later a terrific bang almost blew Miss G's receiver apart. She knew he had done it. With a scream of panic which woke Bappie up—the shot hadn't—Miss G rushed from their bedroom across the living room and into Frank's room. He wasn't dead. He was holding the still smoking revolver and looking rather surprised at the hole he'd blown in the mattress. It was Frank's idea of a cry for help.

Hank Sanicola remembered the occasion with far more emotion. He hadn't heard the shot either. He was awakened by a phone call from Frank. "For Christ's sake, get up here now. Get this mattress out of the way." Hank dutifully raced up the back stairs and carried it back to his room. Frank looked wide-eyed and said innocently, "Shot? What shot?" A few dollars scattered in various directions completed the smoke screen.

The near suicide dramas were far from over. The next occasion was in Palm Springs. Miss G had been spending a few days there with Frank. She returned unexpectedly. I knew something was wrong. I let her finish her drink.

"What happened this time?"

"The usual row, and I stormed off to the bathroom to collect my things and leave." I nodded sympathetically. I knew that scenario well.

"As you know, Rene, Frank always keeps that damned revolver in a drawer by the side of his bed. As I came out of the bathroom into the bedroom, there's Frank sitting on the edge of the bed with this revolver pointed at his temple. Without knowing what I was doing, I ran at him and made a grab for his hand. I got the gun by the barrel and tore it away from him. Probably the most stupid thing I've ever done, because it might have gone off and blown his head off. I just acted instinctively. Frank leapt at me. We both tumbled to the floor in a wrestling match and rolled across the floor to the stone fireplace. You remember it, Rene? Well, the gun hit the stone."

"I remember it," I said.

"I'm screaming at him telling him I think he's a phony and angrily I shoved the gun away. Oh my God, it reacted like a snake…bang! The bullet went ricocheting around the stone fireplace and whizzed out again making a two-inch hole in a solid wooden door. I knew I was wrong. There was nothing phony about that gun."

She paused and gave me a half-hearted smile. "It would have been funny if it hadn't been so dangerous. You see, Jimmy Van Heusen was staying with us."

I knew and liked Jimmy. He had definite appetites for booze and girls, but he was one of the finest songwriters of those years.

Miss G continued, "Jimmy was on the other side of the house, but he heard the shot and came running along the corridor. He flung open the door, not remembering that he'd just jumped out of bed and was stark naked. He looked around and smiled, saying quietly, "Just wanted to know what the shooting match was all about. And then he left."

I remember Miss G telling me, "It was before we were married, and Frank was certain we were going to break up. He was depressed—depressed about me, depressed about the fact that no one seemed to want him during his visit to New York. He brooded all the way back from New York to Chicago. He should have continued on to L.A., but he got off in Chicago and rang me up. God, was he in a state. 'Ava,' he cried, 'I can't stand this any longer. I'm going to throw myself off the train before I reach Los Angeles.'"

"I shouted, 'For Christ's sake!' but he had hung up. You know, Rene, those days I believed him. Later I knew I should have yelled, 'I'm not Lady Bat Woman. I can't come flying low over the tracks from Los Angeles to Chicago looking for your dismembered body.'"

She paused and went on. "Sounds funny now. It wasn't funny then. Rene, I can hardly remember now how often it happened. He almost succeeded in knocking off one of his best friends, Mannie Sacks, when he was staying with him in Mannie's New York apartment. Frank turned on the gas determined to end it all. Fortunately Mannie woke up, smelled gas and turned it off."

Later in our lives Miss G would sit back and try and work out what had gone wrong. Miss G knew they suffered from a commonplace lover's complaint—they couldn't live without each other and couldn't live with each other either. They thought living in happy sin without Frank's divorce from Nancy would solve their problems. It didn't. They thought after they got married a holy bliss would envelop them. It didn't. Somehow they had to work out their own salvation.

10 TEARS AT SANDS HOTEL

In every respect, 1951 was a year of change. After Miss G returned from Spain, we were still enjoying our house in Nichols Canyon. Lena Horne and her husband, Lennie Hayton, who was conductor of one of MGM's resident orchestras, lived down the road, and the three of them became good friends, especially when Miss G started her singing career in *Show Boat*. It was also during this year that Miss G decided we should move closer to the sea, and she rented a lovely house in Pacific Palisades. We kept the house at Nichols Canyon for Bappie to live in.

Mainly I remember Miss G's excitement when she came back to our dressing room in the MGM studios and said, "Rene, honey, I've made it at last. I've got two great songs to sing in *Show Boat*."

I gave her a questioning look. "Miss G," I said, "in all the movies you have made, except when you sang that pretty little song in *Pandora and the Flying Dutchman*, you've been standing there opening your mouth and somebody else's voice has been coming out."

"This time it's different," said Miss G.

"How different?"

"George Sidney, the producer, is the difference. He's listened to my voice and said I can sing both of Julie's songs, 'Bill' and 'Can't Help Lovin' Dat Man.' As he says, it's a different sort of singing, half spoken and half sung. Both are soliloquies with Julie dreaming of her no-good, gambling husband. The sounds must match my acting voice. Makes sense, uh?"

"Sure does."

George was a reasonable, friendly guy who headed MGM's speech-drama section. He was married to Lillian Burns, and together they had certain clout at MGM. It was also George who had vetted the very first film test of Miss G when it was sent across from New York to L.A. George had recommended that Miss G should be offered a contract.

There was no stopping Miss G's enthusiasm. "Of course, Lena should really have been given the part of Julie in the first place. She's already done a marvelous recording of *Show Boat* singing Julie's songs. She's perfect for it."

"She's black."

"She's no more black than you are. She's a golden honey brown like you are. All this black stuff is bullshit. People are all sorts of colors and come from all sorts of nationalities. Lena told me once how many she came from—French, Italian, South Sea Islands, African and God knows what else. She's one of the most beautiful women in the world, inside and out."

Show Boat was about the good old paddle-steamers sliding up and down the Mississippi in the days when gentlemen wore top hats, frock coats and striped cravats, and ladies wore crinolines, carried parasols and talked just like Vivian Leigh in *Gone With the Wind*. At least in MGM films they did.

Black laborers, just freed from slavery, pulled ropes and loaded the cotton bales and sang songs like "Ole Man River"—"body all achin' and racked with pain,"—which was probably closer to the truth than any other aspect of the movie. For *Show Boat* was a romantic fairy story hoping to send people home happy with just a little tear in their eye for poor, haunted Julie.

Julie was a half-caste—beautiful, desirable, but an outcast in those southern states because there was black blood in her veins. Julie pretended she was white. She married a handsome gambling man who made a living at cards on the paddle boat, *Cotton Blossom*, and that was her big mistake. Someone told the sheriff about her, and he threw them both off the steamer. Disgraced, her husband abandoned her, and she sank down into alcoholism and poverty.

Even before the film started, Miss G started working to really be able to sing. Through Lena, she found a fine teacher who had worked with both Lena and Dorothy Dandridge. Eventually Miss G produced a tape in which she sang both songs. I heard it, and it was very good. Lennie Hayton thought so too. So it was with a fair amount of pride Miss G arranged an interview with Arthur Freed, the MGM executive who was the God Almighty in terms of production and whose verdict was absolute.

"Mr. Freed," she said nervously, "George Sidney thinks I should be allowed to sing Julie's two songs in the film, so I've brought this recording along for your approval." Arthur took the tape and looked down his nose at her.

"Ava," he said, 'in this movie we shall be using the best singing professionals in the world—Kathryn Grayson, Howard Keel and that wonderful black opera singer William Warfield, plus others. You are up against superb professionals. MGM would never take the risk of using an amateur."

Miss G should have been put in her place, but she wasn't. She was not only disappointed, she was furious, especially when Lennie Hayton, who was conducting the seventy-five piece orchestra and recording the Oscar Hammerstein and Jerome Kern melodies, had told her the singer MGM had chosen to dub over Miss G's own voice did not match at all. Producer George Sidney also informed Arthur Freed of this impasse. It was Lennie who suggested a solution.

He knew Lena had coached Miss G for weeks to teach her the correct tempo and phrasing for the two songs. Then Miss G had made her recording and given it to Arthur Freed. If Lennie could get that tape back, he could steer the new girl singer through the part, and they'd probably get away with it. They did. It worked more or less, although Miss G thought the whole thing was a botch-up. In an interview she gave, she made her anger quite clear.

"I wanted to sing those songs. Hell, I've still got a southern accent, and I really thought that Julie should sound a little like a Negro since she's supposed to have Negro blood. Those songs like "Bill" shouldn't sound like an opera. I made a damn good job of the track, and they said, 'Ava, are you out of your head?' Then they substituted her voice for mine, and now in the movie my southern twang stops talking and her soprano starts singing. Hell, what a mess. They ended up with crap."

Miss G had the final and last laugh. MGM, after the film's release, decided that the entire music score and songs would go on sale as a record. How an enormous factory like MGM did not know that if you sell a record like this, you cannot use the picture and the name of the artist concerned unless it is her actual voice. Unless they used Miss G's own tape they couldn't use Miss G as part of the publicity. Miss G was called back to record again with the voice of the first singer now wiped from the tape.

The *Show Boat* record was released with Miss G's voice singing her two songs. Then the real foolishness of MGM's actions was shown. Miss G's songs were the only melodies "lifted" from the main record and issued as singles. Even today, you can occasionally hear them on the radio. Miss G received small royalties for the rest of her life.

The premier of *Show Boat* was held at the Egyptian Theater in Hollywood. Bales of cotton were stacked all over the foyer, and little black children danced on them wearing straw hats and gingham dresses. One of the staterooms of the *Cotton Blossom* had been reproduced so we could feel as if we were on a voyage down the Mississippi River. I can tell you, Hollywood in those early fifties was pure bunkum. Miss G arrived looking like the Queen of California instead of looking like Julie, the poor little half-caste heroine. She wore a dress designed by Irene, a black and green satin creation, an emerald necklace given to her by Frank to match her eyes, and the Sidney Guilaroff hairstyle set her off to perfection.

With the completion of *Show Boat*, Miss G's seven-year contract came to an end. A new contract had to be negotiated, and Miss G was in two minds about what she should do. Much later, she understood that this was a period when the other stars were beginning to negotiate individual packages in which they could dictate their own terms. At that time she had tunnel vision. Somehow she had to help Frank to start climbing again. After all, he had sacrificed a lot for her. She had not broken up his marriage—that had fallen apart years before—but now she was the one who did all the supporting.

For a considerable time, she had been seeking a film in which she and Frank could star together. She believed she had found the property, *Meet Me in St. Louis*. With this in mind, she approached MGM. If they would agree to make this picture in the near future, she would sign on for another seven years. They agreed.

I don't think Frank was fully aware of what was going on. He was very proud, even if very broke. I felt he went along with Miss G's idea without realizing how much she was trying to help him. The outcome was sad. The picture was never made, but Miss G was hooked into her contract with MGM. When MGM finally decided to keep their end of the bargain, Frank had already won his Oscar for his performance in *From Here to Eternity*, and he was too busy.

It was without any doubt one of the biggest disappointments of Miss G's life. In the same way that Frank never forgave her for sliding into bed with Mario Cabre, Miss G always held it against Frank that he had been responsible for letting her in for another seven years of MGM tyranny.

MGM had pulled off a great bargain, and they knew it. In the new contract Miss G was going to make seven pictures, one a year for seven years, at a salary of $50,000 a year. Before the contract had been signed, MGM had already loaned her out to Universal for $100,000 for a few weeks' work. With the new contract signed and sealed, they announced the loan-out fee for Miss G would be $120,000. Oh well, just call it smart business. When she finally realized what was going on, Miss G was livid.

Looking at Frank Sinatra today, knowing he ranks as one of the greatest artists of the 20th Century, it is difficult to imagine that in the early fifties he seemed to be on the verge of total eclipse. He lost his voice and his self-confidence after suffering with a throat infection at the Copacabana in New York. Then he was consigned to working in second-rate Reno and Lake Tahoe clubs—a real comedown.

One of the first turn-ups in Frank's fortunes began when he got the nightclub spot at the brand new Sands Hotel in Las Vegas. Ava was now renting the house at Lake Tahoe, which was our base. On the morning we set off to drive to Las Vegas in Frank's black Cadillac convertible, the atmosphere in the car was cool, if not icy. Frank was grim-faced. Miss G was withdrawn. They had had one of their constant rows, and they were not speaking to each other. Great! Rags and I sat in the back and tried to look as if we were enjoying ourselves.

Things did not improve as we reached the outskirts of Las Vegas where the roads were wide and straight. We met more traffic, including a few cars full of teenage kids who were looking for fun. They spotted Miss G—not Frank—in the open convertible. Oh boy, were they thrilled.

"Gee guys. See who that is–Ava Gardner! The real Ava Gardner! Hi, Ava! What ya doing here? Where are you going?"

They ranged alongside, still shouting about their discovery. Ava laughed and waved at them, but Frank was far from pleased. Eventually he braked and yelled across at them. The kids laughed, and no one really minded. Only Frank minded.

We reached the Sands Hotel. It was huge, new and unfinished. Open spaces that would become areas of green lawn were now wide stretches of red mud.

The nightclub spot Frank had been engaged to fill had previously been occupied by Billy Eckstine, the talented pianist and singer. I was about to learn, like he had, that when you were black, management of the Sands Hotel had very little time or space for you.

Frank and Miss G were treated like royalty and shown to a huge suite. A room for me somewhere near by? No way. They were building small duplex apartments around the back. That's where Mr. Eckstine had stayed. I had my room there too. Mr. Eckstine had been allowed into the nightclub for his act. I had no act, so I was not allowed even into the lobby of the hotel or the hotel pool to hand Miss G her towel. No point in protesting. That was the life as it was in Las Vegas in the early fifties. It got very uncomfortable there. I couldn't even go shopping. There were signs outside every shop prohibiting blacks from access. Rags had more seniority than I did.

After a few days I said to Miss G, "Honey, I'm supposed to be here as your maid, and I can't even get into the hotel. I think it's better if I take Rags back to L.A. and keep the Pacific Palisades house going." Miss G agreed, although she had done her best to champion my cause, something hard to do because she had to be on Frank's side too.

She said, "I'll ring Bappie and get her up here. She has nothing else to do but look after that old drunk of hers, Charlie Guest." Bappie raised hell. Didn't anyone know that the races were on? She wasn't coming over to Las Vegas when she could go racing every day. Bappie was a great drinker, and Miss G always maintained that Bappie could drink her under the table. She was also a great user of strong language and a compulsive gambler.

The only thing that broke her determination was when Miss G retaliated in loving sisterly language, "For Christ sake, this is the gambling center of the world. You can play cards and shoot dice for twenty-four hours a day. So get up here, or I'll throw you and Charlie out of Nichols Canyon." Miss G won.

Bappie arrived. She looked around and said, "Rene, let's take a walk and see if we can find a drink. I might even find a craps table." Bappie loved craps tables. I had seen her perform at both Reno and Lake Tahoe. She could shoot craps like a man with all the finger popping and jumping back as she threw the dice. We didn't find a craps table, but we did find a bar with a big sign outside which read, "Everybody Welcome."

"That's us," said Bappie, and we went in and sat down at a table. The waiter came over, and Bappie ordered two dry martinis. A few minutes later he brought one drink and set it before Bappie. She sipped it absent-mindedly, then looked across and said in surprise, "Where's yours?"

Before I could even answer, there was this big guy–plainly the owner–glaring down at me and saying, "Doncha know your sort ain't allowed in here. Out of here–now–before you're thrown out!"

I got up and left and went out into the sunlight and the pavement. I realized I was crying. I didn't want to cry. I began to walk back towards the Sands trying to be realistic saying to myself that crying would do no good. It had happened before. It would happen again. Stop crying and just go back to your room.

Bappie caught up with me and walked alongside and said, "Rene, I'm sorry." Then she said, "You're crying?" and I said, "No, I'm not, I've just got something in my eye."

We just walked together in silence after that. Bappie knew what I was crying about, but she knew she couldn't do anything about it either. I went off to my room, sat on the bed, and cried some more. Rags jumped up beside me and licked me as if I was a real human being, so he got a few tears dropped on him too.

The door opened, and Miss G came in and began, "Bappie told me…" Then she stopped and sat on the bed with me and took me in her arms and held me the same way I had done so many times for her.

She said, "Rene, you are not staying in this place. I've got to stay because Frank's performing, but you're going back out of this junkyard. Rags is going back with you because he can't stand it either."

We went back to Pacific Palisades where the sound of the sea drowned out any crying I had left. It didn't happen often. I don't know why it got to me there.

Bappie and me in a restaurant in Rome. We were outside the U.S., so this time I was allowed to stay.

11 THE QUARRELS

By the time Miss G and Frank came back from Las Vegas, they seemed to have resolved some of their difficulties, but once back in Pacific Palisades they were at it again. Trouble was, they were both insecure and neurotic. Both of them had a sense of guilt, and both were aware the media were probing and saying nasty things about their relationship. A love affair under the glare of such unwelcome attention becomes something of a nightmare. Fights were part of their lifestyle and certainly a part of mine and Hank Sanicola's.

I would hear the quarrels start, hear the voices raised, hear Frank take umbrage and storm out of the door shouting, "Rene, Rene, call Hank! I'm leaving!"

I'd call Hank. As soon as he heard my voice, he'd groan and say, "Jesus."

"Hank, Mr. S wants you to bring the car around and pick up his clothes."

"Not again!"

Hank would bring the car around, and I'd be waiting with the broom handle, which was our local means of transportation for Frank's clothes. We'd trudge up the stairs and hang Frank's suits on their hangers along the broom handle and take them back to the car. Hank would fill a suitcase with Frank's bits and pieces and put that in the car. It was all very serious—no laughter, no jokes. This was the end of the world. They would never meet again—ever.

Occasionally, very occasionally, Frank would say, "Don't take them all. Leave that and that." We would know this was really nothing more than a lover's tiff. If he said, "Take the clothes back Hank, and then come back and fetch me," we knew that was THE END. But, of course, it never was. Often next morning Frank, not having left and not having been picked up, would say in a slightly puzzled voice, "Rene, where are my clothes?" I would say with a forgiving sweet smile, "Why Mr. S, they are around at your office."

Hank was less patient than I was. He'd hiss at me, "Jesus Christ, Rene, I take the clothes back, I come back for Frank, and they're back in bed together."

"Hank," I would explain, "it's their love play."

"Couldn't they invent something else? Judo wrestling or something?"

"Love," I repeated, truly meaning it. "No one could stand the sort of torture

65

they're going through without being madly in love."

"Umph," Hank would say, "Let's abolish it."

It was during this period of unhappy ecstasy between Frank and Miss G that Frank's children now entered our lives. Nancy had played the family angle for all it was worth. Although one might say who could blame her, I certainly could. She'd known her marriage had ended, but instead of cherishing the years she'd had with Frank she decided to hit back. By the time Nancy and her lawyers had finished with Frank he was flat broke, and Nancy was a very rich woman, her fortune due to Frank's talent. I felt this was mean.

Miss G left all her three husbands without ever extracting more than a grubstake–a used car from Mickey and nothing from the other two—although Frank was very generous once he'd started to make millions. After the divorces, the three well-heeled guys walked away with practiced, well-satisfied smiles— Artie Shaw with the broadest. Miss G was never mean to her past husbands and never bore them malice, although she could be a teeny-weeny bit difficult to live with.

For a time, Frank had to go home to visit his kids and would return dejected and depressed. Miss G would immediately jump to the conclusion that he couldn't live without them, so he couldn't live with her. A good subject for any discussion.

Through his lawyers Frank got visitation and other rights so the three kids could come and pay us a visit at Pacific Palisades. I should have hung the house in black. In that first visit of Frank's kids, Miss G got so mad she flounced upstairs and slammed her door shut with an eloquent vehemence. Frank gathered the kids and took them home. When he got back the fight was on. The way they were in and out, banging doors, I was surprised we were left with even one door latch that operated. One sulked in one room, and the other sulked in another. I can't remember if I rang Hank.

Eventually, Miss G softened to the children's presence and would go overboard to make their visit something akin to Disney World. (Okay, I know it hadn't been invented then, Miss G was just a little ahead of her time.) Everything was done to please the hearts and light the smiles of the three little monsters bearing down on us. Chocolates, fruits, cakes, ice cream, soft drinks, toys, games....

They arrived with washed faces and pretty little dresses on the girls, and little Frank, Jr., was cute as a button in his outfit. Nancy, eleven, was the biggest monster because her mother had put plenty in her head. Tina was the youngest and like any other little kid with her feet dangling. If little Frank or Tina wanted to do anything or eat anything, little Nancy wouldn't let them. She ruled the roost. Frank walked around like a sick cat, homesick, children sick, everything sick, knowing that nothing was going to work.

Miss G beamed and smiled and laughed and joked and knew that nothing was going to work with little Nancy's "No, thank you," and "No, Tina doesn't like that." Pretty soon she announced, "Daddy, I think it is time we went home."

In the years to come, Miss G and Tina would form a real living friendship, so much so that on one occasion in New York a handsome, admiring young man on a building site shouted down, "Hey ma'am, that's a real beautiful daughter you've got there with you."

I must say I had a great deal of sympathy for Frank during this period. To me he was always a gentleman—pleasant, considerate and understanding, never treating me as anyone other than an equal. Even in his low, low days he would always manage a smile and a "thank you." I could understand well why Miss G loved him.

What hurt him immensely was his pride. He had been Frank Sinatra, top of the heap, and now he was down to living off a woman. Of course, he could not bear this. Frank couldn't change his spots and devalue his status. Inevitably, it was devalued. The clubs he played were insignificant—so insignificant that we didn't bother to go to them since that would only heighten his humiliation. I remember he had three shirts only. He would come home at night, and I would wash and iron them so he always had clean shirts to change into through every performance.

On November 1, 1951, Frank finally got his divorce. News that he and Miss G were now heading for the altar was released.

By this time, it seemed to me that the marriage was doomed even before they got within walking distance of an altar. Left to themselves without media attention, they might have had a chance—a slight chance—of reconciling their incandescent love affair with the realities of their different lifestyles and possibly making a go of it.

Marriage, I thought, would kill any chance stone dead. I couldn't see how in their turmoil of quarrels they'd even have time to get married, but they did.

Miss G and I decided since Bappie was going to be in attendance, fussing around like an old hen, that there was no point in me making the quick return trip to New York only to have Miss G and Frank fly off immediately on their honeymoon. Nevertheless, we spent days and weeks arranging Miss G's expensive and beautiful trousseau.

The wedding should have been a quiet affair, if one could ever imagine anything quiet between Miss G and Frank. It was scheduled first of all to take place at the Philadelphia home of Isaac Levy, an old friend of Frank's. Then the press got word of that location, so Frank decided to double-cross them and slide it to another venue—the home of another friend, Lester Sacks. Naturally, the press got hold of that location too. Frank would never learn that the press was part of the air he tried to breathe.

The party that assembled was small and select: Frank's parents, Bappie as Miss G's attendant, plus a few of Frank's show biz friends—Dick Jones, Alex Stordahl and his wife June, Ben Barton and a few others. All was humming along like a sewing machine. Then the needle broke.

"God Almighty," recalled Miss G afterwards. "That evening before the wedding, Bappie and I were sitting happily in our suite having a couple of drinks when there was a knock on the door. Bappie went to see who it was. Couldn't be Frank–not allowed to see the bride–right? She brought back a letter delivered to the hotel by hand with the request that it should only be handed to me personally." She took a breath before the next hit.

"I opened it, all happy and sweet, expecting it to be from a movie fan wishing me well. It was from a prostitute. She made that clear in the first few lines to get the dirt properly spread. There were some sexual facts about Frank and her relationship with him I should know. They were sick, sick, sick! Some of them were too close to the mark. How could she have known some of these things? How could she have known anything? God! I almost threw up. I did know one thing–in the face of this evidence, there was going to be no marriage tomorrow. There was going to be no marriage ever!"

I could understand Miss G's outrage. Looking back now, I could have told them that at that particular moment no one was going to get Miss G to reason. The shock was too intense. Of course, Bappie and the group threw up all the reasons to proceed. It was too late to change now. All the arrangements had been made. They would be the laughing stock of the world if they stood up a real preacher man.

So the parade started. It was a situation a bit like the San Francisco uproar years before with Howard Hughes. Bappie was the go-between, bearing threats, accusations and bombshells from Miss G to Frank and the assembled cast and returning with denials, excesses, rationalizations and pleas for common sense from the group. Eventually common sense simmered Miss G down to a reasonable heat. Of course, everyone agreed that the letter was a deliberate and obscene attempt to ruin the wedding and their relationship. Some foul bastard had concocted this false, blackmailing letter. No one bothered, at that moment, to wonder which particular "bastard" it might be. At a later date, Miss G and I worked out that it could only have been one crazed individual–Howard Hughes. This was long before anyone realized that he was a morphine-addicted loony. As I said earlier, Howard Hughes never gave up. This was only the beginning of a long and hectic campaign that Howard would mount.

The wedding went ahead as planned. Miss G descended the wide staircase on the arm of Manny Sack's brother. She looked gorgeous in the Howard Greer-designed cocktail dress of pale pink marquisette, buffed out with pink taffeta and strapless. With a pearl necklace and diamond earrings, no bride had ever looked more beautiful. Dick Jones was waiting at the piano to play the "Wedding March." He struck Mendelssohn's magnificent opening chords and nearly died of shock. The piano had not been tuned, and the sound was horrible. No one noticed, or if they did their faces did not show it. An altar had been set up, and Judge Sloane, standing behind it, beamed. Everyone knew their cues, and it was a lovely ceremony.

Once hitched, the bride and groom made a dash through the photographers lining up outside and made it to their limousine, which took them to a private plane waiting to fly them down to Miami on the first leg of their honeymoon. Miss G rang me from the Green Heron Hotel, happy and laughing, "You'll never believe this Rene, but Frank hasn't taken a swing at a single photographer, and they've almost left us alone down here. You know what, and you'll never believe this, we dashed off in such a hurry that I left the trousseau suitcase behind."

I screamed, "Miss G, after all our work, after all that money! What are you going to do?"

"Don't worry honey. I've been walking along the beach in Frank's jacket. I left wearing the Christian Dior outfit–you know, the brown dress with the matching mink stole. Was Frank's wedding present. We're off to Cuba now. The luggage will catch up with us eventually."

They spent three happy nights in Havana cruising and boozing along that wonderful main Avenida that cuts through the heart of the city. In those Batista years, with happy American tourists filling the place, outdoor orchestras and jazz bands played on either side of the street. With tables packed, the noise incredible, and consumption of margaritas and rum-and-cokes practically endless, it was hard not to have a good time. They didn't even have time to have a quarrel. For them everything had changed. And for me–for the time being–everything was going to change also.

They flew from Havana back to New York, then on to L.A. for their California wedding reception in Pacific Palisades. Frank was determined to make a big splash and engaged a pleasant black lady to take over, who apparently had been in charge of all Barbara Hutton's socialite parties.

She was very pleasant and certainly knew what she was doing. All I had to do was show her where all the materials were. It was a good party. Pacific Palisades was a big house made for parties, and from then on there were quite a few of them, with Miss G as the hostess who could, if necessary, drink any of the guests under the table. We were also being helped at this time by a middle-aged black couple. They were very sweet people who had been around us for a long time and were anxious to get jobs.

It was now that I began to realize that with a married couple living on the premises who could handle all the household affairs and look after Miss G and Frank as well, that I was really a bit redundant. This became clearer every day.

I knew that Miss G was a bit embarrassed about the situation, so I helped her out. I said, "Miss G, maybe I should go back to St. Louis for a few weeks' holiday and see my folks again. You can always get on the phone if I'm really needed." Miss G looked me straight in the eye and knew exactly what I was doing. At this point it was the only sensible thing to do.

We both knew that the chances of her marriage succeeding were not even fifty-fifty. This was a never-spoken, deep-down thought that slid between us. The marriage had to be given a chance–a huge chance, a great boost. Who knew? It might suddenly take off and ricochet among the stars.

I said goodbye to Miss G and Frank and said the usual silly things. "Have a great time. I'm just taking a few weeks off. I'll see you again soon." Miss G gave me a great hug that said more than words could. I packed my bag, and Miss G took me to the station. I looked out of the window and didn't see much that was going on out there. I thought, "Oh God, how can I live without her laughter and her chatter and Frank and their rows and the drama and the uproar?" Then I swallowed very hard and looked out at the scenery again and thought, "Well, maybe it won't be all that long."

Back home in St. Louis my parents welcomed me as the successful daughter. You know, the one who works for The Miss Ava Gardner. My mother and Miss G really got on like a house on fire. They'd met and hugged, and Miss G, I swear to God, thought she was as much her mother as she was mine. It was my mother who Miss G would ring up and talk to about my health and where I was and what I was doing. My mother was the same. "Now Rene," she'd say, "you be certain that you look after that girl." I'd groan and say, "Mama...." Then I wouldn't say anything. I suppose I got them both stuck in my heart.

I was hoping I wasn't kidding myself about the phone calls, but I was pleased when the first one came from Miss G not long after I arrived in St. Louis. Naturally, I had to get my mother unglued from the receiver before I could get a word in edgewise, but then we chatted together.

I said I was enjoying meeting my old friends and spending all my money and seeing all the old familiar places, which weren't quite as pretty as those along the Pacific coast. Miss G said she was starting *The Snows of Kilimanjaro* and that it was great working with Gregory Peck again. Henry King was a wonderful old producer, a gentleman of the old school. He was giving her a lot of help. He'd started in films in the silent days of the twenties and thirties.

The phone calls between us continued. I suppose it was about eight weeks before Miss G said, "Rene, what are you doing out there? You can't stay on holiday forever. Come back to Hollywood and have another holiday here. Rags is missing you too."

The dogs, oh God, the dogs. It was Frank who started our dynasty of dogs. When I arrived, she told me everything about it from the day they got married on November 7, 1951. Exactly one month later on December 7, 1951, they flew from New York on a jet bound for London. They were both excited. Frank was asked to appear at a Royal Command Performance at the Palladium in London—something he couldn't miss. Actually, while he was there Frank discovered that the whole point of the show was motivated by the Variety Club of Great Britain, an enormous group of actors of all sorts, shapes, sizes and ages. They combined their talents to present a show before the Royal Family to aid a charity which helped needy or sick children.

Frank learned this sitting in his dressing room at the Palladium, a stone's throw from Oxford Circus, and said, "Hell, why don't we do the same thing in America?" When he came back, he started a similar sort of charity in the U.S. which still functions today in league with its British counterpart. Frank gets a lot of bricks thrown at him, but he did a lot of things to deserve pats on the back.

I am digressing. Back to the stars. At that time, Princess Elizabeth and the Duke of Edinburgh had been married for some time. The Duke threw a cocktail party for all the American stars who appeared at that Command Performance. Among them were Orson Welles, Janet Leigh, Tony Curtis, Frank and Miss G. Miss G was not overwhelmed by the atmosphere of royalty, but she was enthralled by the Duke of Edinburgh's dancing. In total admiration she said, "He was one of the best samba dancers I've ever danced with."

The second surprise? Somehow the royal Corgis got into the act too. With their shiny black noses, sharp ears, intelligent eyes and four little feet that trundled them around in doggy anticipation, they captivated Miss G. What was

Frank's present as they left London? A small, furry bundle–another Corgi puppy they named Cara. He joined Rags, and they were the first two in a long line that were to inhabit Miss G's household until the day she died.

12 MOGAMBO AND THE PREGNANCIES

In the first of Mickey's autobiographies, his firm opinion was that Miss G was terrified at the thought of having a baby. He was absolutely right. After her arrival in Hollywood and a quick look around at what was going on, she decided to proceed cautiously with her duties to God, husband, and adding to the world's rising population. The only time in her life her conceptual longings overcame that native caution was in the year before I joined her during her courtship and marriage to Artie Shaw. She told him she wanted a baby.

Artie was not remotely interested in producing anything so commonplace. Artie didn't like himself all that much anyway, so why expect another small creature to go through all the trauma without having any choice in the matter?

After that blunt rejection Miss G applied herself to making a living in the film industry where at least God had equipped her with the face and figure that enabled her to stay in employment. A darling little baby would put her out of work. When interviewed by pressmen or gossip columnists, Miss G always made the right noises, cooing sadly how she would have adored that great blessing to have occurred and not believing a word of it.

During her marriage to Frank there were three pregnancies. It is difficult to know exactly what she would have done differently under different circumstances. In those first years of their association she was the breadwinner, and no one could hazard a guess when Frank would be producing bread in any quantity again. That was point one. Point two was Frank already had a family of three, so did Miss G want to add to that total? I don't think Miss G ever thought that through completely, and we never discussed it. We were always too busy.

I went to St. John's Hospital with her during the first pregnancy when things were solved very easily by what is referred to as a D and C. In a campsite in the middle of the African bush things were not quite so easy.

MGM's decision to remake *Red Dust*, which years before had starred Clark Gable, Jean Harlow and Mary Astor, delighted Miss G. She was given the part played by Jean Harlow, Clark Gable was back in his original role, and Grace Kelly was playing the Mary Astor part. And they changed the name, too, from *Red Dust* to *Mogambo*.

The director, John Ford, was a veteran in the movie business and one of the most successful in Hollywood history. Who could forget *Stagecoach*, or *The Grapes of Wrath*? The screenwriter, John Lee Mahin, was highly talented and innovative.

Instead of following in the footsteps of the old movie, he changed the location and got rid of the stereotyped, cardboard characters. Sure Clark was never stereotyped. He was always rock-solid, twenty-three-carat gold, irreplaceable Gable. Jean Harlow had been the predictable tramp and Mary Astor the East Coast prissy dame.

Mahin knew about Miss G, her ability as a comedienne, her mischievous mind and occasional gusts of self-righteous anger. Ava was a Tar Heel. She was a no-nonsense girl, passionate, devastatingly pretty, with a quick dart of the eye that augured well for the adventurous male. When Miss G, playing Eloise (Honey Bear) Kelly, stepped off the up-river steamer in Central Africa barefoot, wearing a white blouse and water-soaked skirt complete with pearl necklace, a parasol clutched in one hand, and her suitcase under her arm, she needed no fictional mannerisms. The real Ava Gardner would do.

As one observant critic pointed out, "Chewing gum or standing against a lighted doorway in her negligee, Gardner is enough to start any African tom-tom thumping loudly, much less Gable's virile heart."

Miss G had her sights set upon the up-standing big game hunter portrayed by Clark. Even when Sir Donald Sinden arrived as the dull and earnest anthropologist, accompanied by pretty wife (Grace Kelly) who falls in love with Clark, the romantic outcome was really never in doubt. Honey Bear would get her man.

It was, one had to admit, a glorious African location set on a high bluff in the virgin African bush above the Kagera River where the rapids roared and hippos and crocodiles flourished. The Kenya Press called it the greatest safari of all time. Miss G had lots of critical things to say about MGM in terms of salaries, contracts and suspensions, but when they put their mind to making an epic, they found an epic location. To start with, an airstrip more than a mile long had been constructed. Supplies and 200 white and 400 black workers were ferried by plane between the camp and Nairobi.

The tented village was enormous, and the accommodations for stars and high-class personnel were superior to those of many luxury hotels. Running water was the only luxury not on tap. There was a hospital unit, a sport's area, kitchens and bars, even a prison for those who might raise hell after a drinking spree.

At times one felt that Africa itself was more colorful than the story being filmed. It had lions, leopards, snakes, buffaloes, antelopes, war-painted warriors shooting the rapids, native witch doctors rattling their magic bones, and handsome, well-paid, white big-game hunters patrolling at all times in case a hungry lion came in to take a bite out of one of the cast.

Honey Bear arrives by river steamer, Grace Kelly arrives over land, and both fall in love with big-game hunter Clark Gable. He dillies and dallies with both of them until Grace gets fed up with his philandering and takes a pot shot at him with a revolver. Naturally he only receives a slight nick in his upper arm. In fact, has anyone ever heard of Clark Gable being killed in his movies?

In real life Grace really fell in love with Clark, and he took a great shine to her. Whether this love affair was ever consummated under those huge golden African moons, only Grace and Clark will ever know. Miss G knew, but she wasn't telling anybody or hazarding any guesses.

Miss G's own love life wasn't all that romantic because after a few weeks on that location she found she was pregnant. This, of course, was difficult because they were going to be on location for a long time and Miss G's stomach was going to advance from the concave to the convex. John Ford had to be informed.

John was of Irish extraction, with a fiery temper and an antipathy to pretty doll-like Hollywood actresses with minds obscured by their makeup. As a very senior director who had wanted Maureen O'Hara to play the part of Honey Bear but had been overruled by MGM's financially skeptical executives, he looked with a jaundiced eye at Miss G, who didn't have a good Irish name like O'Hara.

This antagonism seeped into the first few shots when filming began. He reacted with venom to one of Miss G's light-hearted cracks about one scene being a bit of a mess up. He was outraged and asked if she would like to direct the film herself.

Clark Gable, who thought John had gone too far, walked off the set. Working on the principle that the show must go on, they all got together again. John Ford discovered that Ava was half Irish, that she could cuss, argue, and reason in a very un-Hollywood fashion, and they started an enduring friendship.

When Miss G revealed that she had to go back to London to get an abortion, John, a good Catholic, tried to reason her out of this. She was married, so there was no disgrace about such a natural outcome. As her condition became more apparent, he would shoot all her scenes in a way so that it would not be noticed. John was wonderful, but the production of babies was not on Miss G's list of priorities. She went back to London, got her abortion, and returned a few days later to go on filming.

During those entrancing African evenings they sat outside their tents drinking long, cold drinks and discussing life, Miss G keeping an amiable eye on Grace. The concern was necessary, as Grace got a bit upset about Clark. In her distress she was liable to run away into the bush to have a little weep. For Grace that love affair was really serious. They were both unencumbered. Grace had no dream of a future in which she would marry a prince and live in a palace in Monaco, but she was aware that for Clark there were few dreams left after his much loved wife Carole Lombard was killed in a tragic plane crash.

Frank came over to spend Christmas with them bearing the great news that he had got the part of Private Maggio and that shooting would start in a few weeks. Frank never knew Ava put up money for Harry Cohn as a guarantee if Frank flopped.

Frank could not have been more friendly and helpful. He took over the Christmas festivities, becoming very absorbed by the intricacies of African songs and the booming harmonies that accompanied them. He even trained an

African choir to sing Christmas carols. This created a little furor among white African-born contingents who were not quite attuned to the realities of racial harmony.

Frank's best present to Miss G and Grace, however, was to enlist the aid of the camp carpenter to build a little hut and to supply a pump and rubber pipe that would bring water up from the river to run a shower. It delighted them both. And he got Miss G pregnant again. That meant another trip to London.

Overall, *Mogambo* was a great experience for Miss G. She did not adore Africa in the same way that both Clark and Grace did. It was too big and wild, too primitive, and there was violence toward animals, as well as human beings, that she abhorred.

She did make two great friends. Grace and Miss G became bosom buddies, and in the future Miss G was always popping over to the palace in Monte Carlo to attend some princely function and enjoy a little gossip. Miss G also kept in touch with John Ford and visited him in Hollywood regularly. Later when he was in the hospital and dying, she became a constant visitor, helping his days along with talk about old times.

For the first and only time in her life Miss G was also nominated for an Oscar. She was really very pleased when Audrey Hepburn won the award for *Roman Holiday*. I mean, really pleased. If Miss G had won, how could she have gone on protesting that she knew absolutely nothing about acting?

A radiant Miss G at the premiere of <u>Mogambo</u> in Los Angeles.

13 OLD LOVE...AND NEW LOVE

Miss G flew back to London to finish the last few studio shots of *Mogambo*. True to the financial philosophy of MGM to keep their payroll artists working, she found she had another part in *Knights of the Round Table*. Miss G was playing Guinevere, the lovely damsel loved by that fearless noble knight Lancelot, played by Robert Taylor. As far as Miss G was concerned, her co-star had lost all his noble knight stuff long ago and was now relegated to the chilly status of past friend.

The film should have been enchanting. It read wonderfully on the printed page. It had been an evocative legend. It had been a poetical, magical conception of long-past history. How hard was it to recapture through the camera's lens? Pandro S. Berman, the producer, did not think so. He had already made a great success with a film adaptation of Sir Walter Scott's *Ivanhoe*, starring Robert Taylor and Elizabeth Taylor. Pandro also knew on the back lot of MGM's British Borehamwood location stood a real big and beautiful castle that they had used in *Ivanhoe*. Dust it down, stick it up in the countryside, and King Arthur could be recreated. All you needed was a lot of extras dressed in shining armor, waving swords and shields about and orating like Hollywood Hamlets. You'd get real class. Get them on horses draped in old carpets, chasing up and down hillsides, and cowboys and Indians would have real competition.

The film illustrated Pandro's thinking with great accuracy. Unfortunately, wherever they filmed in England it rained. The extras demanded more money, and they had a point. Sitting on a horse in heavy armor in the pouring rain was no fun. They moved those scenes across to Ireland where the government allowed them to use the Eire army for little more than the price of a few pints of Guinness. The rain was even heavier. The mud was thicker. The nightlife was non-existent. Afterwards one critic wrote, "Reflecting her disinterest in the role, Ava played Guinevere with a wooden graciousness, looking tired and uncomfortable in many scenes."

"God Almighty!" said Miss G. "What was I doing in costume drama anyway?"

Between the English and Irish locations Miss G got time off to take a short

European concert tour with Frank. From London she rang me, saying, "Rene, honey, I've just got to spend more time with Frank. We've got to spend more time together or else this marriage is going to drift apart from lack of use."

Frank's concerts began in Naples, wandered through Germany, and ended in Sweden. They were a total disaster. No one in Europe seemed to want to see or hear Frank in concert. Everyone wanted to see Miss G in the flesh to make up their own minds if this was the most sexy and sinful woman in the world or just another Hollywood doll. Frank got this message very quickly. In Scandinavia he decided to quit, and they returned to London.

I got another phone call from Miss G. "Frank's flying straight home. I've still got some dubbing to do, but Frank's had enough and is not waiting for me to finish. It's one of the 'I've got my own career to consider' situations. I guess you can say we're still apart."

It did not take a great deal of intelligence to understand that their marriage was slowly and painfully drifting to a close. It was not difficult to identify the incidents that caused the final break. One of these took place about two years earlier. Miss G and I had been staying at a rented house in Lake Tahoe, going for solitary walks in the woods. When Miss G prefaced one of those walks with my full name, "Mearene, let's go for a walk," I knew she had something serious to discuss. We hadn't gone far when she said, "Frank wants me to lend him nineteen thousand dollars."

"Have you got nineteen thousand dollars?"

"No, but I guess I can raise it from Charlie Feldman." At that moment he was her agent.

"What does he want it for?"

"It has something to do with his Palm Springs house. You know how he loves the place. He's paying off the lawyers or paying off Nancy from taking it over. It's about all he's got left."

That conversation took place even before they got married. Now we're in 1953, and things are falling apart pretty rapidly. Rumors say Frank might be nominated for an Oscar for his role in *From Here to Eternity*, and his record sales are recovering. Frank's beginning to climb high again. Miss G comes into one of the rooms in Pacific Palisades, and Frank's talking on the phone. As she enters she hears him say, "Well, if only I can get rid of her, it will all work out." Oh baby, Miss G is certain he is referring to her, and Frank didn't even deny the charge. Miss G was very hurt.

She said coldly, "I'll tell you how you get rid of me. Just pay me back my nineteen thousand dollars, and I'll go and file for divorce." It was a pretty dramatic confrontation. It was not one of those "Rene, I'm leaving—tell Hank to bring the car around" moments.

This time it was serious. Frank did not move back to his office. He moved into a rented house in one of the canyons. It was from there that he rang Miss G and said, "I've got your nineteen thousand. Why don't you come around and collect it?" She went across, and Frank was waiting in the lounge. He had a bunch of dollar notes in his hand, and as she walked in he threw them up into the air so that they scattered all over the floor.

When she was telling the story I said quickly, "I hope you had the good sense to pick them all up."

"You bet your ass I did," said Miss G. "Every one of those dollar bills. Then I left, probably for good."

The final break came when again Frank rang up and was apparently in bed with one of his floozies. He taunted her with that fact. "You're always accusing me of being in bed with some dame. This time you are right; I am." It was after this incident that we made our usual exit to Palm Springs in order to "finally get things worked out," to quote Miss G's own words.

We talked about Frank and what she should do in this situation. We wondered if this was really the end. She said sadly, "Rene, I don't know what love is, do you? We have outrageous fights and say dreadful things to each other. I'm certain I'll never speak to him again as long as I live, and if I see him on the street I'll throw up. Then he comes into a room, and those blue eyes look across at me, and he's smiling that smile, and there's that tenderness between us again. How can you explain our ups and downs, sudden hatreds and angers? Then comes the calm in the eye of the storm. Rene, why can't we make a go of it?"

I said, "I don't know. I really don't know." We discussed Frank's great success in *From Here to Eternity*. I said, "He must have worked so hard on that film."

"He sure did," answered Miss G. "Frank can be a real asshole on a set. He doesn't want to rehearse. He only wants to do one take. It is okay for him. Before *From Here to Eternity* he never had a director who wanted to control him or anyone who wanted to oppose him. Then Fred Zinnemann did in *From Here to Eternity*, and Frank began to think, 'Well, there may be something in this stuff.'"

"Funny, really, Rene. Fred was the director on that early film I did, *Kid Glove Killer*, and he gave me the very first line I spoke in a movie. Frank's no fool. You know that Rene. This time he was working with three great pros, Zinnemann, Burt Lancaster, and Montgomery Clift. He saw what they did–how they chipped away and carpentered and sweated time and blood and brain over what they were doing. Frank loved them and set up great friendships. He worked with them and learned from them. Frank wasn't going to be left out as the booby. He was going to be as good as they were. For almost the first time in his life he was working with and as a team. Rene, the man's an actor. The greatest love of his life is singing to an audience. Then he's acting; he's wooing them. He's acting his part with the lyrics and the cadences with that beautiful phrasing of his. He's acting for you."

I always thought that Miss G knew Frank much better than anyone else in his life, including his mother. Miss G was more in love with him than any other man she ever knew; that includes Mickey and Artie and all the lovers. It was now all dissolving, and there was nothing she could do about it. Tears did not help.

We returned from Palm Springs as Miss G had made up her mind. She knew that MGM was about to rent her out to United Artists and Joseph

Mankiewicz to play Maria Vargas in *The Barefoot Contessa*. Its locations in Rome and other parts of Italy would keep her away for several months. It was emotionally impossible to keep up the pretense of a happy relationship and still move around in Hollywood society. Miss G wanted out. Rome was as far out as Miss G could get for the time being. She knew that even there she would have to make a decision. It was better to make a clean break and end the marriage.

For that purpose, she went to see Howard Strickling, MGM's veteran and well respected head of publicity. He agreed with her opinion. The usual diplomatic statement was issued: "Having reluctantly exhausted every effort to reconcile their differences, Ava Gardner and Frank Sinatra can find no mutual basis on which to continue their marriage."

Miss G had kept her vow. She had not left Frank when he was down. After the immense success of *From Here to Eternity*, helped by the furor it created with the love scene between Burt Lancaster and Deborah Kerr rolling in each other's arms in the shallows of a Pacific beach, Frank had begun his climb back to what would become fantastic prosperity and success.

It was not a climb back to happiness. He could not believe that he had lost Miss G. Within days, rather than weeks or months, Frank began to realize what had happened and was desolate—much more than Miss G, who had been realistic when it came to the collision point. Frank had just let it ride, basking in his return to public favor, thinking it would all come out right in the end. He returned to his easily accessible entourage of men, a group Miss G hated. We called them the "Gee, you were terrific Frank" men. Their self-serving applause was sweet music in Frank's ears.

Frank had indeed lost Miss G as a wife for one simple reason. Much later in an interview she summed it up: "I was happier married to Frank than ever before in my entire life. He was the most charming man I'd ever met–nothing but charm. Maybe, if I'd been willing to share him with other women, we could have been happy."

She had put her finger squarely on the reason for her almost insane jealousy — Frank's apparent need to bed every girl that came into sight. One has to admit it is a commonplace masculine obsession. Most men applaud such ambitions, and maybe a few girls do too. Miss G, in my opinion, deep down was old fashioned about infidelity. When you were married you were faithful. What else was the point of marriage? If you didn't want to abide by that definition, as far as she was concerned, you were not welcome in her bed.

Divorced, a second group of rules came into play. What was good for the gander was also good for the goose. Miss G was certainly one of the prettiest geese around. Miss G was lucky. She had the beauty and the money to adopt this attitude, and as the years went on she did make the most of it. Tens of millions of women around the world are treated as cattle and have no hope. Miss G was the one that got away.

Before she left for Italy to make *The Barefoot Contesssa*, Miss G took me aside. She knew I was a bit disappointed about being left behind. "Rene," she said, "you're being left in charge here because you have got work to do. Important stuff."

I blinked a bit and said, "Such as?"

"You are going to sell the house in Nichols Canyon."

"Bappie's house?" I replied, realizing at once that I'd made a mistake.

"It ain't Bappie's house," shrieked Miss G. "We only loaned it to Bappie and Charlie because we moved into Pacific Palisades with Frank, and now that's more or less over. What the hell do we need two properties for?"

"But Nichols Canyon is already being sold by a realtor."

Miss G spread her hands in despair. "You know what Bappie does. She tells anybody the realtor sends that the house is not for sale."

"But Bappie...."

"Bappie is insisting on coming to Rome with me. She'll play the grand dame in whatever place we rent. When you have sold the house you can rent an apartment for Bappie and store all her stuff there."

"Bappie will go stark raving mad," I said.

"I hope so," said Miss G.

Bappie was twenty years older than Miss G and myself and used the experience gap as a mallet to drive her opinions like nails into our misinformed skulls. As time went on, we got tired of her dictatorial attitude. In her youth and middle age Bappie was an attractive woman. All five Gardner girls were attractive and got their warlike independence from their fiery Irish mother. None were as gorgeous as the last little creature to appear from her mother's womb, Ava Lavinia. If fireworks were needed she would supply them.

Bappie was bossy, vociferous, dogmatic and self-righteous. She was also cheerful, optimistic, level-headed, and reliable. I guess Bappie thought she was just a sweet, normal woman. When Mama Gardner was sick and faced with the fact that her young and beautiful daughter was being lured away to Hollywood, Bappie gave up her husband and her good job in New York to go with Miss G as guardian angel. Within six months of her arrival, Miss G was married to Mickey Rooney and after that looked after herself. One difference between the two daughters was that while Miss G never looked at Hollywood through rose colored glasses, Bappie took one look at the waving palms, sunny skies and shining Pacific Ocean and decided that her hat would hang beside it forevermore. She took trips like the one she was now taking to Rome, but for the rest of her life Hollywood was home.

I started off high on Bappie's list of undesirables. At the top of her list stood niggers, Jews and Dagos. As she grew older, this got a little complicated, as Hollywood contained a lot of highly talented, friendly Jews and her soon-to-be Dago friend Frank Sinatra. That left me. As time went by I became part of the general wallpaper of her life, and I don't think she even noticed my color. Occasionally we were even co-conspirators, in the nicest way, in steering Miss G away from some of her more hare-brained plans.

But even despite Bappie's strong personality and our fears that she'd push back, selling the house in Nichols Canyon was no great hassle. The realtor was overjoyed at having someone in the house to show clients around when they knocked on the door. Within three weeks, it was sold.

I also found an apartment and moved Bappie's belongings across. The moving men had obeyed my instructions to the letter. Included in the load were three huge cases containing half empty bottles of gin which Charlie had secreted away as comfort in his hours of need.

For *The Barefoot Contessa*, MGM loaned Miss G out to a new company formed by Joseph Mankiewicz, who was collaborating with United Artists. Joe and his older brother Herman were thought of as whiz-kid geniuses of that period. It cost Joseph two hundred thousand dollars and ten percent of the profits after the first million. Miss G heard about that from Joe halfway through the film, and, as she was getting only sixty thousand dollars, her admiration for MGM slipped even lower down the scale.

Miss G did make one slight slip at her first meeting with Joe when she said, "Well, have I got pretty feet?" as if they were going to appear on the billboards instead of her beautiful body. Joe responded without a trace of humor, "Ava, I think the movie will need a little more than that." Although the film did take a long time, Ava and Joe got on well.

In the film, Joe had himself portrayed as the witty, satiric man-of-the-world observer, looking at Hollywood's cloud-cuckoo land with revealing intensity and showing what a foolish place it really was. Humphrey Bogart narrated and played that part in his usual scathing manner, giving Miss G pep talks and warnings from time to time. His voice-over explanations were a cumbersome way of telling the audience what was going on.

The buzz in some film circles was that Joe was going to make dummies out of various Hollywood operators, such as Rita Hayworth, Howard Hughes, his henchman Johnny Meier, plus Porfirio Rubirosa, the international playboy. That didn't work either. Warren Stevens, Edmond O'Brien, and Marius Goring played their parts looking like Warren Stevens, Edmond O'Brien, and Marius Goring, and no one really understood the satiric subtleties Joe had planned.

The climax of the film–involving disillusioned Maria Vargas, the Spanish nightclub dancer-turned-movie-star–was more farce than tragedy. In some scenes it was pure soap opera. Maria married Rossano Brazzi, who was playing the Italian count. On their wedding night he confesses that during the war he was badly wounded and lost the ability to procreate the son and heir he longs for. Maria, a resourceful girl, slips into bed with his handsome chauffeur. She becomes pregnant, thinking it will delight the poor old count. It does not. He shoots both Maria and the chauffeur. The film ends with Maria's funeral and Bogart trying to patch it all together with dignity. Jack Cardiff's photography was superb. Edmond O'Brien won an Academy Award. The critics remarked on the carnal quality of Miss G dancing in a tight sweater and even a tighter skirt around a gypsy camp fire.

During the months it took to make the film Miss G had been making regular visits to Madrid. Her affection for Spain was becoming more and more evident. Some of that attachment, as I learned later, was caused by the arrival of Luis Miguel Dominguin, another bullfighter in her experience.

The love affair between Miss G and Luis Miguel was one of the happiest experiences in her entire life. She truly loved him, but this relationship also ended sadly.

They met in Madrid during the time Miss G made *The Barefoot Contessa* when she was whizzing about Europe, separated from Frank, and feeling no obligation to any man. Luis Miguel arrived in her life at a most opportune moment to fill that gap. He was tall and slender. He was debonair, handsome, unmarried, and in that period recovering from an injury inflicted in the bullring. He had temporarily retired from that dangerous sport.

He hardly spoke a word of English, and Miss G was similarly handicapped regarding Spanish, but as Papa Hemingway noted, they managed to communicate in the old fashioned way as lovers. They did not waste any time in becoming that. In fact, they were in bed together in a small Madrid hotel when Miss G began to experience the most virulent stomach pains of her life— complete agony, pain beyond belief. She was passing a kidney stone.

Luis Miguel was knowledgeable about belly pains. The horns of fighting bulls keep matadors aware of such practical matters. He rushed her straight to the hospital. It was run by nuns, and when her condition was diagnosed as not life-threatening, all they gave her to alleviate pain was aspirin.

During her convalescence Luis Miguel brought his great friend Ernest Hemingway to her bedside to chat. A.E. Hotchner, who was with Hemingway at the time, reported when they arrived Miss G was yelling down a telephone, talking to MGM in Hollywood and saying that nothing on God's earth would induce her to play Ruth Etting in *Love Me and Leave Me*. She was suffering with an awful complaint in an awful hospital, and now, for refusing to follow orders, she had a suspension by MGM to add to her woes. She saw Papa Hemingway whom she recognized immediately and smiled radiantly. Papa and Miss G became friends for life.

With Luis Miguel Dominguin, Miss G was not so fortunate. We discussed what happened so many times. "I was so stupid," said Miss G. "You remember the time when I got back to L.A. after I'd finished *The Barefoot Contessa*."

I remembered it all right. Howard Hughes had rung us up and said, "I've just rented this big house in Lake Tahoe, and it is very pretty, overlooking the lake. Why don't you go up there with Rene and take a vacation?" We both thought it was a great idea.

There were no strings attached as far as Howard Hughes was concerned, though I'm pretty sure he didn't expect Miss G to take advantage of the idea in the way she did. Howard Hughes had no idea that Miss G had the temerity to fall in love with a Spanish bullfighter and what her next move would be.

With her usual exuberance, Miss G immediately rang Luis Miguel in Spain inviting him to come across and enjoy the natural enticements of both herself and Lake Tahoe. I think he caught the next plane.

Luis Miguel arrived but was puzzled to find he was living in Howard Hughes' house. He was also confused by his continual presence. Miss G could never bother to explain the differing relationships between herself and her ex-husbands, ex-lovers and ex-anything else. She couldn't waste the time. As far as she was concerned at that moment, Luis Miguel was the great love of her life. She expressed those feelings in and out of bed. Couldn't Luis Miguel be happy with that? Why did she have to explain Howard Hughes to him?

Trouble was that Luis Miguel's command of English had not improved much, and Miss G's command of Spanish was equally sparse. So the nuances, subtleties and disagreements attached to their relationship remained unresolved. Miss G said, "Who cares?"

Luis Miguel did care. Was he sleeping with Howard Hughes' mistress? The drama heated up when they went gambling at the casino. It increased on the car drive home and came to a head when Miss G flounced off to bed and slammed the door. Miss G was very good at using a slammed door as a full stop. It was the first and only serious disagreement they ever had. Unfortunately, it was also the last.

Down in the lounge Howard Hughes and his side-kick Johnny Meier were chatting. The sight of Luis Miguel did not amuse them, and their remarks were not welcoming. Howard also realized that this might be his best chance of getting rid of an unwelcome rival. The remarks became pointed. Luis Miguel was far too proud to be patronized by an American multi-millionaire with about as much sense of humor as a lamppost and a contemptuous disregard for anyone who opposed him. If Miguel had fallen out with Miss Gardner, said Howard, and was unhappy in this house, then he was quite free to leave. Transport could be arranged for him within a matter of minutes. A car would take him to a nearby airstrip. A light plane would fly him to an international airport. He could be back in Spain within a few hours.

When Miss G came downstairs the next morning, no one seemed to know what had happened to Luis Miguel. He had just decided to leave. Miss G knew better.

"Somehow, that bastard Howard Hughes insulted him," she said to me. "I shouldn't have brought him here to have to put up with Howard." She rang Luis Miguel and tried to explain, but it was too late. The love affair between them survived for several months afterwards, but it was not the same.

Luis Miguel eventually went back to Spain and married Lucia Bose, whom he met when she and Miss G were together. At his farm in Spain they raised three children.

Miss G pretended that it didn't matter. I knew that it did. Luis Miguel got as close to her heart as any man did.

"Rene," she said in our conversations long afterwards, "he was so gentle, so caring. I should have done more to protect him from Howard. Maybe I would never have understood Luis Miguel unless I'd had that time in the hospital. I think there was a great frustration in his life. He hadn't started out rich. His father was a bullfighter, but there wasn't a great fortune in that in those days. Luis, because of his artistry and skill, made a fortune. Money wasn't his objective. He didn't know what that was. There was always this ache in his life that he should have made more of his intelligence. He had wonderful friends: Papa Hemingway, Picasso, and many more who encouraged him to do more than fight bulls." She began to remember all the fun time they had together, and she began to laugh.

"Even when I had the screaming heebie-jeebies in that hospital from the pain, he'd tell me a funny story and make me laugh. Mind you it was his sort of funny story, and he was lying his head off. He swore he was in the ring one time and was gored so badly they had to pick his balls up off the sand and stick them back in again...that was his perverted sense of humor." The memory flooding back caused her to scream with laughter.

After she'd stopped screaming with laughter, I said, "Miss G, after such a serious operation, how was the results?" The laughter had dwindled to a chuckle, "Yeah, the results were good. I'm sure it never happened even though he was badly gored a lot of times." She paused and went on, "I sure did love him; he was so different."

She paused again to arrange her thoughts. "You know he even loved the bulls he fought. Lots of bullfighters are bold and brave, but they are also stupid. Just being brave isn't enough. Just having heart and courage isn't enough. You've got to have understanding and intelligence, and that was Luis Miguel. He loved animals, all animals."

"He took me to his farm once–his finca where he raised fighting bulls. What do you think he had for a pet? He had a wolf. The wolf adored him, and he adored the wolf. When the wolf understood that I loved Luis Miguel too, the wolf loved me as well."

14 FLYING BLIND WITH HOWARD HUGHES

With Luis Miguel back in Spain and Miss G still suspended by MGM and free as air, we continued our "Move and Booze" vacation at Lake Tahoe. Everybody in the west knows that Lake Tahoe lies between California and Nevada and is huge and beautiful. Certainly, the unbelievable shimmer of its blue surface lured Howard Hughes to say, "Ava, for a girl of such perfect beauty, I must find a ring of that color to match your looks."

I don't think Miss G did anything in response but smile. In due course, he gave her the most wonderful ring, a blue sapphire stone mounted between two large diamonds on a slender band of gold. She took it, smiled again and said, "Well, thank you, Howard." Most ladies would have drooled in ecstasy.

Practically every night when he was there, which wasn't all that often, he would escort Miss G and me to the casino for a gambling session. Get it straight, my appearance there was simply to stand behind Miss G as she sat at the tables and keep her equipped with dollar bills to wager. Usually, she started with a stake of between fifteen hundred to two thousand dollars. I had strict instructions that when she slipped down to five hundred I would react like a red stoplight signal and say, "Miss G, that's it. We are through!"

On one occasion, however, Miss G arrived at the casino, and this night we were without Mr. Hughes. She was liquored up to the eyeballs and started throwing dollar bills around the table as if they were confetti. She was on a losing streak and getting cross. Fifteen hundred dollars clicked into the croupier's hands. My red warning light was now blinking with the speed of a police car signal, and I was hissing, "Miss G, Miss G, you've reached the limit. Stop! Stop!" I could have been talking to the wind. Miss G was having none of it. She turned, not only furious, but as an accuser.

"Rene, what have you done with my money?" This statement she made in a very loud voice. "I want to go on playing. Where is it? What have you done with it?" Her voice must have reached every corner of the casino. Looks were hostile. Who was this strange black girl trying to steal Miss Ava Gardner's gambling stakes?

At speed, I handed over the last five hundred. At equal speed Miss G lost it. The bank then refused to grant her any more credit. Ava Gardner or not, they had seen too many of these dumb, drunk broads before. They knew they could gamble on until they lost their blouses, pants and garters in their efforts to recoup their losses. Next morning they would accuse the casino of scandalous behavior in allowing them to gamble so unwisely. So we went home.

Next morning, a trace of resentment still tingling in my veins, I repeated the story to Miss G. "I did what?" she exclaimed and laughed so hard she nearly fell off her chair.

I said reprovingly, "Miss G, I was the only black face in that whole casino. You could have gotten me lynched." She laughed even louder. To the end of her life, she crowed with laughter remembering that incident. I even get to laughing about it myself these days.

Howard Hughes, who never drank more than one rum and Coke at any meal or gamb
ling session, also scared me to death with his gambling. He would spend between twenty and twenty-five thousand dollars a night trying to work out their system and break it. I don't think he ever succeeded, but Miss G always said, "Don't worry about Howard. If he loses too much money, he'll just buy the casino and get it all back."

I tried to take that into consideration, but found it hard. Once I said, "Miss G, do you really understand Mr. Hughes?" Miss G did her usual quick gurgle of laughter.

"Rene, honey, nobody understands Mr. Hughes. Sometimes I don't think Mr. Hughes understands Mr. Hughes. Everybody understands the orders he hands out and does what he tells them to do."

I was still trying to work out Mr. Hughes, the enigma. I said, "Bappie says he's the richest man in the world, and certainly he's got all these houses everywhere."

"Houses!" exclaimed Miss G. "Before your time, when I first knew him, he had this enormous great house in Beverly Hills. He didn't own it, he rented it. I don't think Howard has ever owned a house anywhere, ever! He just rents them."

She went on with her explanation. "You've seen the suit he wears? Shiny at the elbows, the sleeves damn near frayed and two inches too short. The trousers equally short, worn and shiny. His luggage, you've seen that too. Cardboard boxes made of pasteboard, the cheapest things you can find. They're not even glued together. Howard is allergic to glue. As far as I can make out, Howard is allergic to about ninety percent of the world's components, so he ties his boxes up with string. He even keeps his shaving gear in one."

Many years in the future, Miss G and I would often discuss Howard Hughes and wonder what had happened to him. It was always clear that Mr. Hughes had enormous power and an enormous amount of money. He was vibrantly pro-American, violently anti-communist and when immersed in aviation projects he was a near genius. He also possessed powerful friends in the armed services, the government and the CIA. We read in the newspapers that in 1974 the CIA and U.S. Navy had spent six hundred and fifty million dollars from a secret fund for the operation code named "Jennifer." As it turned out, Howard had something to do with it.

The U.S. Navy was aware that a Soviet submarine prowling off the coast of Hawaii had suffered an internal explosion and had sunk with the loss of all hands in 18,000 feet of water. That was a fantastic depth to even consider attempting salvage, but they wanted that submarine. They wanted the Soviet secrets. The drawback was that a diving operation of that nature was bound to attract media attention from all over the globe, including Soviet attention. How could they keep it secret?

Someone thought of Howard Hughes. Everyone knew Howard Hughes was an eccentric billionaire, always attempting outrageous exploits and nearly getting killed, but most of the time making a large profit. Supposing Mr. Hughes, apparently of his own volition, formed a company ostensibly devoted to dredging rich mineral deposits from the ocean bed near Hawaii. There was a precedent. A great fortune in diamonds had already been scooped off the seabed near the coast of Namibia. It was just the sort of long-shot operation that would appeal to this adventurous Texan, and the public would believe it.

The report went on to explain that the whole scientific world and the media had been completely spoofed by this operation. It was not until the U.S. Navy, with its polite naval etiquette, sent the bodies of the dead Russian crew to the Soviets that anyone knew what had really occurred.

No doubt, Mr. Hughes was one of the most puzzling and secretive men in the whole wide world. Who else on some sort of whim would build the largest wooden seaplane in the history of aviation and with the comparatively low-powered engines of those days expect to get it off the water? Mr. Hughes did just that. Agreed, he only made one maiden flight lifting it off the ocean for a short distance, and it never flew again.

He took Miss G to see it when it was still under construction. She came back exclaiming, "God Almighty, Rene! It's the biggest thing I've ever seen. Each wing is as long as a street. It's as big as a block of flats!"

She also related how in the very first period of their association (when certainly Mr. Hughes had her separated out as a possible future bride), he used to fly her to various meetings he had on the East Coast. At one rendezvous in a posh house in Washington, D.C., Miss G, Howard, and a high-ranking general were together and had a first drink.

"Suddenly," said Miss G, "there's a loud ring on the doorbell, someone opened it, and into the room walks Veronica Lake—the real Veronica Lake. Who could forget during the early war years that lovely, young actress with the flowing golden hair and the radiant smile? What the hell was she doing in the general's house with Howard? Was she there to plan some great war deal, or was it supposed to be some romantic tryst with me making up the foursome?"

"So what did you do?" I said.

"I just left. I am good at leaving. Washington is full of hotels."

Whether Howard invented drama like this or just didn't know he was engaged in drama, I would never know. As I said, he was a puzzling man.

Therefore, when in the middle of our leisure period in Lake Tahoe, Mr.

Hughes reappeared and announced it might be a great idea if we all flew down to Argentina, we were not at all surprised. Miss G had no objections, and where Miss G went I went. I didn't have any objections either. Mr. Hughes was probably arranging a revolution, but what the hell?

Around this period MGM remembered that they had an actress named Ava Gardner on their books, and keeping her suspended wasn't doing them a whole lot of good. They began to make vague mutterings through the agencies about a novel they had just purchased named *Bhowani Junction*. They were considering how they should handle this big project.

It was set in the pre-1947 period when India was about to become independent of the British Empire. Miss G was to be cast as the beautiful, half-English, half-Indian girl torn between those two different cultures.

Miss G was still on her high horse, miffed that MGM rented her out for an exorbitant sum to United Artists for *The Barefoot Contessa* and then suspended her. As far as she was concerned, they could go and jump into the Pacific. Her immediate thought now was Argentina.

"Okay, Howard, when do we take off?" was her reaction.

According to Mr. Hughes, we had to make one stop in Miami for undisclosed business reasons. We flew in a huge, empty plane. Howard and his co-pilot, Glen Odekirk, were up in the cockpit. Traveling with us were a steward to serve drinks and a clutch of seven young men, all crew-cut and gray-flannel-suited, who were part of Mr. Hughes' staff. I got along with one called Butch, who was friendlier than the others.

Miss G settled down to some happy drinking, and the word came back that if we felt like it we could come up to the cockpit and watch what was going on. We did. I was fascinated. Indeed Mr. Hughes was very pleasant to me, pointing out various landmarks and explaining the various weather reports and navigation details that came in through the receiver. Miss G soon got tired of this and went back to dry martinis. I stayed on, never dreaming that within the next few hours I was going to be scared out of my wits.

Flying down over Florida and plainly nearing Miami, Glen said, "Mr. Hughes, shall I clear our landing with Miami airport?"

"No," said Mr. Hughes. "We're landing at the U.S. Army military air base. You know where that is."

"Yes, sir," said Glen, and on we go. Suddenly a suspicious and irritated voice comes over the speaker. "You are approaching a U.S. Army airfield. Will you please identify yourselves? Over."

"Shall I identify, sir?" asks Glen.

"No," said Mr. Hughes.

Glen's voice choked a bit, but he replied, "Yes, sir."

The military voice clips back at him. "Repeat. You are approaching the landing strip of a U.S. Army air-base. Identify yourself at once. Do you read me? Identify yourself at once. Over."

"No," said Howard Hughes flatly.

Glen said, "Mr. Hughes, sir, we cannot land on a U.S. air base without identifying ourselves. Sir, we could be shot down." Mr. Hughes made no reply.

He was perfectly under control.

If you could attach a color to a human voice, you could say that the army base officer's voice was now purple, shot with crimson. He was enraged. We were now obviously losing altitude for our long approach.

The voice snaps. "This is a warning. If you intend to land on this air strip without identifying yourselves, you are liable to be arrested or shot. Identify yourselves!"

Glen said quickly, "Mr. Hughes, if we don't identify ourselves, I am going to lose my license."

Mr. Hughes' sharp retort was unforgettable. "If you do identify yourself, you will lose your license anyway."

Glen clenched his teeth, gripped his wheel, and brought us down onto the runway. We slowed to a halt. The engines were switched off. The door was opened, steps lowered. Miss G, unaware of any trouble, came forward and followed Mr. Hughes down. I could see soldiers collected there. A military-looking car was also there.

When they were out of earshot, Glen said in a tight voice, "The bastard obviously had it all cleared from higher authority even before we took off. No one told the control tower. I expect the tower was ringing up to get permission to open fire with anti-aircraft guns when they got told it was important brass arriving."

Big deal—I lost at least ten pounds of weight through sheer apprehension. Miss G and Mr. Hughes drove off in their car. We all descended and found there were other cars waiting for us. They drove us to a nearby villa complex Mr. Hughes had rented. He held his meeting in the lounge of the biggest house and gave no explanation of what the hell he was up to.

"We shall be here for a few days," he said in his quick, clipped Texan accent. "And I don't want anyone to know about our visit. Got it? We'll all use fictional names."

I thought that sounds like real spooky, international stuff. Any more landings like that, and I'll go back to St. Louis. My pseudonym was Miss Mearene, my first name only. Miss G was Ann Clark, the name Robert Taylor had adopted for their clandestine association.

Mr. Hughes then gave me the real stern secret agent look. "Rene, you are allocated one of the guest houses overlooking the swimming pool. Lock yourself in. If anyone calls, answer no questions. Tomorrow morning lock your door behind you, and come over here."

How right he was. Next morning, the door bell rang with loud intensity, and there was an elderly lady with gray hair outside giving me a steely look through gold-rimmed spectacles. She sounded irritated.

"Who are you, and who do you work for?"

I lied like a born-again secret agent. "Ma'am, I've been recruited by an agency. Just told to stay here and show up when required."

"Well, how many people are there in your party?"

"Your guess is as good as mine."

"How'd you get into this villa?"

"The door was left unlocked for me."

"Who's paying for all this?"

"I've no idea. The agency settles all that."

"I want to come in and inspect the house."

"Sorry, ma'am, that ain't allowed. I am not allowed to let anybody in this villa."

The old bird, who I guessed was some sort of caretaker, looked at me straight in the eye through her shiny spectacles for a good ten seconds. Then she said. "You're either the smartest god-damned nigger I've met or the dumbest." She walked away.

I smiled and closed the door. I knew which description I preferred. Hell, if Miss G fired me, I might join the CIA.

I met Miss G by the pool. She was calm and rested. We had coffee and splashed around. Mr. Hughes seemed to have disappeared. We stayed there for five days, doing nothing but drinking and splashing in the pool. Food was sent in from this little restaurant Mr. Hughes liked. Steak, baked potatoes with sour cream, peas, and salad became our fixed diet. We didn't even wonder where Mr. Hughes was.

On the fifth day he reappeared. We had new orders. Apparently Argentina was out for the time being. A boat was waiting at a nearby harbor to ferry us to a seaplane which would fly us over to Nassau in the Bahamas. Mr. Hughes had rented a house there which once belonged to Sir Harry Oakes.

Butch knew something about Sir Harry's background. He had made his millions, vast millions, when he discovered a gold mine in Canada. Moving to England, he made something of a mark in British society, gave extensively to all the right causes, and was knighted for his charitable works. Eventually he retired to the Bahamas. There on this little known British colonial possession, he built a huge, rambling manor house in Nassau and settled down to become master of all he surveyed. One dark and silent night he was murdered in his bed. The murder seemed motiveless. There were a couple of suspects and eventually a trial, but the crime was never really solved.

"You mean to tell me Mr. Hughes has rented that house!" I exclaimed in shock. "Isn't it haunted?"

"Probably," said Butch. "Mr. Hughes likes mysteries."

So off to Nassau we flew in the seaplane. After my recent experience of approaching a U.S. Army air base without being shot down, I was now quite hardened to Hughes Aviation Travel, Inc. Flying into Nassau, we could see the island from the air. It was flat, the coastline indented, with beautiful beaches and palm trees everywhere.

We skimmed above the sea and splashed down not more than a few hundred yards from Sir Harry Oakes' manor house which stood in green lawns amidst shady trees. A motor boat puttered out to take us ashore, and was it hot. By the time we got to the landing jetty and into the shade of the old fashioned building we were gasping for drinks. They were served by white-coated waiters on the wide veranda that provided a breeze from the sea. Mr. Hughes had certainly pulled strings to rent this corner of the British Empire.

Everything about it was a bit heavy and stuffy. There was an air of quiet relaxation about the place. The estate was run by a black overseer, a sort of butler who served first under Sir Harry Oakes and then under the Duke and Duchess of Windsor. The Duke was the Governor of Nassau at the time. He seemed to think that his position gave him baronial privilege. A short distance from the main house was a collection of cottages where the servants lived. The overseer thought I should stay in one of them. I made it clear that as Miss G's maid I was attached to her by threads of gold. I would sleep in the room next to hers. He came around to my point of view without argument.

I went in to see Miss G, who was fanning herself because it was so hot. She said, "Well, why don't you turn on your fan?"

I said, "I haven't got one."

"I'll call Howard," said Miss G. "He'll fix that."

Two minutes later Mr. Hughes called back. Miss G laughed and put down the phone. "Howard called the overseer. He told Howard that servants were not allowed fans in their rooms. Howard told him that unless a fan was in your room within fifteen minutes, he would be seeking another job." The fan was in my room in ten minutes.

I did feel sorry for the poor guy. His whole life had been run around timetables. Both Sir Harry and the Duke and Duchess had insisted upon breakfast, lunch, and dinner at precise times.

I told him that Miss G's idea of a precise time was imprecise. She would wake up shortly after lunch and start on her first large gin and tonic with a twist of lime. After a few of those and maybe a swim or a walk, we would probably be ready for dinner. For the whole week we were there, the poor guy was always running to me saying, "Rene, we must get organized. We simply must get organized." He had no hope.

We saw Mr. Hughes from time to time, but mainly he was out doing business, about which we knew nothing. At the end of the week, without warning, Mr. Hughes decided he was going to fly the seaplane back to Miami for more hush-hush business and was taking Miss G with him, but leaving the rest of us behind. That included Glen Odekirk, the co-pilot, and the posse of seven guys. We had to pack up and meet them back in Miami by ordinary airlines.

Packing Miss G's eighteen suitcases was no problem, as I hadn't unpacked more than a couple of them anyway. Some of the others contained only one beautiful and expensive gown. Miss G loved trailing those around with her. There was also her jewelry case of which I was the sole custodian.

I had a lot to think about because, so far, I had been flying around America and the Bahamas under a false name, offering no identification, and I had no passport. How the hell was I, a black person, going to get back into the land of my birth? Everybody else had passports. Butch and Glen, who knew their way around, said we would manage it.

Landing back in Miami, the fun started. Our immigration official could have passed for public executioner. Who was this black dame with eighteen suitcases and no passport trying to enter the U.S. of A.? How the hell, on the spur of the moment, Glen thought up the idea, I'll never know. I never really wanted to know.

Glen was standing in line next to me. The immigration officer fixed him with steel-pointed eyes, "Are you with her?" The "her" sounded as if I were a female rattlesnake.

"I'm her manager," said Glen coolly. I mean Glen was an upstanding, clean-cut American whom everyone could trust.

I thought, "Oh, God, manager of what?"

The customs officer thought the same thing. "Manager of what?"

"This lady is a famous recording star from South America."

"Yeah?"

"She doesn't speak any English." I'm taking her to our recording studio."

To my total terror, Glen then turned to me and winked. The customs officer couldn't see him. Then Glen said, "Gorra-manchku-ch-chatta."

I got the idea. What a great new invented language. I gulped and answered, "Gorra-chutta-chatta-me." I sounded great, I thought. Glen turned back to the officer without a trace of hesitancy. "The lady wishes to know if you want to open her cases and examine her–the–er–costumes–she wears for her operatic performances."

"Yes," said the officer.

I thought, "Oh God, if Glen goes on like this, he'll have me singing an aria from Tosca before I know it."

The officer fingered Miss G's gorgeous dresses. A couple came from the Fontana collection which she wore in *The Barefoot Contessa*. They were convincing. He looked suspiciously at my jewelry box but seemed reassured when Glen said it contained only costume jewelry, all worthless trinkets. The immigration officer tagged all the baggage and let us through.

Outside, Glen grinned and said, "Only got a couple more hurdles to clear before we're through."

"Tell me," I said weakly.

"We've received a message that Mr. Hughes has booked the whole floor of a Miami hotel for us. Being Mr. Hughes, he has not revealed where he is, only that when he's ready he'll call us, and we can rejoin him and Miss Gardner."

I said, "Good, I need a shower."

"Trouble is," said Butch, "they don't allow colored guests in the hotel, so we've got to figure out a way to get you through the foyer, into the elevator and up to a room."

"You could pack me in a bag," I said.

It now became something of a Marx Brothers comedy. I was escorted by seven big guys. A couple of them signed in and signaled when the coast was clear. Then, sandwiched between four of them and hidden from view, I was hustled through the foyer and into the elevator. There was an elevator operator, and we thought we had fooled him. We hadn't.

The phone rang, and Glen answered it. The voice on the other end said, "I understand you've got a nigger girl up there in your rooms. Nigger girls are not allowed in this hotel. She will have to leave at once."

By this time we were all a bit fed up and harassed by our journey. A little fed up with childish games.

"Listen bud," Glen said, "our boss reserved and paid for this entire floor. The lady you're talking about is one of our group, and we are waiting for instructions from our boss. Get it straight. We'll stand for no more of this nonsense from the front desk. If we get any more of it, our boss who you may or may not know, will buy the whole hotel and fire everyone on the staff. Do I make myself clear?" There were no more phone calls.

Later that afternoon we rejoined Miss G and Mr. Hughes in another villa complex he had rented. There was a huge modern house surrounded by huge gardens with swimming pool and guest cottages. It probably cost him a fortune, but what was a fortune to Mr. Hughes? He was not very amused when we retold our story of getting through customs. We were rather pleased with ourselves. We thought we had done rather well. Mr. Hughes didn't think so at all.

"You mean they bought that story?" he said.

I said, "They sure did."

"No wonder our country is in such a sad mess," said Mr. Hughes and walked out of the room.

Once more we settled down to our sunbathing, swimming pool, and gin and tonic existence, while Mr. Hughes disappeared on his regular business deals. By now Miss G was getting rather bored by the lack of excitement. It came to an end quite abruptly.

I had noticed that another of Mr. Hughes' bodyguards seemed to have joined our ranks. We didn't see much of him, but he would appear around lunch time. I'd offer him a glass of beer in the kitchen, and we'd chat. One day in the middle of drinking his beer, I saw him looking at me in a very cold manner. I said, "Anything up?"

He took a deep breath, as if he was going to make some important confession, then said abruptly, "Can't you get that dame of yours to go to bed with Mr. Hughes?"

It was my turn to take a deep breath. "Are you being funny? Are you kidding?"

"No. I'm dead serious. I'm asking, can't you influence that Miss Ava Gardner of yours to fall into bed with Mr. Hughes?"

"You're out of your mind," I said.

"Maybe you're right. I am out of my mind. You'd be going out of yours too if you were in the same situation."

"What situation?"

"I'm stashed in a motel room around the corner," he said.

"So what?"

"I'm there twenty-four hours a day. I only get a couple of hours off occasionally when I'm replaced by another guard."

I said, "What are you talking about?"

"I keep a loaded revolver at the side of my bed day and night. I'm guarding this priceless diamond and pearl necklace which belonged to one of the Russian czarinas. Don't ask me which one."

A ray of light entered my head. A priceless necklace? First, the sapphire ring and then the necklace?

"The night that Ava Gardner gets into bed with Mr. Hughes, that is her big reward."

"How do you know all this?

"Everybody knows it. It is no big secret. Everybody on his staff knows it."

I thought to myself, only Howard Hughes could think up a scheme like this. Here he's been flying us around America and Nassau for three weeks, doing his usual business deals, but all the time thinking that this is his big chance for sex with Miss G.

The poor guy went on. "I can't go to a bar. I can't date a girl. All I do is sit guarding that necklace and waiting for your girl to fall into bed with Mr. Hughes."

I said, "I think you are going to grow old and gray before that happens."

"You don't think she will do it?"

"I know she's not. If she were, she would have done it years ago."

"Mr. Hughes doesn't understand women," said the man sadly.

Of course, I told Miss G the story. She smiled, but was not very amused. "Rene," she said, "we're getting out of here."

To lighten the atmosphere I said, "Miss G you've got the sapphire ring. Does this mean you're giving up all claim to the Czarina's necklace?"

"He can stick them both up his jumper," said Miss G.

"When are we leaving?"

"Tonight, before dawn. To hell with all the luggage. He can take care of that. We'll just take a bag or two and we'll ring for a taxi, steal down, and do a bunk before Howard knows we've gone."

It sounded so simple. We didn't go to bed. We rang for the taxi, crept down the stairs, and there was Mr. Hughes waiting at the bottom.

"Oh, hallo," he said, as if it were the most normal thing in the world to see his guests stealing away at the break of day.

Miss G confirmed our position. "We're leaving," she said flatly.

"I wish you wouldn't do that," said Mr. Hughes.

I decided to leave the drama for them to work out, saying, "I'll put the bags in the taxi Miss G and tell him to wait."

When I came back I found that Mr. Hughes was holding a heavy lamp in his hand. I have a good idea that he might have hit her with it if I had not come back. He put it down as I arrived on the scene.

In the taxi she told me that she had thrown the sapphire ring back at him. I could, therefore, understand he had a certain right to be annoyed.

The taxi driver asked, "Where to, ladies?"

"The airport," said Miss G.

I said, "Where are we going?"

"Cuba," she said. "I've got a standing invitation from Papa Hemingway."

15 LOVABLE PAPA HEMINGWAY

Various other incidents prevented us arriving in Havana until late that evening. We bought our tickets and went to inspect the departure board, discovering our flight was delayed. For the next eight hours every flight to Cuba was delayed or canceled. Miss G swore it was the diabolical intervention of Mr. Howard Hughes. I protested, "How does he know we are going to Cuba?"

Miss G nodded across at a newsstand. The guy who was supposed to be guarding the Czarina's necklace was now scrutinizing a Miami newspaper.

"Howard's sly," said Miss G. "You can bet your bottom dollar Howard got that guy to follow our taxi. Howard's got more power in the airline business than any man on earth. He can fix a few delays."

Another troubling incident had already occurred on our drive to the airport. Miss G wanted a hamburger. She wanted to breakfast on hamburgers. The taxi driver knew a place open twenty four hours a day and stopped outside it. I joined the queue.

When my turn came, I saw the man behind the counter was regarding me as if I'd just crawled out from under a rock.

I said, "Sir, the lady I work for sent me in for six medium rare hamburgers. She said would you please toast the buns."

He looked at me and reached down in this bin where he'd thrown away all the stale buns. He took six that were so hard you could hear them crack. Then he reached into another bin and took out six hamburgers that people must have rejected and put them in the buns.

He said, "That will be six dollars."

I said, "My employer wants six hamburgers medium rare and will you please toast the buns?"

He said, "Nigger bitch, if you say one more word to me I'll kick your ass. You've got your nerve to even come in this place. Get your ass out and you take these hamburgers or none at all."

"Well," I said. "I'll take none and here's your six dollars." I threw the six dollars at him.

He was livid. I swear he was going to jump over the counter and come and get me. I was too quick for him. I ran out the door and jumped into the taxi. The driver moved off as soon as he heard the door slam behind me.

Miss G said, "Where are the hamburgers?"

I told her what happened, and she yelled to the driver to pull over. She was going back in with me to give that bastard hell. I said gently, "Miss G, it's no good. That guy's a founding member of the Ku Klux Klan, a real piece of garbage. He'd just as soon hit you as hit me. Miss G, we've had enough action to start one day. Let's save our emotion." We moved on.

Our wait at the airport was helped by the fact that I had stowed a bottle of cognac in my large handbag, so we could take turns to slip into the ladies' room and have a swig. This sustained us until about eight in the evening when one of the airlines decided to take off for Havana. Miss G had spent her honeymoon there with Frank, so she knew all the best places. We caught a taxi to Trader Vic's and stuffed ourselves with chicken livers and water chestnuts wrapped in bacon. I can remember the taste to this day. Funny how some meals stick on your palate and in your mind forever.

Then we went to the Hotel Nationale. Not only did the management remember Miss G, they were delighted to see her. They gave us a two-bedroom suite. We both took showers and then fell into our beds. Never in my life have I been so glad to see a bed. The last fifteen hours or so had drained me completely.

When we woke next morning, we started working on what we termed our strategies. Usually, they were only concerned with where we should go for lunch, what we should drink before lunch, where we should go shopping after lunch, and whether it was too early to start before-dinner drinks.

This time we had real serious plans. We'd been incarcerated in luxury villas far too long. We needed freedom. Miss G knew about a pleasant hotel half a day's drive away at the famous Varadero Beach. We would go there for a couple of days, cut down the drinking, swim, get sun, walk on the beach and get ourselves fit enough to ring up Papa Hemingway and go to visit him and Miss Mary. I had never met either of them.

After a few days at Varadero Beach, we returned to the Hotel Nationale, called Papa Hemingway and arranged to meet him at the Floridita Bar. Every taxi driver knew it. Miss G knew it because she and Frank had made it one of their favorite stops during their honeymoon. It was a large, old-fashioned Spanish bar and seafood restaurant–fans whirring on the ceilings and a clutter of small tables served by nimble-footed waiters. The bar was long and massive, backed by mirrors and stacked bottles. There was a brass rail for your feet and an ample supply of tall bar stools.

Papa was waiting for us, looking very comfortable. Sun-tanned, bearded, and fit, he gave me the impression of enormous stature. I was introduced after he kissed Miss G on both cheeks. The smile he gave me was big and approving. My kiss on the cheek was also welcoming. Papa ordered frozen daiquiris, the main ingredient of which was white Bacardi rum. Papa had invented his own Papa Double, drunk extensively by tourists forevermore. Expanding his alcoholic vision, he had now concocted a jumbo sized daiquiri which one could almost take a bath in. Any favored guest of Papa's had his or her ability tested by his capacity to drink daiquiris level with Ernest, and we did. Miss G and I made ladylike efforts, and Papa was pleased. Then, slightly disoriented, we took a taxi back for dinner at Papa's farmhouse, Finca Vigia, a short drive from Havana. The sun shone, the sky was blue, and the air was balmy. I felt fine. Papa had downed probably twice as many daiquiris as we had and was in an expansive mood. There were fifteen acres of wilderness, he explained, waving at his property. Still there was room for a swimming pool, vegetable garden, vines, and more species of mango than anywhere else in Cuba. There were about five million cats, as far as I could see, along with dogs and chickens and cows that gave the place a friendly atmosphere.

Mary Hemingway, "Miss Mary," was on the veranda ready with more drinks, inevitably cool, collected and welcoming, letting Papa hog the conversation. Of course, Papa did have things to talk about and opinions to express.

The house was wide and airy. A huge lounge with the heads of various animals Ernest had shot on his African safaris were perched on the walls, carpets and comfortable furniture and beautiful original oil paintings. Some of them were very valuable French impressionist works, most of which I'd only seen on posters. It was a place to relax, a house to talk and drink in. It was an oasis from the outside world.

Late that night in our taxi driving back to the Hotel Nationale, Miss G said happily, "Rene, honey, I think Papa's taken a real shine to you."

A couple of days later, Papa took Miss G and me down to the mooring where he kept his powerful ocean-going cabin cruiser, *Pilar*. Miss G was quite right. Papa had taken a serious shine to me–so much so that I had a dodgy time avoiding his busy hands when we were down in the galley together. The main trouble was that I felt seasick, and Papa was gentlemanly enough to see this and save his more serious passes until later.

Papa used the *Pilar* mainly for fishing, but I think he could have circumnavigated the world in it if he had wanted to. It was a bright, windy day, and we bounced over the waves with the sun on our hair and sea spray in our faces. Papa, the expert fisherman, with his crew baiting his lines, trailed them overboard, but we didn't catch anything. Maybe the booze we were drinking had something to do with that. We had a very good trip.

I suppose I should have welcomed the attentions of the most famous author in the world, but when you're on the high seas and feeling lousy, only one's feet on dry land brings relief. In my condition at the time, I could not even have appreciated William Shakespeare.

For the next few days we were regular visitors at Finca Vigia, spending a lot of time in the swimming pool. It was there that Papa's pursuit really started, and fending off Papa's bristly beard, wide smile, busy hands and his evocative dialogue suggesting that we end up in bed needed real diplomatic handling. After one flurry in the shallow end, I protested, "Mr. Hemingway!"

"Papa," said Ernest affably.

"Papa, I'm very flattered, but your wife, Miss Mary, who is a very sweet lady, is in the house not more than fifty yards away."

"Rene, Miss Mary understands these matters."

"Papa," I retorted, "Maybe Miss Mary understands these matters, but I don't."

"Rene," said Papa, gently trying to unhook my concrete grip on the pool rail. "I have always been very fond of ladies of color."

"Papa," I replied. "I'm sure you have been very fortunate with them. But this lady of color does not have any intention of going to bed with you, whether or not Miss Mary approves, or is standing at the edge of the pool yelling, 'Take your hands off that girl.'"

Papa was not at all put off by my resistance. During the next few days he told me at length of his intrigues with ladies of color in far-off Kenya. He was certain he had produced a son by a pretty Masai maiden probably on the pretext that the boy might enjoy writing novels instead of wasting his time running around killing lions. One of his ladies of color had apparently become so fond of Papa that she wanted to share his grass hut back in the United States. Papa had to be quite firm in rejecting that idea.

I suppose Miss G and I were in agreement that Papa Hemingway was one of the greatest writers of our century. That didn't mean we had to join him in bed. We both thought he was a wonderful bear of a man who, when he entered a room and felt like it, could bring intensity, brightness, euphoria, and expectancy to all who were there.

He loved Cuba and never stopped talking about it. He told us how he'd first discovered the island in 1928 on a crossing from France to the USA when the British boat on which he was traveling had put into Havana harbor. He was then 29 years old. His first marriage to Hadley had broken up, and he was then married to Pauline who was pregnant and anxious to reach Key West to have the baby. Papa settled in Key West and wrote what I—just one of a million readers—think to be his finest novel, *A Farewell to Arms*.

The country had caught our minds, too. We wallowed through our days of doing nothing, and every night we went back to the Hotel Nationale, where we rested in preparation for another day of inaction. But one night the phone started ringing. "Who?" said Miss G, listening with an attentive look on her face. "Okay, Okay. Ring me tomorrow at lunchtime, and I'll tell you what I think. Yeah—it's an exciting idea."

16 PUBLICITY CHIEF DAVID HANNA AND THE SOUTH AMERICAN SCANDALS

While we had been enduring Howard Hughes' tour, David Hanna, publicity director for *The Barefoot Contessa*, had been worrying about what direction his campaign for this movie should take. The film had been edited and was safely shelved. Investors associated with its success had previewed it, and few were wildly enthusiastic. Rumor suggested this was not a Joseph Mankiewicz smash hit like the award winning *All About Eve*. This was a "well, we'll have to see" production.

David Hanna's job was not to act as critic or doubter. It was to generate the greatest possible amount of media attention to the movie, hopefully to build it up as one of the best movies to reach the screen since the camera was invented. The gala premiere had already been planned. United Artists was already issuing statements about it being their enormous smash hit of the fall season. How could it fail when it was written and directed by the great Joseph Mankiewicz, with Humphrey Bogart heading the cast, divine Ava Gardner playing the female lead, and many other famous stars involved? David thought they were right about Ava Gardner.

David knew one thing for certain. Until he saw her arrive at Rome airport, he had known little about her except that publicity suggested she was just another Hollywood sexpot who leapt from husband to husband and bed to bed and exhibited not the slightest ability as an actress. Then he saw her standing at the top of the airplane steps smiling down at the enthusiastic crowd and looking so radiant that she almost glowed.

The crowd went wild. David went slightly numb with disbelief. As a movie man who'd been in the film business for a long time he knew without any doubt that if he hadn't seen a great actress, he had seen a female of dazzling intensity and a woman movie fans loved. David Hanna's certitude never wavered in all the years he spent with Miss G.

His time with Miss G in Rome added to that first impression. No one wanted to know about Humphrey Bogart or any other member of the cast. They only wanted to know about Ava Gardner, to see her, to be near her, to cheer her. If he could implicate Miss G in this publicity build-up, his worries would be over.

First of all, getting her to attend the gala premiere would be a good start. If he could coerce her into spending a week before the opening giving press and photo sessions in New York that would be an added bonus. He expressed these ideas to Joe Mankiewicz and other United Artists personnel. With alacrity, they agreed.

Where was Ava Gardner? Did MGM know? Did her agents know? Did anyone know? The voices boomed at David Hanna. "You're the publicity guru. You find her. You bring her back to New York, not dead or alive, but wholly alive and beautiful!" David started work.

He found that she was rumored to have been seen in North Carolina, Lake Tahoe, Palm Springs, Miami–even as far away as Nassau in the Bahamas. His starting point must be the West Coast. David arrived in Hollywood saying he felt more like a wartime secret intelligence agent than a movie publicist trying to track down a famous star. MGM was frosty. They had no idea where she was. Still less, they didn't care. Ava Gardner was still under suspension.

David, however, had one ace in his pack. During those months in Rome he had made great friends with Ava and become equally friendly with her older sister, Bappie. If anyone on earth knew where Ava Gardner was, it was Bappie. He was right. A phone call to Bappie enlisted her help. No, she couldn't reveal Ava's whereabouts without first consulting Ava. If he rang back in an hour, she would probably be able to give him that information. David rang back in 58 minutes. Yes, Ava would talk to him if he rang her in Havana.

"Havana!" cried David. "What the hell's she doing there?

"Only Ava knows," answered Bappie cheerfully. "Ring her at the Nationale Hotel. She's staying there under the name of Miss Gray."

In our suite at the Nationale, Miss G put down the phone and said, "That was David Hanna."

I said, "Oh?"

"United Artists and Joe Mankiewicz want to do a gala premiere opening at the Capital Theater in New York in October. They want me there as Queen Bee."

"Will MGM have words to say?"

"To hell with MGM," said Miss G. "I like David. He was a great help in Rome. Now I'm considering these publicity ideas of his. David thinks that if I cooperate they can really give old Barefoot Contessa a real lift." She turned to me with a big smile on her face. I could see she was hatching something. "Want to go to South America, Rene? We didn't get to Argentina with Howard Hughes, did we?"

"I don't know," I said.

"David's often talked about the time he spent in South America. He's told me how popular I am in those countries." She paused, frowning.

"Miss G, what's on your mind?"

"We've done a tour with Howard Hughes that wasn't worth a damn. Why don't we do a tour for United Artists and have a lot of fun seeing South America? Let's make a change. What about it, Rene, honey?"

I said, "Great idea. Do you think David and United Artists will buy it?"

"They'd be crazy if they didn't," said Miss G. They bought it all right. David could hardly believe it. What other famous star would offer to do such an arduous tour for free?

United Artists' foreign sales manager began to work out tour schedules immediately, while David took over the actual day-to-day details. Miss G would hold court at two receptions in each city, one for the local big-wigs and one for the press. Where and when was the tour to start? "From where you are and now!" said David on the phone. "I'll come across to Havana, and we'll fly from there. We haven't got a lot of time."

I put in a word there. "And we can stop in Miami to pick up the other sixteen suitcases from Howard Hughes?" We did.

The tour schedule was Havana, Miami, Lima, Santiago, Buenos Aires, and Rio de Janeiro. Caracas had to be left out because Miss G had to get back to New York for the gala opening.

It was thought better to leave Rio until last. There had been some sort of scandal in Brazil suggesting that due to U.S. intervention President Vargas had committed suicide. The country was still under martial law, and U.S. citizens were not all that popular.

In the plane flying south to Lima, Peru, David warned Miss G that she should expect thousands, rather than hundreds, to gather at the airport and that they would not be as well behaved as the crowds she usually encountered in the United States. Even David blinked when he saw the mass of spectators gathered at Lima airport. There was even a military band. We landed, and a United Artists representative informed us our landing coincided with that of the President of Peru returning home after a foreign visit.

Nevertheless, the crowds cheered. They were there to see one person only, and that was not their president but Ava Gardner. The police were polite and helpful, and there were no dangerous crushes. Miss G waved and smiled as she was led through the barriers and signed as many autograph books as she could. The cavalcade of cars was cheered as we passed through the streets, and David said, "Incredible, we could be royalty."

The two receptions were orderly, and Miss G was surprised and happy. With one more day left and only one more luncheon for the local dignitaries to attend, Miss G made her big mistake. The evening before, she was introduced to a drink called Pisco Sour. She liked it. She didn't care what the drinks were made of–she liked them and as far as I could see, see drank about a couple dozen. I sipped far more gingerly, as did David.

Next morning, I took in her coffee to find a very unhappy and hung-over Miss G. She groaned, "Coffee? Horrible! Take it away and just leave me alone."

I said, "Miss G, we've got a celebration drive through the streets to a local function. Crowds will be there to cheer you up."

"Rene, nothing will cheer me up except death. Go away."

I took the coffee into the next room and drank it myself. David came breezing in with his daily worksheet. As this was South America, he followed local custom by calling Miss G "Senora."

He looked surprised. "Isn't the Senora up yet?"

"No, the Senora is not up yet, and I don't think she is going to get up."

"Rene," he said sternly, "you must go in and wake her."

"David, I've tried. You go in and wake her."

David looked suspicious. He moved cautiously into the bedroom leaving the door open. His light-hearted approach was received with contempt.

"Senora, Senora...wake up...we've got lots to do." There was no reply.

"I think if you wore the red dress today, it would look absolutely great."

A rebellious voice from under the sheets growled, "I am not wearing the red dress. You wear the red dress. I am not going anywhere. I am not doing anything."

"Senora, you are the guest of honor at Lima's swank Jockey Club. You've got to present a Gold Cup to the winner of the big race."

"No."

David wailed. "But I've got to take you to the reception."

'You are not taking me to any reception. I've quit."

"But what are we going to do?"

"Take Rene. She'll be a great stand-in. She's pretty, and she will do it." Miss G's head poked out from under the sheets and she saw me through the door. "You'll take my place, Rene, won't you?"

Miss G was submerged beneath the sheets again. We retreated to the outer room.

"Jesus!" said David in a voice similar to a man being strapped into the electric chair. "What do we do now?"

He took a deep breath and began to think and came to a conclusion. "Well, we press on regardless, as they say." He looked straight at me. "Come on Miss Ava Gardner, go and put your best dress on."

"I can't do that," I shouted.

"Yes, you can. It's a closed car, a limousine, so no one can see you clearly. You've got twenty minutes."

We argued, and I lost. With what is known as a sinking heart, I went to get dressed.

The police cars, the outriders, and the limousine arrived. David went out first and held open the door of the limousine. I dived in like a rabbit and tried to submerge myself in the leather seat. We moved off. The crowds on the pavement cheered and waved.

"Sit up and wave," ordered David, doing a rather grim-faced imitation of the Duke of Windsor. "Wave honey, wave!"

I smiled and waved, and we moved at a sedate pace through the streets. I suppose the poor Peruvians had so little to cheer about that even a surprisingly new version of Ava Gardner was enough to give them something to remember. Maybe a few who got a close look were surprised how dark and sunburned Ava Gardner really was, but then the sun in Peru is really hot anyway. I thought that just the idea of seeing a famous film star cross their paths raised their spirits. I was sorry I was a counterfeit.

The luncheon and reception was held at the posh racetrack at the edge of town. As we neared it, David said, "I suppose we can't risk the lunch or the Gold Cup." He smiled at me. "You did real well."

"We can't risk the lunch," I confirmed resolutely.

David nodded and continued, "I'll go up and explain that the Senora is 'indisposed'–that's the best word ever invented by the female professional. I hope the word is just as good in Spanish. They're nice people, and they will understand." They did.

As I've said, David was a very resourceful young man. I was introduced to a small number of guests as Miss G's secretary and shook hands with a lot of pleasant people. The next day, the newspapers went on printing the hundreds of pictures they already had of Miss G shaking hands, holding babies, and looking divine. We had passed the test and without me ever having to do my impersonation again. Miss G did her own personal appearances from then on.

Receptions in Santiago, Chile, and Buenos Aires, Argentina, went well. In Buenos Aires David picked up a scent that Dictator Peron, whose wife Eva had recently died, would welcome Miss G's company as he laid flowers on Eva's grave and perchance maybe Miss G could join him for dinner afterwards. Miss G ruled out both the grave and any perchance immediately.

"David, our engagement book is packed...understand?" David did understand. Strange coincidence though, when we were living in a rented apartment in Madrid, who should be our neighbor but Peron, by then Argentina's deposed dictator.

David, who spent a lot of time in the company of Miss G, was remarkably observant about her. In the book he wrote in 1960, which included details of our South American journey, he wrote one passage which I think identified one facet of Miss G's personality in a way no one else has ever done–her astonishing beauty at any time of the day.

David wasn't the only one who saw it, though. There was an incident that occurred on our flight between Buenos Aires and Montevideo, Uruguay, a comparatively short hop between cities. Miss G realized that she couldn't possibly be ready in time for her usual spectacular appearance at the top of the airplane steps. Worried, she implored David to ask the pilot if he could possibly circle a bit before they landed to give her a chance to complete her star image.

The pilot, a big, tall Texan, knew he had Miss G aboard. He was not the slightest bit phased by the request. In his slow drawl he told David to inform "that sweet, little girl" back there to take all the time she wanted. When she was ready all she had to do was let him know. Just come up to the cockpit and tell him–alone.

What the rest of the passengers must have thought as the aircraft made several wide sweeps around the airfield in a maneuver that lasted half an hour has never been chronicled. A delighted Miss G dazzled the cockpit for at least fifteen minutes and returned saying, "That Texan! He's some fella!"

Flying north to Brazil, David had been worried about the hotel accommodations that United Artists had reserved for us. He knew Rio de Janeiro. He knew that in those years the Copacabana was miles ahead of any hotel in the city. He'd never heard of the place we had been slotted into and had misgivings.

We were not arriving until nine in the evening, which meant it would be dark and the crowds might not be too ferocious. What a hope. News had traveled ahead of us. As we turned off from the main runway, the crowds were already amassed and were so undisciplined that through the windows we could see them trying to keep with our plane's trundling speed. By the time we reached our parking space, we were hemmed in by an ocean of excited human beings. David said, "We've got to wait for them to clear a space. You'll never get through that mob without being torn apart."

The noise of people cheering and shouting outside was scary. The other passengers took their chances, went down the airplane steps and fought their way through. The crowds were getting restless and started chanting, "Ava, Ava, we want Ava!" They also chanted a lot of other things in Portuguese which conveyed the same message.

It was Miss G who said, "If the United Artists representative isn't going to show up, we are stuck. Hell! Let's take a chance. There are policemen down there. The fans will only push us around a bit." Push us around a bit! Hell! They nearly tore us apart.

With Miss G leading, trying to follow an almost submerged policeman, David next and me bringing up the rear, we dropped into that seething mass of excited spectators. I'll never forget the experience with the shoving and screaming, the lunatic cameramen, the TV lights, the exploding flash bulbs, the hysterical waves of sound. At one point Miss G lost her shoe but with one despairing dive managed to fish it up. There was no chance of her getting it on again. We were dragged, pushed, and shoved but fought our way through to a television hut. There we clung, all on the verge of collapse. Miss G was near hysteria. The noise outside was still appalling.

At last someone located a back door. Someone else summoned an old taxi. We piled in, and the taxi moved off. The taxi driver didn't seem to know what he was doing or where he was going. David yelled the name of our hotel a dozen times. Then to help his concentration, Miss G in complete exasperation and rage hit the poor man over the head with her shoe. It didn't seem to faze him, but it broke off the heel of her shoe. We eventually reached the hotel. The neighborhood seemed crummy, the façade of the hotel dilapidated. We scrambled out of the taxi, and a barrage of flash bulbs popped again. We hurried inside. "Christ!" said David.

The manager and a dozen staff appeared. They were about as elegant as the crowd we had just escaped from. We were taken up in a creaking elevator and were steered along a worn carpet into a suite that must have seen not better days, but better centuries. The bedroom was equally dismal. In order to sooth us, a tray of martinis stood on the table. Miss G seized one.

I heard David say, "Jesus Christ!" a second time. The furniture was old and stained. There was a stench of tobacco and cigarette burn marks everywhere.

The United Artists representative, Gilberto, had now arrived. David led him aside for a quick and forceful discussion which we overheard.

"For God's sake, who booked this accommodation? Miss Ava Gardner can't stay here."

Poor Gilberto blustered, "The new office of United Artists. They said there could be no cancellation."

David raged. "I cabled them personally to change us to the Copacabana."

"I had no authority...no authority."

"Well, you've got authority now. Go telephone them. We want a suite and two rooms."

Gilberto hurried off. Plainly he also alerted the manager, who appeared flustered and alarmed. Poor little guy. Later we realized he must have been only a small cog in a well rehearsed plot.

He waved his hands in despair. If Miss G left his hotel his reputation would be ruined forever. What reputation did a dump like that have to lose? Then the truth, or at least a particle of it, emerged. The hotel was paying for the cost of both of Miss G's receptions in return for her staying in the hotel.

That did it. Miss G, who had been cool, calm, collected and apologetic for not being able to stand his awful hotel, blew up. She threw her martini on the floor where it smashed to smithereens. She stormed into her bedroom shouting, "I can pay my own bills. If United Artists can't pay theirs, it's too damned bad!"

We finally made it to the Copacabana hotel, which was great. It was clean, modern, luxurious, and efficient, with great views from all of our rooms. It was late, but the Copacabana nightclub was open until the small hours. So we went to eat dinner and watch the show.

Miss G simmered down. We all heaved sighs of relief. All the heaving sighs, however, did us no good. When I made contact with David the next morning, he had the newspapers spread out before him. Although he did not admit it until he wrote his book long afterwards, he plainly knew a double cross when he saw one.

Pictures of the suite in which we had spent no more than an hour were given front page prominence. If David, aided by Miss G, myself and a couple of staff had been given a week in which to smash up that place with axes, we could not have done the job better. A wrecking crew had gone to work. It was a disaster. They had torn the place apart. They had broken every mirror, gouged furniture, walls and beds. Whisky and wine bottles and smashed glasses were everywhere. The headlines told the story. Ava Gardner had arrived drunk, barefoot, and disorderly. She had thrown glasses at her manager, and her conduct had been so abusive and outrageous she had been thrown out of the hotel. The headlines and the pictures were very convincing. There was a picture of Miss G, disheveled and clutching her broken shoe, entering the hotel. The pictures of the bedroom offered decisive proof that hurricane Ava Gardner had passed through.

What was even more diabolical was that, given adequate notice, this entirely false story had been wired by the news agencies to papers all over the world. Miss G cruelly and systematically had been set up. When David Hanna immediately rang the United Artists publicity office in New York, he was greeted with cries of joy by one of its senior staff. David reported that conversation in his book. "Congratulations!" they screamed. "It's great...just great!"

David replied angrily, "Are you out of your heads? This is a madhouse here. I don't know what to do. I'm sure Ava is going to cancel, and I think damned well she should."

"Stop it. You're breaking my heart. How did you ever get her to take off her shoe? The whole thing is terrific. Just keep it going and get Ava to New York."

I remember a wise politician on TV once declaring. "When a lie is first propagated, it tends to become accepted. Once accepted, it takes on a life of its own."

This is what really hurt Miss G. Everybody believed those lying newspaper reports. She read them and got pieces translated. She said to David. "Get the press here right away. I'll be ready for them."

She was not furious. She knew she had no hope of denying them worldwide, but she was determined to give her side of the story to the Brazilian press. David rang every newspaper and agency in Rio, telling them Miss G was giving a press conference in an hour. They all turned up. Miss G, looking lovely and composed and about as far removed from a room wrecker as the sun from the moon, denied all the charges.

Calmly and quietly, she told them what had happened. The entire Brazilian press printed her story that evening or the next day. Not a single word of it appeared in newspapers outside Brazil. The outside world had gotten the story they wanted. Later in the day a timid, courteous consul official arrived at the suite and apologized for what had happened. As a small token of consular consultation, he also presented Miss G with a beautifully cut topaz stone about the size of a playing card.

The damage had been done. Miss G was blamed for this incident for the rest of her career. David later heard that the hotel booking had been prepared by United Artists publicity department with the thought in mind that, "maybe there will be a blow-up."

Who needs "good" publicity? If you're going to publicize Ava Gardner in a movie, you will get more coverage with scandal and outrage.

When we left the hotel to drive to the airport, the photographers followed us in hordes, driving dangerously and swooping in and out between cars to get shots of us. Once inside the immigration building, you would have thought we were criminals trying to flee the country. First our passports were confiscated. Then we were separated and led into small rooms to be harangued and cross-examined by hard-faced immigration officials. I didn't know what had happened to Miss G or David. All I knew was that I was alone and under threat. They interrogated me ruthlessly. What was I doing in Brazil? Had I entered Brazil illegally? How could I prove I hadn't? What sort of work was I doing? Did I expect them to believe my lies? They knew all about people like me. They knew what to do with them. There were severe penalties for illegal behavior. The interrogation went on and on.

God, they were awful. It was so unexpected, so unfair. The badgering and intimidation went on for hours, it seemed, though it couldn't have been anything like that long. They reduced me to a sobbing, terrified wreck. Eventually I was escorted out to the aircraft, frightened that Miss G and David were still being held in custody. I was pushed up the aircraft steps and shown to a lonely seat.

David and Miss G were given the same rude treatment. None of us knew whether the others were on the aircraft or had been left behind. Our passports were only returned to us when we were in our seats. Once airborne, the decent and friendly Brazilian staff, free of the immigration officials, hurried to our assistance. They sat us together and did all they could to soothe our feelings. We flew on to Caracas and then to New York, and rarely had any of us felt more relieved or appreciative than when that imposing New York skyline came into view under the aircraft's wings.

Miss G, David Hanna, and me in a hotel in Venezuela during our <u>Barefoot Contessa</u> promotional tour. What a trip!

17 THE SAMMY DAVIS DISASTER

We took time to settle down after South America. Miss G disappeared into our suite at the Drake Hotel for something over twenty-four hours. David, of course, ever on the go, was trying to protect her but had to try and fix one important *McCall's* magazine photo session by Richard Avedon, featuring her and Joseph Mankiewicz. Not even that got past the telephone receptionist's implacable answer, "Miss Gardner is not to be disturbed." Letters, telegrams, and notes piled up outside our door. We were resting.

Eventually, Miss G rejoined the world, and I answered a phone call in our suite. It was Sammy Davis, Jr., and his voice was jubilant. "Hi there, Rene. How's things? How's life? How ya doing?" Then, without waiting for a reply, he asked, "Ava there for a quick word, honey?"

I knew that Miss G liked Sammy very much. She remembered the time when Frank was rock-bottom, and Sammy was one of the few friends who stuck around. Always ready with a supportive upward heave-ho. I did not doubt his exceptional talent, but I was a bit suspicious of his motives. His total devotion to Frank Sinatra, who he thought was the greatest singer ever, amounted to reverence, and Frank's continuing friendship was important to him. I also knew Sammy was a black guy desperately trying to claw his way to the top in a white entertainment world. That wasn't easy.

Today people cannot comprehend the difficulties of being a 'black anything' in the forties and fifties. Admittedly, there were lots of black musicians and artists playing in their own black groups, but none with white artists. Artie Shaw, to his credit, was the first to use Lena Horne in his band as a black vocalist. He also used black trumpeters, drummers, and horn players.

I'm sure Sammy was well aware of this situation, so there were no holds barred in his devouring ambition to attain world fame and acceptance. Good luck to him. Above all, Sammy Davis craved Hollywood. Frank Sinatra was Hollywood. Ava Gardner was Hollywood. Therefore, I always sensed a potential danger to Miss G.

Miss G told me what Sammy had wanted. He'd said, "Ava honey, every time I walk the streets of New York, I see the great billboards, 'Ava Gardner in

The Barefoot Contessa.'"

"It'll be a flop," Miss G had replied cheerfully.

"Come on, Ava, it's terrific. You're at the top. I bet those United Artists publicity guys can't do enough for you."

Miss G said, "I didn't tell him what I really thought about what those United Artists publicity guys had done to us back in Brazil."

Sammy went on, "Feel like doing a little favor for an old friend, Ava?"

"Sure," said Miss G without hesitation. "What is it?"

"I'm doing an act up in Harlem...the Apollo, 125th Street. You know the old song and dance stuff. It's the usual routine."

"Nothing routine about your act, Sammy."

"Thanks a lot Ava, but listen. If you could spare a few minutes one of these night to drop by, just before my act, walk on the stage and say, 'Folks! Sammy Davis is an old friend of mine, and I'm here to wish him luck and watch him sing and dance.' It would bring the house down. What do you think, Ava? It might even add to publicity for *The Barefoot Contessa.*"

Miss G paused in her account, and I prompted her, "What did you tell him?"

"Okay Sammy, I'll check it out with United Artist and get back to you."

Miss G looked across at me, and I said, "Well?" It was a pretty long "Well..." and my "Hmmm" was equally as long.

"He's an old friend."

"I know," I said.

"You're feeling the distrust vibes too?"

"Sure am."

"Tell you what I'll do, Rene. I'll give Bill Williams a ring and sound him out. He'll know."

Bill Williams was an old friend of Miss G's. He was a New York disc jockey who had his own radio show, and his specialty was showbiz. He was always chatting with up-and-coming guys and gals in the entertainment world and giving them a boost. He told Miss G, "Ava, you know as well as I do that Sammy's got great talent—really great—and he's going places. He can't wait, and he's got a lot of fast moving friends who are also on his bandwagon."

"So, Bill, what do I do?"

"Tell you what, Ava. Why don't I chaperone you out to Harlem and check out the skyline with you?"

Ava was grateful for the offer. But what we didn't know at the time was that Bill Williams had his own suspicions about Sammy. For the Apollo visit, Miss G really dressed the part. To start with, she wore a white Fontana skin-fitting gown. One of the luxuries she really enjoyed as a film star was to be able to buy gorgeous, fancy-priced clothes. She really fitted into that gown and loved wearing it. Standing in the wings, diamond glints flashed in her hair as she waited for Sammy to introduce her to the audience. She looked dreamy.

Sammy started off, "A big surprise for you tonight, folks...." That was a bit of an exaggeration because when Bill Williams and Miss G arrived, the street outside the theater had been jam-packed. The word had spread. Indeed, they needed a police escort to reach the stage door.

Sammy went on with his build-up. "She is a beautiful young lady who lives in Hollywood. She's been called the Love Goddess of the World. Certainly, there's no one more beautiful...and she's a pal of mine...ladies and gentlemen...a big hand for Miss Ava Gardner!" Squeals, shrieks, whistles, feet stamping and applause amounted to bedlam.

"Rene, you should have heard that noise," Miss G said, and went on, "But I'd had a couple of drinks with Bill Williams, so I was sort of relaxed." She tripped on to the stage and put her arm around Sammy's waist and gave him a bit of a hug, which got an even bigger cheer. Then she said her little piece about Sammy being a great entertainer, dancer, singer—the usual plug—and a great chum. Then, as instructed, she got in the fact that *The Barefoot Contessa* was in town and then started talking about bare feet. "Mine feel a bit pinched," she said, "so if you don't mind I'll take my shoes off." Then she took her shoes off, and from the noise you would have thought she'd taken off her dress. She blew them a kiss, and off she ran.

Next day, Sammy rang again to say thanks a million and to tell us that United Artists was pleased and was releasing a publicity blurb about the visit quoting all the nice things Miss G had said about him. Great!

Not so great was another phone call from a friend of Sammy's who worked for *Ebony* magazine. He too had a great idea which would help Sammy's career and give *The Barefoot Contessa* such a boost that everyone in Harlem would flock downtown to see it. *Ebony* was putting their Christmas edition together. "Would Miss G be photographed in a Christmas scene?" they asked. Sammy would dress up in a Father Christmas outfit, white beard, red robes, and all that jazz, looking down in a fatherly fashion at Miss G as she made out her Christmas wish list. It all sounded very harmless, but Miss G rang Bill Williams again. He said, "Ava, don't do it."

Ava argued, "Bill, if I don't do it, it will get about that I'm against black people, and I'm not. I've been mixed up with black people since I was a girl, and the last thing I am is prejudiced, and I sure don't want to have that reputation."

Bill hemmed and hawed and again didn't tell Miss G what his real suspicions were about Sammy. Finally he said, "Okay, Ava, but be careful."

Sammy and his team arrived at the Drake Hotel. It was almost an entourage—two photographers, a publicity guy from United Artists, and one or two others. Bappie was there with Ava and me. What could be bad about that? I didn't know why they wanted to pin up a large sheet of red paper against one of the walls. It would be really like Christmas, they said. Only much later did we understand its special significance. There were no drinks, not even coffee. Sammy got into his Father Christmas outfit, and Ava had on an ordinary dress, nothing the slightest bit sexy. The whole session took about an hour. They were just about to leave when Sammy made his request.

He describes it exactly as he remembered it in the autobiography he wrote about ten years later. Jokingly he said to Ava, "I still ain't got that autographed photo you promised me."

To which Miss G allegedly replied, "I've only got glossy studio stills here in the hotel, but you can take pictures right now if you like." They did like. There didn't seem to be anything unusual about the shots. Sammy had changed into street clothes. He sat on the arm of Ava's armchair smiling at her—that sort of thing. Now comes the suspicious bit. In his book, Sammy admits he asked the photographer for the roll of film. The photographer shrugged and said, "I'll develop it for you."

Sammy then replied. "Well, look, please be careful. Don't let it get into the wrong hands. It could make trouble for her."

That was the second suspicious bit. If Sammy had the slightest idea that the photo session might cause trouble for Miss G, he had no right to put her at risk. And she was in trouble, big trouble.

Howard Hughes was the first to bring the trouble to her attention. He flew into New York and invited her to dinner, telling her it was of considerable importance. After their dinner Miss G arrived back at the Drake, green eyes flashing red signals. She fell into an armchair, thrust out a hand, and demanded, "A drink!"

Always ready for such emergencies, I hurried to the kitchenette where a pitcher of dry martinis were already marinating in the fridge. Miss G shouted after me, "Do you know what that little bastard Sammy Davis, Jr., has done to me?"

I called back, "Miss G, Bill Williams did say not to do it."

I returned with the pitcher of martinis and two glasses. Miss G swallowed her first drink as if it were cold tea. I refilled the glass and she drank half of that in one gulp. That meant she was very upset.

I said, "Miss G, honey, how does Mr. Hughes get into this thing between Sammy and you? What's Sammy done to him for him to be concerned?"

Miss G took her time and finished her second drink. She was seething. "Rene, I'm sitting there watching Howard carving up his eternal steak and balancing his little green peas on his fork, when suddenly he turns to me and says in a nasty voice, 'Ava, what have you been up to with that little rat, Sammy Davis, Jr.?' and I said, 'Hold on there Howard, what the hell do you mean?'"

Miss G held out her glass for the third martini and said, "Howard went on, 'You've heard of that magazine *Confidential*?'"

Miss G says, "'Everybody's heard about that filthy, lying, pornographic rag. What's that got to do with Sammy?'"

"'They have got a front cover picture of you and Sammy looking very friendly with a headline which reads, 'What Makes Ava Gardner Run for Sammy Davis, Jr.?' Inside there are more pictures and a story saying you've been sleeping with that nigger, paying visits to his flat for a long time, and that he's the greatest male stud you've ever met!'"

Miss G paused for a breath. I could not believe it. It was now my turn to sink a martini in one gulp. "That's impossible, Miss G. It's the worst lie I've ever heard," I said. Then it dawned on me. "You mean when you did that photo session with Sammy for *Ebony* at the Drake Hotel?"

Miss G was still rambling on about Sammy. "I can't believe Sammy would do this. Remember, Rene, those days just before Frank and I married, Sammy gave me earrings engraved with A.S. for Ava Sinatra. That was the first time my married name really stuck, and I loved his thoughtfulness."

I changed the subject for her. "Miss G, the magazine isn't published yet. How come Mr. Hughes knows so much?"

"Because a year or so ago, *Confidential* did the same sort of hatchet job on him. You know, wealthiest man in the world has a string of beautiful broads stashed away all over Hollywood. He treats them as sex slaves."

I said, "Well, Miss G, we both know the broads stashed away is true. I'm not sure about the sex bit. Besides, if he's the wealthiest man in the world he can sue them or buy them up."

"Rene, they would love it if he sued. He'd probably win a million dollar lawsuit and get five dollars' damages which they wouldn't have and they would have countrywide publicity. If he bought them out, they would move two blocks down the street, open a new magazine called Bedroom Secrets, and pay one of those stashed broads for an article called 'My Sexy Nights with Howard.' It's a no-win situation, Rene."

"Have you talked to Bill Williams?"

"Sure, I called him from the restaurant. He said, 'Jesus Christ, I should have warned you more strongly about Sammy and the friends he mixes with. This black guy-white chick sex scene is right up *Confidential*'s alley these days. I believe that Sammy could be cooperating. I know Sammy pretty well. I've been to his apartment and seen enlarged photos of Hollywood heartthrobs— Marilyn Monroe, Kim Novak, among others, on the walls. I was not amused by Sammy's little grins and innuendoes suggesting he'd had a good time with these ladies.'"

Miss G stopped talking, and we looked across at each other in silence. Very carefully I shared what was left in the martini pitcher between us.

I said, "Miss G, so what evasive action can we take now?"

"Don't know. I've called Howard Strickling, MGM's publicity chief, and they are setting up a meeting with the top brass and me as witness and injured party."

Miss G came back from the meeting with a serious face. Everybody had been outraged. Everybody screamed they would sue *Confidential* for every cent they had. Howard Strickling had talked and brought them around to his solution. They would ignore the entire episode.

He maintained, "Who reads a lying, salacious magazine like *Confidential* anyway? Don't give them world publicity with a lawsuit. In a couple of weeks the entire episode will have been forgotten."

Of course, he was right. No other newspaper or publication picked up or dared print the allegations.

Oh yes, *Confidential* came out with their cover and headline. Inside were more photos which the photographer had shot to ensure the highest possible degree of intimacy. They were against a red background as positive proof that the shots had been taken in Sammy's bedroom. He maintained he had posted the pictures to *Confidential* instead of *Ebony* by mistake. There was also a short article based on the United Artists publicity blurb circulated when Ava visited Sammy at the Apollo Theater. The article had been tampered with. Sentences had been shortened and twisted. The wording was given spurious and sexy implications, with lines added such as, "Some girls go for the gold, but it's bronze that sends sultry Ava Gardner." The photos presented plausible, but totally lying, proof that Sammy and Ava were passionate lovers.

Then something terrible happened. Before the Christmas edition of *Confidential* appeared in November 1954, Sammy had been playing the New Frontier in Las Vegas. The Will Mastin Trio, consisting of Sammy's Uncle Will, his father, and Sammy were pulling down seven thousand five hundred dollars a week. That was a lot of money in those days. Sammy had bought himself a new Cadillac convertible. Things were going great for Sammy, and normally no one would applaud more than me and Miss G.

As he drove along one day listening to his first hit record, "Hey There," a car swerved and turned in front of him. Sammy wrenched at the wheel, hit the car and smashed into oncoming traffic. In the collision Sammy's right eye hit the cone in the center of his steering wheel, and his sight in that eye was gone forever.

Sammy was still in the hospital recuperating when his father entered the ward with a copy of *Confidential* and silently laid it on his bed. Seriously and reproachfully his father asked—as between father and son—if there was any truth in the story. Sammy was indignant and said vehemently, "Dad, are you losing your mind?"

Sammy's first worry, however, was not what either his father or Miss G might think about *Confidential*'s allegations, but what was his good friend Frank Sinatra going to think about it? After all, Frank and Miss G, even though separated, were still very much in love and closely associated. Sammy's own explanation in his autobiography was that it was inexcusable that he could have put Ava in a position so that such a thing could have happened to her. It sure was!

Sammy's further explanation was that he rang MGM's publicity department offering apologies and was told that Ava was ignoring the entire episode and that if he was thinking of suing *Confidential* he should think again because a lawsuit would only attract more disgraceful publicity.

Sammy's first worry was quickly removed when Frank arrived at the hospital bearing gifts and kind words. He believed Sammy's denial of any implication. There was no way Sammy could be involved in such a stunt. Miss G also gave Sammy benefit of the doubt and sent him a get-well card. But the more she thought about it, the more she began to change her mind. The divergence of opinion between Frank and Miss G soured their relationship for a long time afterwards and created many heated quarrels.

Bottom line, Miss G did not believe Sammy's story. She was bitterly hurt that someone she had always rated as a real friend should betray her. The fact that sheets of red paper matching the wallpaper in Sammy's flat were pinned on the wall of the Drake Hotel suite implied a calculated conspiracy. She and Sammy had been photographed against it to bolster *Confidential*'s claim that she had been Sammy's lover and a regular visitor to his flat.

Other occurrences in the years ahead that sustained her suspicions were Sammy's continual involvements with white actresses. When rumors surfaced about a liaison between him and Kim Novak, one of Columbia's prime money-spinners, the boss of Columbia Pictures, a gentleman not renowned for reticence, allegedly threatened Sammy that if he didn't get himself married to a black girl by the next week he was likely to lose sight in his other eye.

Miss G never forgave Sammy Davis, Jr. She shunned him with a virulence that was very unusual considering her forgiving nature. We both did. I will not repeat the names we called him, but they were very vulgar, and he had earned them. If the story had been given wide publicity around the world, her film career could have been destroyed. It did indeed do a good bit of damage among her friends and family in North Carolina. Salacious lies and sexy innuendos find a ready audience in most societies, and Miss G's home territory was no different. Gossip spread across the Bible Belt that "Ava Gardner was a Hollywood whore after all...and a nigger's whore at that." This scandal deeply distressed Miss G's family, who could do little to counter such vicious gossip. I think that even some of the family was not prepared to give Ava the benefit of the doubt. At the filling station of Miss G's brother Jack, whom she adored, windows were broken, and "your sister is a nigger-lover," was daubed on the walls. (Incidentally Miss G had given Jack the five thousand dollars necessary to start the business).

I, for one, knew there was not a fragment of truth in the *Confidential* allegations. No one in the whole wide world knew more about Miss G's private life than I did. The scandal lingered in the atmosphere, a shadow at the back of every conversation. It was never forgotten.

I think Miss G was dead on target. Sammy was involved. We believed that he cooperated with the people responsible for the article. Maybe he did not anticipate the damage he would cause, and maybe he didn't think that through. For the male artist, black or white, sex scandal is often an aphrodisiac, not a disaster. Not so for a female. In many ways, the whole episode hardened Miss G's attitude toward the press and the media in general from then on. If they were prepared to print such wicked and destructive articles, then why the hell should she agree to cooperate?

I guess black guys and white guys can all pull mean tricks like this when they feel it is to their advantage. I think–I hope–Sammy learned something from this. He got to the top, reached all his ambitions, and maybe mellowed enough to become a more thoughtful human being.

18 THE TROUBLE WITH LOVERS

Miss G was still smarting over the Sammy Davis incident when she attended the New York opening of *The Barefoot Contessa*. By this time Miss G was pretty well fed up with the movie, and half way through the premier she would have walked out had David not pleaded for her to stay until after Eddie O'Brien's big scene. As old friends, they owed that to him.

It was clear that despite the fine cast, the wonderful camera work, the ornamental settings, the marvelous shots of life as lived by the jet set in Italy and the south of France, the movie's drama quotient was limited. It had very little to say. What was to have been Joe Mankiewicz's bitter attack upon the shallow, superficial and greedy Hollywood society had turned out to be more of a soap opera than a satire. The spectacle of Warren Stevens playing Howard Hughes and Marius Goring playing Porfirio Rubirosa, shouting insults at each other forty feet apart in a crowded room did not engender any confidence in their respective intelligences. Humphrey Bogart's insistent narration explaining every bit of philosophy and action was a bore. Miss G, gorgeous as ever but totally miscast, certainly did not live up to the often quoted phrase, "the world's most beautiful animal." Her characterization as "the proud, prowling, restless tigress sure of her powers, yet convinced about their proper uses" was real film speak. Miss G had one slinky dance around a gypsy campfire that gave a hint of those aforementioned qualities, but the rest of the time all she did was stalk around in the fabulous Fontana gowns exhibiting her exquisite profile and giving a performance as wooden as a telegraph pole.

To allow our thoughts to settle and avoid having to live in Hollywood, Miss G decided we would base ourselves in a rented house in Palm Springs. Bappie, who had seniority over me, stepped in, saying it was her turn to go with Miss G while she finished her *Barefoot Contessa* publicity tour in the Orient, so I stayed home in Palm Springs.

In our life at that moment were two love-sick suitors, Howard Hughes and Frank Sinatra. Both hated each other with feverish male venom. Frank, even after the unhappy separation, was back in favor. I had already been told that during the shooting of *The Barefoot Contessa* he and Miss G had spent

Christmas together in Rome. Miss G had decided to forgive and forget their mutual unhappiness during the last few months. They had both enjoyed a romantic week in bed together without a single fight.

Mr. Hughes knew that. Mr. Hughes knew everything, even if he didn't know what to do about it. He had to make a counter offer. Mr. Hughes was still pursuing his lunatic theory that everyone has a price and that for most women it was either jewels or money. Having tried and failed to heap jewels into Miss G's lap, he decided he would have to make a real dramatic, clinching gesture.

Our Palm Springs house was situated some distance from the center of town on the edge of the airfield. At that time, the area was no more than a peaceful, open grassy space. Mr. Hughes would often land there at night. All he had to do was ring up his aides and get them to line up their cars with their headlights blazing to form an illuminated runway.

On this occasion he rang Miss G to ask her to meet him when he landed. Slightly mystified, Miss G drove the short distance to the makeshift landing strip. She met Mr. Hughes as he was leaving his plane. He was carrying his usual cardboard box. He opened it as she approached. It was packed thick with wedges of dollar notes.

"What's that?" she asked.

"Two hundred and fifty thousand dollars," he announced.

"What for?" she asked politely.

"For you."

"For what?" a puzzled Miss G asked.

"We want you to make a film."

Miss G did not say in exasperation, "You brought me out here at this time of night to tell me that?" She only said quietly, "Who's we?"

"Darryl Zanuck is working on several scripts."

"He always is. But what is the money for?"

"It's an advance."

Miss G paused for a few seconds, then gently pushed the box away. "Howard, honey, if you want to do a film, you have got to start with my agent. Sorry, I've got things to do at home. Good night, Howard."

I often tried to feel sorry for Mr. Hughes, but I never could. He wanted to marry Miss G. If only he'd tried Mickey Rooney's technique, "I love you, I love you, I love you. I'm going to go on asking you to marry me until I'm a hundred years old, so you might as well marry me now." If Mr. Hughes had taken that route, he might have stood a chance. Mr. Hughes only offered bribes. He was also possessive to the point of lunacy. He knew Frank Sinatra also owned a house in Palm Springs within walking distance of ours.

Frank might make approaches to Miss G, Mr. Hughes figured, so he came up with a plan to forestall such possibilities. He rang Miss G and told her that he was sending down a car and chauffeur for her exclusive use. He hoped she would be happy with this arrangement. By this time, Miss G knew it was useless to argue with Mr. Hughes. He would send the car and drive down anyway whether she liked it or not. So she just said, "Thank you, Howard." The chauffeur was named Bill. He was young, fresh, handsome, and athletic, with an

American style crew cut, typical of the scores of prototypes that Mr. Hughes used for his handiwork. Bill was willing to oblige in any way he could and bored to tears with just sitting in the car. He became Miss G's chauffeur, butler, drinks server, odd job man, washer upper, cleaner, shopper and general factotum. I've never had more help in my life.

19 LOVE IN LAHORE

MGM had spent two hundred thousand dollars buying the film rights to John Master's novel, *Bhowani Junction*. Its heroine was a beautiful Eurasian girl–half Indian, half British–named Victoria Jones. Masters described her appearance through the eyes of her dazzled first lover: "Victoria is tall, and her eyes are brown and she has the longest legs and thick black hair. She has a figure like a film star, only better. She is beautiful."

The back cover of the book added to the hype: "It is a blazing story of India torn by riot and civil war when a proud Anglo-Indian girl and a hard bitten English colonel faced terror and death on an isolated railway outpost."

MGM production chiefs said, "Dead right for Ava Gardner. George Cukor is directing. He's great with women. He'll love Ava."

"Miss Gardner is suspended," protested the suspension department.

"Well, for God's sake, un-suspend her," said the big brass. "What's the point of having a world famous pussy cat under suspension when she could be making us millions of dollars?"

By this time, Miss G had improved her financial situation because she had acquired a decent agent. First of all, she got more money. Secondly, she had some say in the choice of roles she played. Thirdly, and most importantly, American tax laws offered exemption to actors who spent long periods overseas making films. I would suspect that from that moment onward ninety percent of Miss G's movies were filmed overseas.

The film should have been made in India; however, the territory had been divided into two nations–India, which was Hindu, and Pakistan, which was Muslim. In India they were suspicious of how MGM was going to treat the subject matter. They were even more suspicious when they learned almost the entire cast was British. Also the Indian tax collectors were demanding a large chunk of film profits to be paid in advance, even though MGM lawyers were busily explaining that Hollywood films never, ever made a profit. Profits were always lost somewhere in the labyrinth of production costs. Indian tax collectors were not buying that claim. They wanted dollars before they would allow the cameras to roll. Pakistan, next door, said, "Forget the tax collectors. We'll loan you the Northwestern Railway and throw in the 13th Battalion of the Frontier Force all for free. And as for extras you can rent them out at about a rupee for a hundred.

MGM reached the quick decision to locate the film in Lahore. To get there was quite a journey. The first stopping off place was the capital of Karachi where we were all to assemble. Miss G reached London at the end of her Far Eastern tour for *The Barefoot Contessa*, which had been uneventful compared to the South American tour. I flew from Los Angeles to London where I was delayed for a few days getting a visa. As I was booked into the Savoy, I was not enduring any hardship.

I reached our hotel in Karachi just in time to overhear Stewart Granger and Miss G having an argument. Apparently the British Embassy was holding a reception for King Hussein, and they had invited Stewart Granger, George Cukor, and Miss G to represent the film people and to be introduced to the king. Jimmy, as Stewart Granger was known, being a perfect English gentleman, thought this an honor not to be missed. Miss G didn't think that way.

Jimmy said, "Ava, don't you want to meet a real king?"

"What's he king of?"

"Jordan."

"Where is Jordan?"

Jimmy waved an airy hand in the direction of the window. "Out there somewhere. It is near Israel. Ava, you can't miss the opportunity."

"I can," said Miss G.

Jimmy ignored her comment and went on. "You will have to dress up and curtsy. Can you curtsy?"

Miss G blew a raspberry.

"Curtsy! Let me tell you honey, when I was married to Mickey, we went to a film party at the White House where we met President and Mrs. Roosevelt. She was wonderful and showed Mickey and me all over the White House, even the bed in which President Lincoln slept. I didn't curtsy to the President or her. I am not going to start curtsying to some king from some country I've never heard of."

"Now, listen Ava, love...."

"You curtsy," said Miss G.

Oh God, how we laughed over that later. Jimmy did too. Not that Miss G's absence made the slightest bit of difference to the reception. In the Muslim world women are not noticeably important. Jimmy and George Cukor played their parts and came back to tell us that King Hussein was a really nice guy.

Our main location was the ancient city of Lahore five hundred miles to the north of Karachi. It was the capital of Punjab. Our hotel, Felatti's, was the only one in the city as far as I could see. The whole cast stayed there. It was definitely not of the Hilton standard, but they had done their best. They even put in a separate bathroom for Miss G in our section. Calling our rooms a "suite" would be too much of an honor. It was a low, rambling building with verandas everywhere. We also had a hot-plate which worked and an icebox which didn't. We made friends with some American service people in Lahore. I remember they always had pancakes on Sunday. Their house was like a commissary full of food, which we were happy to share with them.

In the summer season, Lahore was one of the hottest places in India. When we were there it was supposed to be getting cooler, but was it hot—110 degrees! And it sure was ancient. I loved the line in the guidebook that said, "The streets of the old city are narrow and tortuous and are best seen from the back of an elephant!"

"Damn it!" cried Miss G. "We've forgotten our elephant!"

The guidebook also did not mention that the back streets with open sewers, packed with people of a dozen races and religions, stank! There were pinched, hungry faces everywhere. They had gods to take care of you, gods to whom you paid penance, gods of sexuality. It was "pick your own god," it seemed. I also discovered that the young girls of the lower castes were not looked after by much of a god. They could be bought or sold, and for many of them prostitution was a haven.

We were in Pakistan, which was totally bewildering in its customs, full of desperate poverty and a total lack of hygiene. Who were we to grumble? It was their country. The British had established themselves there for more than three centuries and had prospered. The Indians had lived there for thousands of years and survived. Who were we? One white actress and one black girl; we didn't complain. We ate everything–well, practically everything. We did everything required of us. We certainly drank a lot.

The British expatriates to whom Pakistan was home believed that alcohol in a variety of bottles was a sure antidote against malaria, sunstroke, snakebite, typhoid, leprosy, foot-rot, and similar maladies. We did our best to give ourselves immunity. Nobody there was immune to green-apple-gallop—a euphemism for dysentery. We all suffered from it.

I have to say, and I'm certain there would be no contradiction from the cast, that the Lahore location provided us with the most difficult, hair-raising, trying, exasperating, nerve-wracking, disease-ridden potential of any film location any of us had or would ever experience. Of course, there were good memories, funny memories, even though some of them didn't seem funny at the time.

During our first week, I can remember hideous screams emerging from Miss G who was in the bathroom. I mean real hair-raising, "I'm being murdered" screams. Then, stark naked, Miss G came racing out the door. God in heaven, there was a great black flying "thing" attacking the top of her head. She hit the front door leading out onto the veranda at speed. The "thing" was still after her. I realized what it was–a huge, black bat which must have swooped out of the rafters or come through the window.

Many might think Miss G in the nude a pretty sight. For the city of Lahore to be given the chance of assessment was not on the cards, especially since their women were cocooned in cotton from head to toe, their faces covered with a veil.

My decision was split second. Miss G was running in a clockwise direction. If I could exit out of our other door and turn counter-clockwise, I could intercept her. I made for the door, seizing a large towel and a broom on the way. I just managed to cut her off. I smothered her in the bath towel, which cut off her screams and pushed her back through the open door behind me. Then I took on the bat, which was whirling and diving like a Stuka dive bomber. I did not make a single contact, but by now I was aided by members of the staff who had heard the screams. Obviously it had happened before, because they were armed with loopy old tennis rackets. The bat, understanding that the odds had changed, flew off. I can only imagine that it intended to make a nest in Miss G's rumpled black hair.

What about the film itself? It told the story of that period at the end of the Second World War when the enormous subcontinent of India, with its two hundred and six million Sikhs were protesting against the British and against each other. They were rioting, burning, looting, killing and breaking down every barrier of civilized behavior in a crisis that came close to civil war.

Three hundred years of British rule were ending, but who would have believed it could end in such chaos? What would replace it? Independence had a fine ring, and the British were leaving secure in the knowledge that they were leaving behind a nation that would frame its own constitution. Now it seemed no one could agree to frame anything.

Many opposing factions were at loggerheads. The Congress Party, India's major political power, was organizing mass marches, alleging their purposes were only peaceful. Its more passionate supporters were already settling deadly scores against religious enemies–mainly Muslims. The Muslims were retaliating with equal fury. It was heart-breaking. People who had lived side by side for centuries were now at each other's throats.

The Communists, of whom there were many, also played a large part in the general anarchy by encouraging civil disorder and inciting people to riot, and they themselves were always at work in clandestine terrorist activities–anything to promote chaos and allow them to take over.

The leaders eventually worked out their solution. Partition was the only answer. India must split into two nations: India and Pakistan. It was achieved with an enormous cost in human life. For months refugees struggled across the countryside trying to find shelter in their own religious enclaves, which had been apportioned to them. Eleven million people died in that murderous change-over.

The British Army, with their Indian counterparts, did their best to contain the tumult and rioting and defend the network of railways without which the whole nation would be paralyzed.

In the film Colonel Savage's job was to protect Bhowani Junction and the railway lines in his area and maintain law and order.

Against this dangerous and dramatic background, pretty Victoria Jones (Miss G) and her boyfriend Patrick Taylor, played by Bill Travers, were in a quandary. They were both Eurasian, a commonplace situation among a British population that had lived in India for so long. Victoria held a good position; she worked in the British Army offices and held the rank of subaltern. Patrick was employed as a supervisor for the Railway Company.

Patrick was confused and angry as the British began their withdrawal from India, for he was left with a conflict of identify. To which side did he owe allegiance? He had no friends or contacts in England, and since childhood the British part of him had treated the "wogs"–his fellow countrymen–with contempt and derision. How could he become part of an India he despised?

Victoria belonged to the same Eurasian community and faced the same problems. She was more practical and realistic about the future. Nevertheless, was she British or Indian? She decided she was Indian and moved among them. She met a handsome, romantic Sikh played by Francis Matthews, and he introduced her to a culture and religion she hardly knew existed. They became lovers, and she was considering marriage. She realized she could not live that sort of life. Besides, she had fallen in love with that handsome, suave, gallant, mocking, irreverent Jimmy Granger in his role as Colonel Savage, and he had fallen in love with her. Conflict existed between them from the first, and the turbulent background of divided loyalties did not help. Miss G really did like her role as Victoria Jones and felt she and Victoria had feelings in common.

When she stormed at Colonel Savage, "I belong here not as a phony Indian, not as a phony white, but as myself," she was echoing her own philosophy. Miss G did not wish to live as a phony actress, phony ex-farm girl, a phony anything. She wanted to be herself.

The critics applauded: "Ava Gardner has several scenes of extraordinary intensity and power in which her mature gifts as an actress are given greater scope than usual as she rises to the challenge of doing justice to this complex and divided human being. In one sequence when she argues vehemently with Bill Travers over his blind worship of all things British, a whole range of expressions—rage, frustration, and compassion—cross her face in rapid succession, rather than the more frozen beauty she has been required to exhibit in the past. With her loose and flying hair, her body bending free of the erect posture which had imprisoned her in her earlier performances, Gardner is a figure of humane convictions and great emotional force." I agreed.

We both agreed with one other thing also. If we had to single out any member of the MGM *Bhowani Junction* expedition for the award of the British Empire Director's Medal, one man stands out above all others–George Cukor. Not only did he direct the film, he bought the film!

In the middle of riot scenes, rape and desolation, there he was defending himself with only one weapon–his rolled up script bearing details of that day's shooting. There he was battling his way through thousands of violent Pakistanis bent on tearing the world apart, and no one in their right mind could refer to them as "extras."

This small, skinny Hollywood director, who never in his life had encountered a crowd bigger than a queue lining up at the MGM lunch counter, smashed his way through black bearded Pathans, bayonet-armed Gurkhas and raging rioters in blood-stained white nighties as if they were harmless extras in an early Hollywood film. He marshaled them into riot formations, village-burning orgies, and mass horror shows with hundreds lying on railway tracks seeking to prevent trains from plowing through their bodies.

Faced with any sort of disobedience, he whacked the air with his paper baton but always emerged from these scenes breathless, disheveled and alive. The Pakistanis loved him. They had never encountered anyone like him, and neither had we.

From the first day Miss G met George Cukor, she was as excited as if she had discovered Clark Gable number two. "I've never met such a man," she cried. "He can do anything. He watches every detail from start to finish, and he never sits down. I've never been so happy with a director in my life." The only other director she loved more was John Huston.

A problem arose for Miss G. She wasn't going to waste all those hardworking weeks just eating, boozing, and polishing her part as Victoria Jones. Not with all those good-looking young English guys in the cast. She needed attention, affection, and a love affair or two. She called it quits at two.

She had focused her eyes first of all on Stewart Granger. They had met in Copenhagen with an entire evening and night to spend together before boarding the plane bound for Karachi the next day. They ended up spending the entire evening and night on one long boozing session, managing to squeeze a little dinner in between endless rounds of aquavit followed by beer chasers. It was a memorable evening. Eventually Miss G got around to the subject of going to bed together. That caused Jimmy to observe sorrowfully that he had just married his beautiful young wife, Jean Simmons, and was madly in love with her and could not possibly commit adultery.

Miss G cackled with laughter. At that moment, Jean was making *Guys and Dolls* in Hollywood with Marlon Brando and Frank Sinatra, so I guess Miss G had doubts about Jean's chances of staying sacrosanct. That might have been a reasonable assumption, but Jimmy was determined to keep his marriage vows.

The truth of the matter was that neither Jimmy nor Miss G remembered getting out of the taxi which took them back to their hotel. They woke up in their separate beds with hangovers as big as storm clouds over Mt. Everest. Miss G knew that romance had not flourished. She and Jimmy remained great friends forever after.

Miss G soon collected compensation in the shape of two young, healthy, attractive English guys, who today probably have happy homes and kids, so I will disguise them as Harry and Edgar. Both at the time were unaware that their experiences in sharing Miss G's affections ran parallel. Neither of them was the jealous type and just accepted such bits of luck as part of life's little bonuses.

The only really arresting and original event occurred when Miss G announced one morning that we were taking a week off. I sensed a dereliction of duty, desertion from one's post. *Bhowani Junction* was that sort of film. "What's Mr. Cukor going to say?"

"George has given us permission. He's busy shooting at other locations. Besides, he knows we have a trusted friend taking us into the wilderness of the northwest frontier; the hanging-gardens-of-something-or-other and the death defying slopes of Mt. Everest and Christ knows what else."

Miss G's knowledge of Pakistan's geography was minimal.

"Which friend is taking us?"

I got a reproving glance from Miss G. "What do you mean, which friend?"

"Edgar or Harry?"

"Edgar. He's borrowed a Jeep and is filling it full of booze. He was in the army in these parts in the last war, so he knows what he's doing."

"I'll fix a few sandwiches." I said, "And take a few cans of beans."

We bumped and rolled away from Lahore on a track through wild and deserted country. We passed an occasional camel train or a smoky old truck. The old vulture wheeled high in the sky always ready for lunch. We sipped our bottles of anti-malarial gin and sang tribal melodies. The journey took several hours.

It was not as Miss G had thought. The hanging-gardens-of-somewhere-or-other and the slopes of Mt. Everest were not a romantic Shangri-La. It was a stone fort sitting on a high rocky outcrop in the middle of nowhere. To me, it brought back memories of that wonderful Gary Cooper film *Beau Geste* about the French Foreign Legion, with all the poor, dead soldiers hanging over the battlements having been slaughtered by those nasty guys in Arab headgear.

"Here we are," said Edgar. "A peaceful oasis, a whole week for relaxation. Better than active service...uh?" A whole week, I thought. We'll all go mad. We'll get the "cafard," that terrible depression those poor legionnaires used to catch after months in the desert. And that bit about "better than active service"? Well, Edgar seemed to be on active service twenty-four hours a day. On reflection, I can't remember many minutes when Miss G and Edgar were not snug in the connubial bed.

But the damn place grew on you. There was the fort. Below it were a sort of village, palm trees, a water well, a huddle of flat-roofed little houses hemmed in by servant quarters, which were three sticks and a canvas. Even people of modest income, those with one camel and a cooking pot, supported servants. In Pakistan if you were born poor there wasn't much in the way of social services to help you out.

The landscape, once you got used to not being frightened by it, was breathtaking. There were huge vistas, immense skies, far-off mountains marking the untamed borders of Afghanistan. Dawn sun crept over the rim of the world to burn off the mist and fry you alive if you lit it. The air cooled in the evenings. The smoke from the cooking fires drifted above the houses, and there were canvas shelters. There were the sounds of voices, camels braying, and children playing. There was such silence. You pulled the blanket up over your nose and listened to the silence.

As Edgar had packed enough booze to keep his entire ex-regiment drunk through a five-year campaign and there were only the three of us trying to do the same thing, we lived on a wobbly edge of euphoria. As I have already noted, the lovers seemed permanently encamped under the covers. Cuisine didn't seem of much importance. We had beans and more beans.

I shall never forget waking on that first morning, opening a cautious eye and circling the room and encountering two other sets of eyes at floor level, both coal black, watchful and curious. The eyes slid away, and the owners stood up.

Swathed in yards of calico, they belonged to two little girls about eight years old. And then, psst! They were gone. I sat up thinking, what the hell are they up too? Then I heard the dragging noise and two small girls arrived tugging a large bath of water into my room. They exuded laughter and chatter. Their hands fluttered to illustrate washing down, that is under the armpits, down the back and over the rear end. The two giggling little handmaidens were anxious to give me a bath. I enjoyed every minute of it.

Clean and refreshed, I went to look for Miss G. I approached her door cautiously in case Edgar was still on active duty. No, the splashes and giggles coming from Miss G's room told me that a second team of handmaidens was giving her the same treatment. It was a great week's holiday. We returned completely worn out from our experiences.

We flew back to London to finish the final shots and filmed a lot of railway scenes on a disused track in Haslemere, Surrey. Miss G volunteered to do one scene in which a stunt girl would normally have been used. She had to chase a moving train and, as it picked up speed, leap aboard.

When we saw the rushes she almost dropped dead. She would have been dead if she'd missed her footing. "Why the hell didn't George tell me how dangerous it was?" she gasped. She still thought George Cukor ranked close to a heavenly angel.

I said, "Mr. Cukor believes in realism."

It was a second piece of movie realism that shattered her far more than the train. She was trapped in a dark alleyway by a soldier, played by Lionel Jeffries, and raped. Miss G grasped a metal bar and killed him. It was a brutal and terrifying scene. George directed with all dramatic stops out.

It wasn't Lionel's fault, but Miss G was almost sick. You can't play a rape scene as if it's tea with the vicar. It's horrible! Miss G suffered from nightmares for a long time afterwards, but we all parted the greatest of friends.

George Cukor said, "Ava was a gem. She was marvelously punctual and never complained even when it was clear the poor darling was exhausted. She was wonderful in the part."

I could have told him that "the poor darling" was often more than exhausted. She got amoebic dysentery which is a rotten disease and can last a lifetime. You have terrible headaches and suffer from vomiting and diarrhea at the same time. Our medico gave her some tablets which helped, and Miss G was such a good trooper and only missed two days of filming.

Later Miss G said, "Thank God some Swiss pharmaceutical firm discovered a pill that could get rid of the after-effects."

Jimmy Granger said approvingly of Miss G afterwards, "There was no movie star thing with Ava. She never kept you waiting while she played with her makeup like so many others. She was always on time and completely professional and never complained about the heat and the flies. In fact, she was one hell of a woman!"

20 SPANISH FLAMENCO!

"Rene," said Miss G thoughtfully, "Why don't we go and live in Madrid? Really live there, permanently." I knew she had been playing with the idea for a long time now. She'd been indoctrinated during her first trip to Spain with *Pandora and the Flying Dutchman*, heavily influenced by her love affair with Luis Miguel Dominguin and by all the holidays she had spent there during her months filming *The Barefoot Contessa*.

"Why don't we take the plunge? We are both getting old anyway."

"Old?" I protested. "We're both thirty-three next birthday. That is the prime of life."

"Let's enjoy the prime of life then unencumbered by any male. We can pick and choose as we want." I knew she was remembering *Bhowani Junction*.

"What about Walter Chiari?" I said.

"What about him?" said Miss G bellicosely, "He's just a friend."

I didn't know an awful lot about Walter Chiari at this time except that he was a friend of Luis Miguel. I knew he was young and good-looking and Italian. Miss G was into the dark Latin types at this time. He was also a very well known Italian film star and musical hall performer, hardly spoke a word of English, but then neither had Luis Miguel.

"What about MGM?" I said.

Miss G said forcefully, "MGM made enough out of me with *Bhowani Junction*. All the big companies are making money overseas now. It's cheaper. It's not like the old contract days when you had to get a permit from old Father Mayer to even leave Los Angeles. We can live where we like."

MGM was already setting up a future picture, *The Little Hut*, which would be shot in the Cinecitta studios in Rome, and the only reason Miss G thought she could bear it was because of Rome and the fact that Stewart Granger and David Niven were in the cast. We could commute between Rome and Madrid with no trouble.

We flew into Madrid, and Miss G began her hopeful metamorphosis from healthy, radio-blasting, martini-fortified, Hollywood girl into her idea of a Spanish mantilla-hung, Mona Lisa-smile, Castilian lady. I've got to admit she was worth looking at.

She booked a suite at the Hilton Hotel, and Miss G was on her way. She looked around the huge suite saying, "Well, first of all, we've got to learn the language." I did not feel it my place to suggest that no Spanish senorita of any quality would make a statement like that. Instead I said, "That shouldn't take us more than ten minutes if we work hard."

Miss G gave me one of her quick "now don't be cute, Rene" looks and went on. "And you got to tell room service that we don't want three cubes of melting ice once a week. We need fresh ice three times a day."

"Miss G," I said, "the gin and vermouth can't wait to freshen up."

Miss G eyed herself in the mirror and then spun around. "Don't you think I look Spanish, Rene?"

"Sure," I said.

Miss G walked across to the window, pulled aside the heavy drapes, and stared down to check out how the passing ladies of Spain were looking. "After all," she said, seeking conviction, "I'm white-skinned and dark-haired. That is a good start. Yes? I'm a real Celt—both sides of the family. Mama was Scottish Celt; Papa was Irish Celt."

"Miss G," I said, "all you need is a guitar."

Miss G gave her usual happy scream of laughter and then adopted a more serious tone. "Now Rene, we've got to study the ladies. That's the secret. See how they dress and what's chic, what is fashionable. Gee, ain't this going to be fun?"

The Hilton foyer with its reception desks and adjoining offices was her first operational area. An enormous turnover of visitors and citizens passed through. Not many ladies passed through, though. In those early fifties respectable and high-born Spanish ladies did not frequent such places. Those who did were wearing black dresses with short sleeves or sleeves to the elbow, their hair pulled straight back. Miss G was fascinated by the way they wore their hair. Her first transformation into a Spanish lady, she decided, was the hair. She had naturally curly hair, and that had to be altered. With the help of my combs and brushes, a little grease and water, and a bit of tugging, we got her hair pulled straight back Spanish style.

Seeing Miss G making her practice circuits around the Hilton in a little black number, gliding along as if she was on wheels, with the final gesture of a flower behind her ear, certainly created large gaps in conversation. Passing gentlemen missed steps, walked into pillars, and occasionally choked on cigars.

Madrid was glorious. We did the shops, the cafes, and the taverns, leaving our marks on each. We tramped along the boulevards, visited the galleries, and knew every masterpiece in the Prado Museum. That's overdoing it, but let's say we loved every brushstroke. Miss G hired a Spanish teacher and took lessons every day. She introduced him to dry martinis, and why he wasn't killed by a passing taxi leaving the hotel, I'll never know. We gave the concierge and his flunkies a terrible time demanding seats at the opera, the theatre, and the bullfights, and we demanded tables at all the best restaurants. Naturally, we had to experience flamenco. So every night until the dawn broke, we were engulfed—the heels stamping, the skirts swirling, and the howling of maniacal Andalusian artists. We enjoyed every second.

Practically every day scripts were flown in from Hollywood agents, and with equal alacrity Miss G threw them out. Those days were past. Hollywood? Who had ever heard of Hollywood? Wasn't it that quaint little place on the California coast? Miss G had shaken the Hollywood gold dust off her feet and was never going to wear those shoes again.

After a couple of weeks or so hurtling around the city in jaded taxis, Miss G said, "Rene, we need our own transportation."

I thought, "Oh God, Miss G in traffic." Then I thought again, "Rene, don't be a coward, be a fatalist."

So we flew to Paris for a few days. If you can't enjoy Paris in any season, in any year, at any hour of the day or night, you need measuring for an undertaker's tape because Paris is…Paris…and great!

Between martinis Miss G bought a high-powered white Mercedes coupe, which the salesman assured us would be waiting for us on the Hilton doorstep when we returned to Madrid. And it was. This altered Miss G's perception of our lifestyle completely.

"Rene," she said, "We're wasting too much time here in Madrid. There are miles and miles of Spain to explore. Friends have been telling me of this chic new place down on the Costa del Sol."

I asked, "Where is that?"

Miss G answered, "I don't know. We just drive south until we hit it. It's called Torremolinos and just beginning to be a famous resort. We'll help it along. Let's go!"

We took the road south out of Madrid in our brand new Mercedes coupe, its paint job shining in the sunlight, luggage and booze piled in the back, our hair blowing in the wind. Questions to the concierge and half a dozen other people about how many hours' drive it was to Torremolinos produced a consortium of opinions suggesting seven hours.

It took us thirty-seven. We left on Friday and arrived on Sunday at two in the morning. But we had a lot of fun, and maybe there was something wrong with our navigation. Soon we were clear of Madrid's outskirts. Soon we were clear of everything, zooming along an empty main road. "Main road" was a relative term in Spain, where the traffic had not changed much since the Middle Ages. We passed a few carts, many pulled by oxen, some by horses and a lot by little donkeys. These poor little creatures were laden with heavy sacks, heaps of straw, vegetable produce, or household furniture, and the driver with stick inevitably was perched on top of the load.

We tooted, and they waved, as we swept up through lanes bordered by pines or cork trees creating dark shadows, the cork carefully sliced from the trunks to reveal a sheen like gleaming varnish. We passed fields thick with the huge bobbing heads of Van Gogh sunflowers. We swept down from the high ground surrounding the capital to the smooth, contoured brown plains. As we were happy and as the scene suggested it, we sang, "The Rain in Spain Stays Mainly on the Plain…terumpt-tum-rumpt…terumpt-tum-rumpt, and took another swallow out of our bottle. After all, the London version of *My Fair Lady* had just hit its jackpot, and we were applauding not only the song but the sun, the fresh air, our escape from bondage, and the whole wide, lonely, God-given, unspoiled beauty of Spain.

Old and young ladies in black gowns, with straw sun hats fixed to their braided hair by scarves, straightened up in the fields as we passed and waved to us. We gave them our toots to tell them we loved them but that we didn't want to trade places.

The country altered again, we drove through sleepy villages and little towns of narrow streets where smooth-skinned dogs lying in the shade of doorsteps scarcely bothered to lift a nose to look at us. Now we were in flat, well-watered farm lands. On one occasion, since the idea of public convenience had not crossed the minds of the inhabitants, we stopped for a call of nature, pulled off the road into the side of a field beside a clump of bushes. We had just emerged and were adjusting our dresses–as one says–when Miss G looked up, frowned and said abruptly, "What's that?"

Her voice was urgent. I turned expecting to see at least a charging bull, but instead saw a shambling figure stumbling across his wheat field towards us apparently enraged–apparently shaking his fist or something at us. Behind him we could see the tiled roof of a cottage we had not noticed before.

I said, "Think we are in trouble? Is that a gun he's holding? Jesus, I suppose we are trespassing. Let's beat it."

"Hang on," said Miss G, a note entering her voice. "I think it's a bottle."

I had another look. "You're right. It is a bottle, and he's got two glasses."

The old man struggled through the knee-high grass to reach us. He was wearing a farmer's worn clothes, stained, dark blue jacket and trousers. His hair was white, he hadn't shaved for a week, and his stubbly whiskers formed a sort of frill around his leathery face. The two bright blue eyes and the wide smiling mouth, showing a few crooked teeth, expressed a delight and welcome that needed no speech.

He unhooked a thumb from the glasses, handed one to each of us, and then proceeded to fill both to the brim with dark red wine.

We grinned and said, "Salute!" The wine was fresh and good.

He questioned, "Inglesi?"

"No...no...Americano."

"Americano...buenos." Then with a big thump on his own chest he announced, "Espanol."

We had not really thought he was Eskimo, but with introductions now effected it was time for explanations. With his right hand now free for emphasis, he swigged his share of wine from the neck of the bottle. He first dramatized our approach–a hand to one ear as he heard the drone of our engine, a hand shielding his eyes as he saw the car, and a long pointing finger as he indicated the line of our approach along the road. A palm pointing upwards indicated our stop. Like a true Spanish gentleman, he did not waste time on our move into the bushes to spend a penny...but ole! We had arrived. We were his guests, and he was honored.

The sun was high, the leaves green, the earth golden. This was his welcome to his land, his house, and his heart. Why did we not come back to meet his wife and drink more wine? Miss G, bless her, always reacted to that sort of warmth with a similar affection. She laughed and threw up both arms as if she was surrendering to the enemy and indicated, "Thank you, but we must press on." Normally, she would have embraced him, but this was our first meeting, and he was a bit smelly. He refilled our glasses, and we made more toasts. He was very impressed by our Mercedes. It might have been a space vehicle from Mars. He circled it with murmurs of praise, touched it with one finger, and wiped off the invisible fingerprint with the sleeve of his shirt.

Our visit lasted more than half an hour, and it was doubtful if our command of the Spanish language improved at all. But it was such fun. We finished the bottle, held up our palms in gentle rejection of yet more wine, and with multiple "Adios" and "Buenos" and "Muchas Gracias" we restarted our engine, blew kisses, and sailed away.

Miss G said, "You know, Rene, never in my whole life have I ever had an elderly gentleman run across a whole field to serve me wine. He doesn't even know who I am."

"Neither have I," I said. Miss G was dead right. No meeting with anyone in our first few months in Spain gave us more genuine pleasure than that unexpected encounter. Miss G had actually found someone who didn't know her!

Next day on another lonely road we stopped at what we thought was a little shop and asked for coffee. Again the owner was elderly and a bit decrepit, but he produced hot strong coffee. So strong in fact that Miss G, airing her Spanish, asked for "Latte, por favor."

"Si, si." With a broad smile and vigorous nods of his head, off he went.

I had noticed a small tethered goat in the side garden as we walked in. Glancing through the window, I now saw the old gent milking his little goat, the milk dripping into a small jug. He was back and pouring it into our coffee before I had time to warn Miss G of the lack of hygiene. However, when he left us alone, we had time to conceal it in the various pot plants. It might have been delicious, but we were not prepared to experiment. Certainly we did not want to hurt the old boy's feelings.

Another ten or twelve hours later we came down out of the mountains somewhere near Malaga and drove along the winding coastal road with the stars bright above the sea. We had really only stopped for necessities—petrol, car servicing, toilets, and occasionally at a small restaurant for some food. We did more drinking than eating, but there were few patrolmen on the road.

It was about two a.m. when we tried a small hotel which seemed to be close to Torremolinos. A bright young man gave us an outside cottage and led us down to it. In the bedroom he pointed to a piece of string hanging from the ceiling, saying, "Tomorrow, for breakfast, you pull, si."

Miss G woke at 8:00 a.m. the next morning shouting, "Rene, pull that string, and see if anything happens."

We quite obviously were not in a five-star hotel. Telephones in the

LIVING WITH MISS G

bedrooms had not reached this end of the beach, and at which end of the beach we were was anyone's guess. I pulled the string. Maybe it jangled a spoon against a frying pan somewhere in the kitchen, but it worked. Within seconds a young man came running wearing a not too clean shirt, not too clean pants, and bare foot. He did have a great smile. "Café, orange juice? Si, si senoras." He was gone.

The coffee and juice arrived. The coffee was cold, the juice was warm. I poured us a decent shot of Spanish brandy into the coffee. This improved things, but I could tell by the look on Miss G's face that this hotel was going to lose a couple of clients very shortly. Maybe a long, golden beach and a bright blue Mediterranean sea would raise our spirits.

In swim suits we raced out into a splendid sunlit morning. We sure were at the wrong end of the wrong beach. The sand was gritty. The sea had washed up a thick tide line of debris to its highest point: plastic bottles, pieces of old wood, swathes of seaweed which looked like dead carpet, all sorts of nasties. Even the rocks looked ugly. Spain was still in the throes of starting to keep its beaches spotless and to welcome the package tours. We were way ahead of that time. High rises, night clubs, the orange tree-shaded squares, lovely outdoor cafes, and the chic, jet-set people had not yet arrived. We had beaten them to it. Miss G waded in and swam a few strokes. She came back with that look on her face.

"We'd better find somewhere to eat." She said. I knew she didn't want anything to eat. She wanted to get out of the place and fast. I said, "Bags, booze, all packed and ready."

We paid the bill; it was negligible. We cruised through the emerging town. There was no chic anything anywhere. Miss G said, "Let's turn inland and see what we can find in the mountains. Spain's supposed to be so beautiful inland."

Some of the roads we followed were little more than tracks, and very occasionally we encountered a smoke-belching lorry moving at minus miles per hour. There were very few people at all, because we were crossing, without knowing it, the high Sierra Mountains and circling into the region of Granada. The road rose and fell, climbed and turned, and we began to notice small caves in the barren sides of the mountains.

"Caves," said Miss G, who had obviously read a guide book. "Jesus, Rene, do you think this is where the Andalusian gypsies live?"

I stared at a passing couple. "They are a funny-looking lot," I said nervously. Miss G was now thrilled. If these were real gypsies then they could play guitars and sing and dance like the real thing, and Miss G was really after the real thing. We pulled to a halt in a rough open stretch of baked clay. Around it there was some sign of habitation, a store and a bar, and big caves out of which gypsies emerged in scores to see what luck had brought them.

We were shepherded into the largest cave. It was furnished. Carpets on the dirt floor, wardrobes, chairs, tables, beds stuffed in the back corners, charcoal burning stoves, oil lamps. Miss G's anticipation was at fever pitch.

"Flamenco," she said, dancing, snapping her fingers and making a few swirls. An old gent in the corner immediately reacted with a nasal sort of honking, haunting, and wailing that sounded to me as if he were about to leave this world due to an acute attack of some rare Spanish disease. Miss G reacted as if Paganini was just tuning up his violin.

Her next remarks, however, struck through to the heart of the matter. "Vino!" she cried. "Vino!" That struck the bell. "Vino…vino!" many voices took up the chant and fingers began making that whispering movement which suggests "the dough first…huh?" We caught their drift very quickly.

"Rene," carried Miss G. "Give them pesetas and tell them to go and get the wine." We were now on the right track. They took the money and brought the wine, and we started on that long endurance test of flamenco dancing.

The guitars started to twang, and a lot of their cronies arrived. They were all pretty grubby. Very few wore shoes. They wore a variety of gypsy clothes. Everybody was very merry, and everybody drank the wine.

That first night we just sat there being entertained by a variety of singers and dancers, and when the wine ran out they'd go and get some more from the local store. It would arrive in traditional wine skins which they would squib into their mouths with polished accuracy. Several of the women carried babies and whipped out nut-brown breasts to feed them. Somebody plopped a nut-brown baby on Miss G's lap. I wasn't certain whether it was supposed to be a present or just on loan. Miss G crooned over it, it dribbled and laughed, and everyone was pleased. We had no food, not a single mouthful, but that first night passed away so quickly, we didn't need any.

Miss G had discovered paradise–a whole cave full of genuine Andalusian gypsies who were her friends, who taught her the staccato handclaps, who whirled around her as she stamped and pirouetted, looking marvelous with her erect Castilian-like figure.

The sun came tilting through the cave entrance, and we were still at it. From time to time, someone lay down in a corner and had a nap, but not us. We still had no food. We were simply living on atmosphere and wine. That day I noticed if they hadn't worn us out they were damn close to wearing themselves out and were now operating in shifts. I guess there were enough shifts of gypsies in those caves to keep Miss G going for a month. Honest to God, with very short intervals we kept at it all that day and all that night.

By the third morning, after two nights in the cave, we were still at it. Now it sounds unbelievable, but no one can really sum up Miss G's energy when she was dancing the night away. I kept giving them money for the wine and they brought it back and gave me the change. I guess they were making a slight profit out of the deal, but it wasn't costing us much.

I've got to say also that those girls in the caves were really something, and the way Miss G spun and clapped her hands and stamped her feet she could have been one of them. Their skin was brown, so you couldn't tell if that was sunburn, nature or a lack of soap, but they all smelled very sweetly of oils and incenses. They wore the round-necked blouses we all think of when we think of Spanish senoritas, and their breasts like Miss G's were turbulent and pretty. They jangled with bracelets and necklaces, their fingers were latched with rings, and their heavy dancing skirts had metal coins sewn into their hems so that when they spun they swept around you heavy as stiff brocade. Their eyes were black, provocative and exciting. In spite of those wanton looks, we heard that very, very few gypsy girls were ever prostitutes. They had strict moral codes, and those old mamas with bright, gleaming eyes had special powers to lay curses on wrongdoers. They consulted their Tarot cards, and if they had it in for you, baby, you better watch out.

On the morning of the third day I noticed the men looking at us a little suspiciously. Either they were going to make us blood sisters of the group or drop dead from exhaustion. They were getting into little huddles and whispering, and with my newly found mastery of the language I heard them saying, "La noche" several times. To my slightly jaded and suspicious mind, it seemed slightly sinister. Maybe they were saying "Can you believe it, Pedro, they're going to stay for another night!" I decided there might be something going on with this "noche" stuff. After all, "noche" was the time when the ghosts ran through the mountains. All sorts of nasty things happened. I said, "Miss G, why don't we get the wine ourselves and perhaps get a bite to eat somewhere?"

In our best sign language, off we went. Outside I revealed my feelings about "la noche" and gave my opinion that if we didn't want our throats cut we had better jump in the car and exit!

Miss G got the message, and for once she didn't protest. I think she was too tired. Off in the car we went and hit some sort of road with a signpost saying "Granada." That was our cue to change our theme tune from "The Rain in Spain" to the popular song, "Granada," and, with our blood now replaced by red wine, we sang all the way into the old city.

We stopped overnight in a hotel and slept, bathed, changed our clothes and knew we just couldn't make it all the way back to Madrid. We slept like logs but woke early and headed for Madrid once again. The whole journey down and back took six days and nights, and I think we only hit a mattress three times out of the six. I can tell you we were pretty glad to sink into the comfort of the Madrid Hilton.

Back with our friends, when we mentioned our adventure authorities on the gypsies sprang out of every corner of every bar. The gypsies at Sacromonte, where we had spent our last weekend, were apparently one of the last cave-dwelling communities, not only in Europe, but in the whole world.

No one knew where or how the gypsies had gotten there. Legends were endless. Learned authorities had studied their history and come up with a dozen learned dissertations, all different.

Many of the Romany families themselves favored the romantic legend that their origin lay back in the Old Testament with the story of Cain and Abel. Cain had killed Abel, and because of that crime his whole tribe was cast out and doomed to roam the world forever as a wandering nomadic people. They were certainly that.

We also learned with a sense of surprise that Romany is not a written language and that flamenco has no written music. We also realized, as everybody did, that this lore and legend born in a long-ago time in history is sliding away, the mystery of their past unsolved and probably soon to be forgotten by this uncaring century. We felt it was such a pity. The memory of this two-night stint in the caves near Granada we would never forget.

Apparently the paparazzi found us on one of our European jaunts. With little or no make-up and wind-blown hair, Miss G was still a sight to see with her rare natural beauty.

21 A PERSONAL EXPLOSION

No matter how hard Miss G tried to ignore her film responsibilities, she was stuck to her contract with MGM. It was obvious to MGM that there would not be enough time left to make more than another three or four films–Miss G intended to do her best to limit it to three–but they still had the contractual right to summon her to various meetings and discussions, usually in Hollywood, New York, or London.

It turned out to be three: *The Little Hut*, produced by MGM; *The Sun Also Rises*, produced by Twentieth Century Fox with Miss G on loan; and finally MGM's farewell production, *The Naked Maja*.

For the time being we postponed these liabilities. Spanish life had a lot to offer. It is not everyone who gets their basic flamenco training in the gypsy caves of old Granada, and Miss G, having survived that apprenticeship, returned to Madrid confident she could now conquer the flamenco circuit.

From our base camp at the Hilton Hotel we slept all day and danced all night, the sound of heels banging, fingers and castanets snapping, guitars strumming and voices hollering a perpetual echo in our heads. Then to alternate, we danced all day and danced night as well. So days and nights sort of got strung together, and how we survived those experiences I have a hard time remembering.

We were known in every posh hotel, bar, tavern, and restaurant in Madrid. We drank martinis, champagne, whisky, gin, sherry, red wine–anything out of a bottle, flagon, goat skin, spigot or decanter would do. Miss G constantly repeated her theme tune, "I don't like the taste of any of them, but I sure do like the way they make me feel."

Miss G's twenty-four hour desire for flamenco music and dancing did not really endear us to the Hilton Hotel management, but as she was such a spectacular advertisement sweeping around their corridors, they fixed their smiles and counted up to ten. If, on our nocturnal wanderings, she discovered a flamenco group she liked, she would invite them back to the hotel to continue the party in our suite. The sight of the doorman's face as he saw us tromping across the foyer at four in the morning should have been painted by Picasso. I did not even want to hear about the enraged telephone calls that must have reached the desk when the feet started stamping and the singers started honking. I would imagine that, by the time Miss G announced that she was going to buy a house and settle down in the peace of the countryside, the sigh of relief that went up from the Hilton management would have gotten the Graf and Zeppelin airborne.

Newfound friends were willing to help us. One introduced us to Moraleja– a new American-style country club being built about ten miles outside Madrid. Several houses had already been finished, and Miss G chose a ranch style house which was half completed. She bought it for fifty thousand dollars and spent almost as much again in furnishings and changes to her liking.

Now cables were dispatched to Hollywood, New York, and Palm Springs– everywhere she owned a stick of furniture or a treasured painting–with orders to crate them and dispatch them immediately to our house, La Bruja. La Bruja–the Witch–got its name because our weathervane was shaped like a witch riding a broomstick.

Miss G had her own ideas about house furnishing and decoration. She had a flair for it, a great feeling for color, texture and space. She also had the good sense to utilize the skills of a marvelous interior decorator named Harris Williams.

When it was finished it had a swimming pool that gleamed blue in the hot sunshine. Far away you could see low hills, and there were a lot of grass and flower beds. There was Spanish contoured mahogany furniture, a bit heavy for my taste, and Spanish oak and polished walnut. There were lots of shelves filled with books with bright covers. There were more records than we could have listened to if we'd lived to be a hundred. Our collection of Frank Sinatra must have dated from his first baby squawk to his tuneful middle age. There was a big kitchen full of electric devices, polished brass pans hanging on the walls, and big jars and bottles of wine stacked on the shelves.

La Bruja was a bit of a madhouse when the cartons and cases and bundles began arriving from the States and, so it seemed, went on arriving forevermore. At first they were stacked so high in the rooms that even the building contractors couldn't get inside to work.

We had one interesting "adventure" during this period. A rather snobby couple we knew–I shall refer to them as the Senor and Senora because of the complexity attached to this adventure. They owned a yacht, an opulent vessel, and they were going cruising along the North African coast. Would we like to come? We said yes, and there were two other guest couples.

We could have called our voyage "The Mystery of the Ships That Pass in the Night." The only trouble with our ships was they came right in close and nestled against us. To start with, we sailed along very happily. We sunbathed, took trips ashore at the small ports and town, changed our money at the banks, and had a lovely time wasting it on useless trinkets. We drank the local wine and ate meals at a lot of funny restaurants. We had a fine time. Back on board, there were more drinks and a great deal of fresh air.

The first time we were alerted that something fishy might be going on occurred one night after dinner. We were standing on the highest deck looking over a dark sea, the shore lights a couple of miles away, the sky shimmering with stars, and the breeze balmy–millionaire stuff.

"Hey," said Miss G, "isn't that a boat heading this way?" She pointed her finger.

It looked like a small trawler or fishing boat, but its masthead and red and green navigation lights were practically invisible. It came alongside and we watched as one of those special landing ladders was lowered. Two guys carrying cases jumped aboard and slipped in through a hatch two decks below us. Fifteen minutes later they departed with the same silent speed, and the boat disappeared into the darkness.

"Can't be the pilot," said Miss G frowning.

"Special dispatches for the captain, perhaps?" I said.

"They usually use a ship-to-shore radio for that sort of stuff," said Miss G.

Every night after that we went up on top deck for a breath of fresh air stroll and continued our detective work. Other mysterious boats paid us calls. Our shore trips were irregular, but we did notice that the other guests always seemed to be slipping away to "go to the bank."

"For Christ sakes," said Miss G, "they never buy anything ashore and they can't spend a single peseta aboard, so what are they doing?" She paused and then went on. "I think they're drawing money out, not putting it in."

I said, "That isn't unusual when you are on holiday."

Miss G said, "Rene, let's write the plot. Darkened boats come alongside; mysterious men carrying cases jump aboard; mysterious men jump back onto boats and sail off again. Now what is going on?"

"Drugs," I guessed.

"Well, it sure as hell ain't the white slave trade," said Miss G. "That's only still going on in Hollywood."

I said, "Is it any of our business?"

"Honey, we don't want to be mixed up in this sort of scenario if what we think is going on is going on," replied Miss G.

"But we are stuck aboard this boat," I reasoned.

"No, we are not," said Miss G. "Next boat that comes alongside, we are hitching a lift ashore."

"Miss G," I said trying to sound brave, "Isn't that dangerous jumping aboard a drug smuggler's boat? It's something for the movies." Then to make my point clear, "Why the hell invite us for a cruise when they're doing this sort of thing?"

Miss G shot back immediately, "because we are great cover, Rene. Who is going to suspect drug smuggling when this is obviously only a fun-loving cruise with that fun-loving Miss Ava Gardner as one of the party."

"It would make some headline," I said.

"Yeah, and get me barred from the States for the rest of my life."

"Include me in that," I said.

I still did not like the idea of a trip ashore in a drug smuggler's boat. What was to prevent them from tying an anchor around our necks and dropping us overboard? I tried my last defensive ploy. "But, Miss G, what about the luggage?"

"Leave the luggage," answered Miss G, dismissing her eighteen suitcases as if they were something she just carried Kleenex tissues in. "Just bring the jewelry case." The case held Miss G's rings, necklaces, bracelets and the bits and pieces she loved; about ninety thousand dollars' worth in all. It also contained our passports and credit cards.

I guess I sounded dismal. "Right," I said. Miss G recognized my apprehension, but remained resolute.

"Rene," she said soberly, "there's no other way. For all we know Interpol might have a customs patrol boat tailing us waiting to catch us in the act."

I thought that was over-dramatizing it a bit, but it didn't make me feel any better. I've got to admit, however, that when the opportune moment arrived, Miss G handled our escape plan with great assurance. First, she sprung it upon the Senor and Senora at the very last minute–the minute we saw the navigation lights of the "next boat" approaching. The Senor and Senora were in the bar with quite a few drinks inside them when Miss G marched in.

"Can you ask the captain of the supply boat to hang for a couple of minutes to take us ashore?" she said airily. "Rene and I thought we would have dinner in a little café, find a small hotel and start shopping early tomorrow morning. We'll meet you when you come ashore tomorrow. It would be nice to be by ourselves for a few hours, okay?"

So how could they stop us? Two dim innocents going ashore for a bit of fun.

The message was passed down, and the guys aboard the trawler helped us onto their craft. It was hard to distinguish their faces in the darkness. As we chugged in towards the lights on the shore, the breeze was a bit chilly, but as we nosed into the shelter of the small harbor we were pleased to see a circular quay ringed with bright shops and cafes. We had struck lucky. Once ashore, we walked at ease among the strolling population. From that day to this, we have never known exactly where we were. We never did bother about such unimportant details. As far as we were concerned, it was forever "some little joint along the North African coastline."

"We need a drink," said Miss G heading towards a vacant table at an outside open air café. People at the other tables were the normal Mediterranean assortment and seemed quite relaxed and happy. A dark-skinned waiter trotted up, and Miss G ordered anise with ice. Then she said to me, looking around, "A bit like the set of Casablanca, Rene, huh?"

I said, "I've got the jewelry case tight between my knees under the table in case Humphrey Bogart or Sydney Greenstreet happen along."

We both grinned. After the fifth drink we were both relaxed, and Miss G looked at me over the rim of her glass and said, "Glad to be ashore shipmate?"

Our "adventure" was almost over. Miss G waved a hand at the guy behind the bar. " I think that's the patron. He's giving us the eye. He'll know the whereabouts of a cute little hotel." He did, and the hotel was comfortable, the rest of the night uneventful. The next morning, we did not go shopping. We hired a taxi and told him to take us to the nearest airport. Direct flights to Madrid were no problem.

Our sudden disappearance aroused little interest. It was accepted as one of those abrupt turnabouts for which Miss G was renowned. Back in Madrid, our luggage appeared on our La Bruja doorstep about ten days later. Our relationship with Senor and Senora was still affable, but we met them less frequently. No mention of our sudden flight was ever made, and we formulated only one resolution for the foreseeable future: we were sticking to dry land.

A regular feature in our social life during those summer months was the Sunday afternoon bullfights. Miss G had been first indoctrinated by Papa Hemingway and his book, *Death in the Afternoon*. Also, as she was now for all intents and purposes the past mistress of the best matador in Spain, Luis Miguel Dominguin, our status in bullfighting circles was akin to that of royalty. I know that Miss G never ever thought of herself as anyone's mistress; quite the opposite in fact. If there was a jailhouse factor in any relationship, Miss G was in charge of it.

Luis Miguel, during that long love affair with Miss G, had been recovering from a goring he had sustained in the bull ring and was wondering if he should retire permanently. In 1959 he did decide to return to his hazardous occupation and fight in a series of mano-a-mano exhibitions against Antonio Ordonez. The winner was the matador who performed best in the killing of six bulls. He made bullfighting history. They were documented by Papa Hemingway in one of his last books, *The Dangerous Summer*.

We were given the best seats on the shady side of the arena and anesthetized ourselves against the sight of bloody violence by a steady intake of strong drink. It steadied our nerves. It also blunted the inward agony we both suffered at the sight of those magnificent animals being slaughtered.

The pageantry was brilliant, the atmosphere electrifying, the bullfighter's skill often breathtaking. Ostensibly Miss G became an aficionado. She knew all the right phrases. She moved in a clique of other aficionados. She adored associating with this company of men of immense courage. She was hypnotized by the grace of the sweeping capes, the pirouettes, the drama of the killings and the lethal risks. I always believed it was one of her best acting parts, a part she tried hard to turn into reality. I can also remember the occasions when I accompanied her to the ladies' room to be physically sick at the sight she had just witnessed. Long after she had abandoned all association with bullfighting, she said often, "I don't know how I managed to watch it all. I really don't."

We were even admitted to the bullfighters' dressing rooms to watch them arrayed in their ceremonial costumes. I lost count of the number of times when, after the playing of music, the blasting of trumpets and the opening scenes completed, a matador would offer his three-cornered hat and dedicate a portion of the bull he was going to fight to Miss G. It was either an ear, a hoof or a tail. Usually, she got the ear. Oh God, she collected so many ears we could have opened an ear museum. What could we do with them, nail them above the mantelpiece? No way!

I remember on one occasion we arrived back at La Bruja with me carrying three ears. We had hardly got through our front door before a party of her posh friends, hard on our heels, crashed in behind us. We had reached the drawing room, and I gasped to Miss G, "What the hell do I do with these bloody things?"

Miss G gestured at the settee. "Stick them behind the cushion over there. Quick!" I raced across and stuffed two large cushions over the hairy monstrosities. I straightened up as a large and beaming Spanish matron came through the door and headed in my direction. I realized she thought I was straightening the cushions for her. She plopped down between Miss G and me. We managed to weather that incident. Other incidents we could not weather.

With Miss G's arrival in Madrid's social scene as a famous, beautiful Hollywood film star, she began to find she had made a great number of friends. Some were very pleasant people; a few were a pain in the rear end. Two of our nicest friends who lived out at Moraleja near us were Richard and Betty Secrist. They had five kids and were very helpful in every way. Betty and Miss G remained good friends for the rest of their lives.

Other lady friends, many of them ex-patriot Americans, influenced Miss G in a way I hardly believed possible. I suppose I could mark this change in her as beginning on the day when she marched into the drawing room where I was cleaning up and sounded off.

She began, "Rene, I am a film star. Is that correct?"

I put the duster down. "Miss G, you are a film star."

"Rene, you will admit that here in Spain I am treated like a queen?"

I sat down on the nearest chair. What was she up to? This sounded as though it might take quite a while. "Miss G, in Spain you are treated like a queen."

"But over in the States because of the parts I play I am treated like a whore."

This was getting positively loony. I screwed up my face in protest. "Miss G I don't think that's correct."

"Well, I do. And now I know I'm a film star. I'm going to act like a film star." The film star flounced out of the room.

Betty Secrist, an American but very knowledgeable about Spain, had managed to find us a pleasant husband and wife combination who were employed to look after the household in general. My job, as usual, was general factotum looker-after-Miss G and second-in-command. We also had a couple of gardeners and a variety of other people around the house.

Now the newly crowned "film star" took over. In a tantrum one day she sacked the husband and wife team. Over the next few weeks in similar film-star tantrums she sacked a selection of other household staff. I could not believe that this was the Miss G I knew. Even to this day I have difficulty reconciling what was happening during these months. If I had to hazard a guess, it was a Miss G trying subconsciously to face up to the lifestyle she had chosen.

Brazenly and publicly she had abandoned America and her film career. She had given herself no room to maneuver. She had enough money. She was footloose and fancy-free. Now an unknown future frightened her. She had always worked. From the time when she was a tot she had been given small duties which increased as she grew older: picking the bugs off the tobacco plants, helping to get in the wood as winter approached, milking the cow, leading home the mule. Then there came school. Her Mama ran a country teacherage–lodgings and food for eight young school mistresses. Miss G lived with them so she had no chance of dodging her homework or her chores. Mama kept a shrewd eye on her youngest and most precious, seeing that she was busy. Even when MGM whisked her away to Hollywood she was on duty from early morning to five thirty in the evening: makeup, hairdressing, rehearsals, the picture gallery, making movies. Now, God help her, she could lead the life of a film star.

We were still receiving boxes and cartons from the United States containing sufficient household material to equip a small hotel. Confusion continued as Miss G's inclination was to act as if she was the captain of a slave ship in the middle of a hurricane. She also insisted on maintaining her sequence of flamenco nights on the town with me in close attendance. Forty-eight-hour days were commonplace.

Before the final shipwreck occurred, one should know a little about the general atmosphere in Spain in the fifties. Franco, after the bloody and bitter civil war that had started in 1936, was still firmly in power. His dictatorial clout was massive. Law and order and the authority of the Catholic Church were rigorously enforced. Nowadays the sunlit beaches of Spain are crowded with comely topless girls enjoying displaying their nubile body language. In those days such exhibition meant instant arrest. If you stole an automobile in Spain in the fifties you went to jail for fifteen years. The result was no one stole automobiles in Spain. Franco had restored the monarchy and aristocratic privileges. Professional classes were top of the heap. The large and influential middle class that exists today was only very slowly emerging. Servants and peasants were still down in the straw. You could maintain, without much serious contradiction, that Spain was probably the last great European power to be dragged slowly into the twentieth century.

Not only did Spain have a continuity of sunshine that was enthralling, it was easily the cheapest place in Europe in which to settle. You did not need a fortune to live in a style far beyond your wildest dreams and in many cases far beyond your behavioral standards. In other words, there were a lot of bums around. Many of the ladies pirouetting around Miss G had never employed a servant in their lives, but, oh boy, they were now making the most of such opportunities. You can probably guess from the tone of these paragraphs that I thought they were all creeps. Overhearing their dialogue, I often heard opinions that were close to unbelievable. Allow me to report a summary overheard at many gatherings of ladies.

First Lady: "Ava, do you mean to tell me you are paying your servants seventy-five cents a day! That is absurd. It is far too much. I mean, you are spoiling it for the rest of us."

Second Lady: "I agree with Cynthia. I mean many of my friends rarely pay them in cash at all. They are grateful for scraps they get in the household and perhaps for an egg to take home at night."

And my really favorite quote:

Third Lady: "Ava darling, you are a famous film star. If you gave them an autographed copy of one of your photos at the end of the week they wouldn't need a salary. They would be very happy with that."

I was also aware that my own salary was the subject of continued speculation.

A brood of ladies: "I mean, Ava darling, why do you have to have a black maid at all? There are so many country girls needing jobs around here. They know the language. They know how to go to the market. They cook and clean and scrub. They are very hard workers, and you could get half a dozen for the wages you pay Rene."

They were dead right. I knew that Miss G, as a loyal American, with another loyal American working for her would not be swayed by this serpent talk. It did confuse, intimidate, and influence her. That's how the Film Star was born.

Our personal explosion was not long in coming. After a long night boozing with Miss G, I drank more than I should have simply to block out the noise. I woke knowing that it was not my best day.

In the kitchen I faced an assembly line of new cartons that had arrived from the States. They contained all manner of silver pieces, including piles of knives, forks, spoons, and other kitchen implements. I unpacked them, washed them and arranged them in drawers. I was just breathing a sigh of relief when Miss G with her most imperial film star flourish appeared through the doorway. She was exasperated, and her voice was shrill.

"Rene, didn't you hear me calling you? I've been calling you for five minutes, and you haven't answered."

I was contrite. "Miss G, I'm sorry. I just didn't hear you call."

"Well, you should have been more attentive. That's what I pay you for. That's the whole reason you are here. You servants are all alike–inattentive, not caring, lazy!"

I knew she was quoting the lies of her friends, but this was hurting.

"Miss G, I was just trying to pack all this silver away," I said lamely. She marched around the kitchen, her voice taking on an edge of hysteria. There was no stopping her. She had to have servants, real servants. Servants who knew what they were doing, servants who were happy to serve, trained servants. Spain was full of them, so why hadn't she got any. It was a constant flow. I had never seen Miss G like this before.

I began to boil. Here I was a grown-up, tax-paying, flag-saluting American citizen being screamed at in a foreign country by the girl I adored more than any other person in my whole life. She was a girl I would have died for, my close friend, my surrogate sister, my beloved female conspirator, my friend in need, this girl who was a part of my heart, and she was giving me this going over as if I was a piece of stale garbage.

I boiled over. I looked for something to throw at her. There were the weapons–the cutlery, missiles of all varieties. I grabbed a handful of spoons and threw those first. When they had all gone, I started on the forks. Then I didn't

care what I threw: knives, serving spoons, ladles, dishes–crash, bang, wallop–
the lot. Miss G was dodging and diving like one of those girls in a knife-
throwing act. When I'd used up all the cutlery, I looked for something else to
throw because I hadn't made any significant hit on target yet. I pulled out the
drawer and threw that at her and then I pulled out another drawer and added that
to the missile count. I have an idea that I was also shouting things like, "I ain't
taking no more of this film star shit from you or anybody else," and other rude
things.

Miss G fled. I knew where she had gone, off to her bedroom. I marched
across to the drawer lying on the floor and gave that a hefty kick. It didn't hurt
the drawer but it almost broke my toe. I hobbled out to the telephone and rang a
familiar number. "Taxi? Right. Will you send a car at once, no, immediately,
fast to La Bruja in Moraleja? Hurry!"

I limped back to my bedroom and picked up my suitcase. My suitcase was
always packed alongside Miss G's emergency bag because you never could
know when she wanted to take off in any direction or at any time of the day or
night. Now, it was my turn.

I heard the taxi arrive, then marched out and shouted, "Hilton Hotel." The
poor driver looked at me as if I'd gone mad, and I probably had. When I got
there the desk clerk recognized me and smiled and gave me a nice room. That
helped.

I took a bath and changed into a new dress. That afternoon, in a simmered
down condition, I walked around to the Plaza Major–the great stone-enclosed
square that has figured large in Madrid history. I sat at a small café out in the
sunshine drinking endless cups of café negro, spiked with an occasional shot of
harsh Spanish cognac, and watched the holiday makers and the beggars, the old
ladies in black with shopping bags and noses pressed against shop windows,
business men in their smart suits, ladies with their poodles, guard civilians in
their cloaks and three-cornered hats, lottery ticket sellers, horse-drawn carriages
with ancient drivers muffled against the weather, fluttering waiters. Lady
Mearene Jordan, late of St. Louis, Missouri, Lady of Color, was on vacation.

22 ENDING THE FURIOUS FIFTIES

Next morning I heard a gentle tapping at my bedroom door. Opening up, there was Miss G. I didn't expect to see a hostile Miss G or a humble Miss G. It could have been the film star Miss G, but this was the Miss G I really knew–green eyes wide, mouth already smiling, voice urgent. "Rene, when are you coming back?"

I let her in, and I said, "Miss G, I don't know. I just need time to think."

"Okay, honey, let's go and get some coffee. I'm going to keep at you."

She did keep at me. Every morning for the next six mornings, she arrived at my Hilton Hotel bedroom door with the same sweet smile and the same demand. I gave her the same answer. We never discussed the fight. As every reader of this book has already heard a dozen times, we never discussed past dramas.

On Sunday she picked me up at the hotel and took me to the Madrid airport. I'd already told her that I wanted to go back to the USA, take a break and decide what I should do.

"Okay," she said. "I'll still be after you. I'll get you through your Mama, uh?"

We sat in the lounge waiting for my departure time. We had a few drinks. As usual we gurgled with laughter over the look of somebody's Sunday hat or someone steaming through to catch his flight. She chattered away with bits of news.

"I had those buggers from MGM on the phone for an hour this morning. They are still sore about me ducking *Love Me or Leave Me*. They want me to do this crappy thing called *The Little Hut* that is crap comedy. Only one thing good about it is that the three male leads are David Niven, Jimmy Granger, and Walter Chiari. They should be able raise a laugh with that lot even without a script."

Soon I was thirty thousand feet up over the Atlantic wondering why I hadn't tried to say all the things I should have said: "Miss G, you've opened whole new worlds to me. I have been places, seen foreign parts, and known great people. Yes, okay, as your maid, but also as your friend. I've been given opportunities open to very few, especially to a black girl from St. Louis. I know all that. I admit that. It's all been an exhilarating charge across the first third of my adult life. Now Miss, I want to stop and think. Sure, I love Spain, but I don't want to make it my permanent home. I know it is going to be yours. I miss the sounds of America. I miss my family and friends, a good cheeseburger, a thick steak, fried chicken, fried catfish, American autos, and the open and cheerful society. I get homesick for these things."

I think Miss G understood that and let me go. In Spain I had no identity. Miss G loved it because she could blend into the background or blend out of it. She could enjoy publicity if she wanted to but also could escape from the frenzied intrusion of the media. I knew she was exulting in the fact that in the time left under her MGM contract the most they could make her do was three more movies and then she would be her own boss. I had a feeling that I wanted to be my own boss too.

I went from Madrid to Chicago to talk to Tressie. Tressie looked at me with her shrewd, older sister look and said, "You've left Miss G?" A big frown appeared on her face. "That girl needs you just as much now as she always has."

I said, "Tressie, I've got to make a life of my own. I've got to stand on my own two feet."

"Uh." Said Tressie.

I went back to St. Louis and stayed with my folks. My Ma looked me straight in the eye and said, "That girl's been calling me again and again. She wants to know when you are going back."

"Ma, Miss G is fine. She is surrounded by friends and servants."

My Ma didn't hear me. "She wants to know when you are going back."

I wondered that myself over the next couple of months as I took a beautician's course and a couple of jobs in stores before moving back to Los Angeles.

Then one other factor entered my life. I fell in love. I had met a tall, handsome guy–a sheriff with a big Stetson hat, a pistol in his holster, and a big broad smile. He was the same shade of brown as I was and apparently was as smitten as I was. So, between the odd jobs and more beautician courses, I started an affair. For the time being I kept my secret, and it certainly stopped me hurrying back to Miss G's side. There was, of course, the usual drawback. He was married—unhappily married, but then a lot of married men usually are unhappy.

I let Miss G into my secret when she came to Hollywood to talk to her agent and MGM. Bappie was now alone, as Charlie Guest had died. She had bought a little house high in the hills behind Hollywood. Miss G stayed there, and we talked in the alpine atmosphere.

"Married?" she said doubtfully. "Christ, all the nice guys are."

Then she looked at me. "You know I've got to go to Rome to make *The Little Hut*. Bappie wants to go with me now that she's lost Charlie. Why don't you look after this house while we are away? Rags loves you to death. You could act as our Hollywood contact while we are away. See how things work out with the police department."

I agreed. Things didn't work out with the police department. I was back on Miss G's payroll.

The Little Hut was a film adaptation of a long-running London and Broadway play. It had been written by a Frenchman, Andre Roussin, as a farce. A randy male gets cast ashore on a desert island and finds a gorgeous grass-skirted female waiting for him with goo-goo eyes. In his version, three men had been cast ashore with one lovely showgirl swimming ashore with them. As soon as the MGM brass realized what they had bought, the screams went up.

Miss G said, "They thought it was immoral! It was outrageous! Three fully grown men and one girl washed up on a desert island with nothing to do but you know what; and they do 'it' in turns. It was a different guy every night, and it was scandalous!"

"Now, if they had left it to me," continued Miss G, "in the film we were about to make, I would have arranged a suitable time schedule for all three poor castaways."

"Miss G?" I said. "A suitable <u>time schedule</u>?"

Miss G did one of her music hall faces. "You know, Rene, one every other night. Maybe poker games for special Saturday and Sunday nights." Her mirth was outrageous. "You have to realize that Niven, Granger, and Chiari are really nice, sexy guys."

Unfortunately, MGM's editorial alterations obliterated what might have been Miss G's idea of a nice friendly relationship on a desert island which might have added a new slant to the term "ménage-a-quatre." As it was, Jimmy Granger was cast as Miss G's husband. David Niven, who was Jimmy's friend, had to lust after her with no hope. Then just to liven things up, Walter Chiari arrived dressed up in a grass skirt and war-paint shouting, "Boula-Boula," for no apparent reason. He was the Italian chef who had been shipwrecked in the same yacht.

The film was doomed to mediocrity from the start. Miss G looked divine in black lingerie and a grass skirt. Niven and Granger looked absurd in shirt, drawers and socks, and Walter Chiari never stood a chance in his getup.

Miss G's only realistic comment at the end of filming was, "Rene, if I had ducked out of this one and got another suspension, I would still be forced to make films for MGM into the next century."

The film did mean one other thing to her, and that was that Walter Chiari was now seriously into her life. Miss G's relationship with Walter Chiari had started in Rome with an introduction on the set of *The Barefoot Contessa*. Walter was introduced as "one of Italy's leading film and music hall artists." His English was diabolical, but as he smiled and bent over to kiss Miss G's hand, his determination to make up for his lack of English must have been uppermost in his mind. I must also add that, in my opinion, Walter realized a strong relationship with Miss G would be a career building move. I believe Miss G thought that even before I did.

Walter was a different sort of man than Luis Miguel, whom Papa Hemingway described so well in his book, *The Dangerous Summer*. "Luis Miguel was a charmer–dark, tall, no hips…with a grave mocking face that went from professional disdain to easy laughter." Luis Miguel was Spanish; Walter Chiari was Italian. Both were Latin, but with dramatic differences.

Walter was not your usual Italian type. He was fair-skinned, good-looking, athletic and a gymnast of near acrobatic ability, as I was to discover in the future.

MGM didn't waste any time with Miss G, and they quickly had her back at work in an adaptation of Ernest Hemingway's *The Sun Also Rises*. Miss G said immediately, "I know they will spoil the film. There is no way of making a film that can do justice to Papa's books."

I said, "Miss G you aren't psychic, and they haven't got a script yet or even a director."

"Yes, they have–Henry King. You remember he did *The Snows of Kilimanjaro*."

"That was a good film." I said. "You got good reviews. Papa didn't grumble too much about it. You liked Henry King, and he liked you."

I was being a bit dramatic, but I remembered from the reviews and the comments Henry King had made. He had said, "No one else could have given the part the sensitivity, the bruised quality that Ava imparted to it....She had cut out drinking, the late nights and too much Frankie. She had disciplined herself rigorously for the part. She could always do this if she believed in a role, and she believed her part as Cynthia. Sometimes she would come in grumbling in the morning–she hated to get up early and drive to the studio. Once she was actually on the floor, she worked with a kind of desperate involvement and intensity that amazed me."

Miss G said defensively, "I still love Henry King. He is a lovely guy. Christ, he has been directing since they invented films. Papa's books and short stories never really do anything as films. His characters are his characters. You can't match faces to them."

"But you loved playing Cynthia in Kilimanjaro. You matched the fire; you liked the part."

"Rene," she voiced expressively, "it was a part. I could understand her. She was American, and I could understand her. But it was just a part. Now, how the hell am I going to play this young English tramp, Lady Brett Ashley? I love her, and it is one of Papa's greatest books. But I can't be her."

"Miss G," I said, "if you love her, you will play her well. Besides, you have got Tyrone Power as your leading man for the first time."

"Jesus, as Jake how the hell is Ty Power going to play a man with his testicles shot off in the Big War? What am I going to say, 'bad luck?' All the heroes I get in films are testicle-free."

"Miss G," I protested. "It is not true."

"It is true. What happened in *The Barefoot Contessa*? Poor Rossano Brazzi, playing the count who married me, had lost his private parts, and then he shoots me because I want to give him an heir and hire the chauffeur to make me pregnant. A girl has not a chance."

Then she thought about it and added, "The only good thing about *The Sun Also Rises* is that it is going to be made in Spain, on my front door, so to speak. I love Errol Flynn."

It did start in Spain, in Pamplona, a pretty little city that Miss G and I had visited a couple of times in our traveling days. It started in winter which was a bit of a mistake. Somebody had forgotten that Pamplona stands half way up the Pyrenees. Well, maybe I'm exaggerating a bit there, but Pamplona is certainly in the foothills of the high ranges of those mountains. The snow can be three feet deep. The rain can pour for days on end. It isn't sunny in Spain.

They had no alternative but to transfer the location to sunnier climes. They moved it to Morelia in Mexico, and Miss G loved every minute. They rented a fifteen-room house for her with servants, lots of rooms, and a swimming pool. She enjoyed eating and drinking with Tyrone Power, Mel Ferrer and his wife, and Errol Flynn, who was now slightly past his swashbuckling pirate days and more content with a large vodka.

I always liked what Bob Evans, who played the part of Ava's love-stunned bullfighter, said about her afterwards. He said, "I had a real collision with Ava at the outset of the picture. She was determined that Walter Chiari would play the bullfighter." Later Bob became Paramount's Production Chief, so I guess he knew what he was talking about.

By this time, Walter was firmly entrenched in Miss G's life, and she was giving him a helping hand. As she was only on loan to Zanuck and Twentieth Century Fox, she had no hope. Bob went on, "Zanuck and Henry King wanted me, so she was rude and unpleasant to me, which made our love scenes quite an ordeal. Later on she relented and became reasonably friendly. She drank too much, and her language was offensive. I thought her sister had a bad influence on her."

That's about right. Bappie could be a bad influence on anybody. When she wanted to be nasty, she could be really nasty. She was nasty about blacks, Jews and Dagos. But she had lots of good points, many of them difficult to dig out; however, we got on. Bob Evans made one good point: "Ava was wonderful after we got over that first hurdle. When she is in a scene she shoots off electric sparks. The love scenes were so violent that when they ended my teeth were chattering , and she took a half hour rest."

Miss G roared with laughter at that. She thought the rest was pretty accurate.

On one of my visits to Bappie's house on Rinconia Drive after we were all back in California, I met Myra, Miss G's older sister. She was visiting. While there Miss G took me aside to tell me one interesting item of news.

"Guess who rang last night?"

I didn't try. "Who?"

"Howard Hughes. I thought he had given up after all this time. 'So Ava,' he said, 'can I come around and talk to you and take you out to dinner?'"

"'Strange,' I said. 'Howard, you know I'm staying here with Bappie,' I said, 'and Myra is here as well. I'm going out to dinner with them tonight.'"

"'That's fine. Let me take all of you out to dinner. What about the Beachcomer? How is that?'"

"Great!" Ava said. "Bappie will love to see you."

Miss G told me how he'd come around later to pick them up, and before heading out Mr. Hughes had said to her, "Can I have a private word with you before we leave?"

"Sure," Ava said, knowing that at least Bappie would be pleased. "Christ, she never gave up telling me how crazy I was not to marry the richest man in the world."

I was curious. "So what was the private word?"

"He hummed and hesitated and looked at his fingers. Then he plucked up courage and said, 'I've decided to marry Jean Peters.'"

"God Almighty, Rene, I think he expected me to burst into tears or cry, 'Howard, you can't do that!'"

"So what did you do?"

Miss G shrugged. "I'd never met Jean Peters and only knew of her because of her films. I said to him, 'That's great, Howard. Congratulations. I'm sure you will be very happy.'"

"And what did he do?"

"Not much. He sighed, stood up, and said, 'Yes, I suppose so.'"

"And that was it?"

"More or less. The four of us trooped outside. Howard's usual beat-up Chevrolet car was waiting for us. He put my two sisters in the back, closed me into the front passenger seat, and walked around the back of the car to get in behind the wheel. We three girls had been talking non-stop for hours. We went on talking non-stop. Five minutes later Bappie said, 'Where's Howard?'"

"I said, 'Howard? Why I don't know. Well, where is he?'"

"We all got out to look. Howard was lying flat on his back behind the car. Was he dead? No, he wasn't dead. He had blacked out. We sat him up and got him to his feet. He said that he was fine. We brushed him down. No explanations. As usual, his suit had seen better days. Then he got into the driving seat and drove us to the Beachcomer. We all went on talking non-stop. Howard was quiet. We ate all the oriental goodies, and Howard drove us home."

At the time we never quite worked out what happened. We thought he may have had a black-out because of the many plane accidents he had been in. He rarely tied his shoelaces so he could easily have fallen and hit his head on the fender. Now from Miss Katharine Hepburn's later revelations we know some of the reasons for Howard Hughes' eccentric behavior.

Miss G never ever saw Howard again after that night. He married Jean Peters in March 1957. I believe the marriage lasted about thirteen years before Jean filed for divorce in 1970. Howard just went on being a perpetual enigma until the end of his most mysterious life.

Around this time Miss G and I took a trip to see how MGM studios were faring out at Culver City. Half the studios were empty, and they told us it was the same at Warner, Paramount, Universal, and all the other major studios.

"Christ, Rene," said Miss G. "At least we saw the best of it. Who'd have expected fabled Hollywood to close down like this?"

Of course, it didn't. Movie-making was simply moving into the hands of independent producers and independent stars. They were making movies all right, particularly in Britain, France, Italy and Spain. Hollywood never really returned to the eminence it had held since the early twenties.

The film MGM had Miss G lined up for following *The Little Hut* and her loan out for *The Sun Also Rises* was *The Naked Maja*. This time they were renting her out to an Italian company–Titanus Films. Variety magazine accurately described Miss G as the "gold seam that lined the financial package." You could say that again. MGM made millions. Miss G got ninety thousand dollars.

Miss G had no option but to grin and hate it and count the weeks before her contract with MGM ran out. Between us, she was adamant that she was going to spin out the making of *The Naked Maja* long enough for that to happen. It wasn't even difficult. The charming Italians backing Titanus Films seemed to think that films were made by divine intervention. It took them a considerable time to work out that they weren't.

But long before the contracts for *The Naked Maka* were even signed, Miss G made one of the most dangerous mistakes of her whole life.

23 AVA AND THE GOYA NUDE

Miss G was now firmly based in Spain but ricocheting occasionally between Madrid, London, Paris, Rome, New York, and California. I was holding down the fort at Bappie's hillside house in Hollywood. Walter Chiari had his own artistic career to look after but was spending more and more time as Miss G's major escort and bed partner. Unfortunately whenever Frank arrived on the scene he had to relinquish both posts. A demotion he did not much care for.

Luis Miguel was now married to Lucia Bose, and they were spending much of their time at Luis Miguel's finca. Miss G was still closely involved in Madrid's bullfighting circles and had no intention of quitting her senior position with the aficionado in-crowd. Little did she know how quickly it would come to a spectacular and career-threatening finale.

She was invited to visit a huge ranch down near Seville. Its wealthy owner was renowned for breeding the great fighting bulls used in the corridas. She was invited to visit for a celebrated and revered tradition called a "torea a caballo," which was the testing of young bulls for the courage and spirit they were expected to display in future appearances in the bullring.

It was staged on the ranch in a specially built bullring which was a much smaller circle than the huge arenas of Madrid and Seville and surrounded by only a modest tier of seats. At intervals a feisty young bull would be released into the ring to spot a horseman leisurely circling its perimeter. The young bull would be affronted– enraged. What was this pain-in-the-derriere doing confronting him? With a stamp of hooves and a flourish of horns, he would charge, determined to toss horse and rider into the next county. The horseman and his steed were experienced and wily. The rider was armed with a long lance with a tip of solid, black rubber. Its use was not to injure the bull, but together with expert manipulation of the house to fend him off. After a lot of energy expended in forays and violent collisions with the barricade, the young bull, his courage exhibited and charted, would be shooed back into his ringside pen by the cape swirling handlers.

It was a fascinating spectacle and a time honored festival attended by many of the bullfighting community. There was a lot of drinking, a lot of speculation, a lot of betting, and a lot of noise.

"Then," she said, remembering the occasion with vivid clarity, "I got the buzz. All my so-called friends started dropping hints, little taunts. 'Hey, Ava, you're so keen on bullfighting. Why don't you have a go? Nothing to it. A couple of circles of the ring and that's it. Just hang on and the horse will do the rest.'"

I said to her with alarm, because I had also witnessed one hell of a lot of bullfights and knew a bull was dangerous from the time it could stand on four legs, "Miss G, you must have been out of your mind. Luis Miguel would never have allowed you even to get on the bloody horse, let alone go into the ring. You've never ridden. You know nothing about horses, let alone bulls."

"Dead right, Rene. But Louis Miguel wasn't there, and I was. I was also full of booze, and booze makes you do stupid things. I could hear the onlookers picking up the idea. 'Ava's going to ride. Ava's going to ride.' I'd got my audience. How could I disappoint them? 'Okay,' I said, 'I'll give it a try.'"

"They helped me up into the saddle. 'Hold the reins like this. Hold the lance like this. When you see the bull, just point the lance at him, and the horse will heave him aside.'"

"I went sailing around the ring a couple of times and felt pretty good. Then they let the bull out and the rest got very confused. I saw the bull come charging across the ring. I think it came straight at the horse. I think the horse reared up and the bull went underneath him. All I really knew was that I was shot straight over the horse's head. I remember the bang as my face hit the dirt. Then I was out cold. I remember feeling people picking me up and carrying me somewhere. Then I was dazed, but beginning to function again. I felt bashed up but okay. I was taken back to the farm and it was only when I looked in the mirror and saw my face that I said, 'Christ, what is that?'"

As Miss G would soon find out, "that" was a hematoma, a blood-infused lump the size of a large plum on her left cheek.

Miss G went on remembering. "We left next morning to fly from the local airstrip back to Madrid. The famous owner was waiting there with a large bunch of flowers. With difficulty, I stopped Bappie from stuffing them down his throat."

"You were set up?"

"Completely, honey. A professional cameraman had been positioned correctly. The entire 'Have-a-go-Ava' crowd had been briefed. I don't suppose they were trying to injure me, just joining in the fun. Nobody cared very much what might happen. The magazine, *Paris Match*, paid seventy-five thousand dollars for a set of pictures showing the incident from start to finish. Christ knows what it fetched syndicated around the world. I was the fall guy, darling. The mug!"

Someone or some clique had set up the entire affair, but it was a very long time before Miss G could raise the courage to face the cameras again.

The famous British surgeon Sir Archibald McIndoe, who had operated upon hundreds of badly burned pilots and who she was advised to see, became a great friend of hers during this period. He insisted, "Don't touch it with a knife. Don't have it operated on. It will disappear. I promise you, it will disappear. Heat treatment and that's all. It will take time. You must be patient. Wait! Wait!"

Frank, trying to be helpful, gave her the name of a famous New York plastic surgeon. Miss G went on. "I got an appointment and went to see him. He said, 'You should have come to me earlier; however, I can remedy it with one small operation.' With hardly a pause he added, concerning his fee, 'I have a new hospital branch opening in New Mexico. They would appreciate a donation of one million dollars.'"

Miss G smiled without much mirth at the memory. "I should have told him the place to stick his million dollars was the same place I should have told that famous bull breeder to stick his lance."

Miss G started her next picture convinced that her face was ruined forever—a conviction she maintained for years to come. It was total nonsense figuring only in her fertile imagination. For the blemish left by the facial hematoma was too small to notice. Anyway, she need not have worried. That next movie called for a far larger exposure of Ava Gardner's flesh than a spot on her cheek. It's title, *The Naked Maja*, made that clear.

Prior to the beginning of this picture Miss G and I were quite certain we were authorities on the life and times of the great Spanish painter Francisco Goya. I do not suppose the art world would have confirmed this supposition, but we didn't care about that. We adored Goya. We'd become familiar with his work during our first Spanish period when we spent weeks constantly returning to the Prado, prowling its corridors with our eyes out on beanstalks. Francisco Goya gripped the imagination and the hearts of us both.

To start with, his great canvases of the Spanish Royals stopped us in our tracks. Those long, shallow faces framed by black curling locks were enthralling and mesmerizing. Those full lips, black mustaches, sword-pointed beards, those cruel, long-nosed faces, contemptuous and arrogant, looked out at you with chilling comprehension. Among them was the face and full length figure of Ferdinand the Seventh, the tyrant who forced Goya to flee from Spain in order to save his life.

Kings, queens, princes were all royal masters perpetuating decadent luxury. Their navies were looting gold from the New World, their Jesuit priests burning and destroying ancient civilizations and always enriching their mighty empire. One could understand from Goya's portraits that the females were only minor players. They were imprisoned in the same sumptuous attire–silks, laces, stiff jewel-laden brocades–but they were bland, moon-faced creatures exhibiting few signs of the sexuality that had produced their children. The children were dressed in the same raiment, wooden as marionettes.

Goya had preserved them in pigment forever. But he did more than just give the royal line immortality. Progressing from the patronage of the court, he mirrored the horrors of his time, the massacres, firing squads, executions, and the misery of the common people in the series of paintings, engravings and cartoons. It was really ironic that his consummate artist's fame should rest to some degree on a reclining portrait of the Duchess of Alba in the nude.

"I'll bet," observed Miss G before the movie started, "that Goya never dreamt that MGM was waiting for him two hundred years in the future. I also bet you that some smart ass producer had his thought of the year when he saw a reproduction of that painting. Gee, a masterpiece and history! Who can say it is pornography? A beautiful dame stark naked on a bed; superimpose the face of a super sexy actress on top of that body…now let's think." I joined in the laughter as we synchronized in, "Ava Gardner!"

It should have been made in Madrid, but the aristocratic Albas who were still in power got wind of the idea. Who could blame them for being horrified at the thought of great-great-great Auntie Alba about to be exhibited without her nightie? They accepted that she had been revealed naked for two hundred years, but that was art. Who could anticipate what that scarlet woman, Ava Gardner, might do with her portrayal?

Certainly one of their high-voltage friends rang General Franco and blew the whistle, knowing of the Spanish dictator's support for hereditary principles and Spanish dignity. The film company got the message. The location was moved to Italy, and the project was inherited by Titanus Productions. Titanus was operated by two charming Italians, probably intrigued by the title and the thought of Ava Gardner in the nude. Unfortunately, they had very little understanding of the production needs and costs of a movie like *The Naked Maja*, and the film came close to collapse. It was rescued when United Artists became interested. MGM guaranteed distribution and made a binding agreement that Ava Gardner would play the Duchess of Alba.

Miss G thoroughly enjoyed another stay in Italy. She made her headquarters in Rome. Walter Chiari was a constant companion, and she saw more of that beautiful country than ever before. Every few days a newspaper would report that Ava and Walter were planning marriage, but Miss G was quite certain that Walter himself was spreading this news. No church bells were heard. Walter was very useful to her, but never at any moment did Miss G contemplate getting hitched for the fourth time.

Eventually the shooting of *The Naked Maja* commenced, directed by Henry Koster. Miss G looked totally dreamy in black lace mantillas and beautiful gowns designed by Fontana. Anthony Franciosa played Francisco Goya. They got on well together. Miss G thought he was a very nice guy and a very fine actor. Tony thought the same way about her. He did get disturbed when the Italian newspapers, in between announcing Miss G's imminent marriage to Walter Chiari, informed their readers that Tony and Miss G were having an affair. As Tony was securely married to Shelley Winters at that time, he was not amused.

Tony was a method actor. Miss G didn't know what a method actor was. Tony spent a lot of time researching Francisco Goya's background. Tony understood that Francisco Goya was a passionate man, an eloquent man, and at times a manic, screaming man, right or wrong. Tony wrapped himself in all those emotional skins of feeling. Miss G talked about this with a slightly worried look on her face.

"God Almighty, Rene, there we are on the set, cameras ready to roll and where's Tony? He's behind a bit of scenery sticking his finger down his throat to make himself nearly sick and groaning and moaning to get his self in the right psychological mood. Jesus, sometimes it's more like a wrestling bout than a film scene."

I think Miss G tended to exaggerate, but the script was so soap-like, the dialogue so moronic that Tony's ambitious interpretations were wasted on the sheer banalities of the scenes.

Miss G also suffered for far different reasons. "That very first scene was in a church. The church was full of Goya's paintings. Goya was standing there with a smile on his face. All the crew and cast were Italian. The script was in English. Many of the Italian cast didn't speak English. They learned their lines in what they thought was English, but I couldn't understand a word. I didn't know when a sentence ended and when it was my turn to talk. I stood there like a deaf mute ruing every scene. Director Henry Koster, who had a script, knew where the Italian gobbledygook started and where it ended. He thought I was either drunk or daft. This created problems, but," Miss G paused to raise a slender finger to emphasize her command of the situation, "What was I to do? I decided not to listen to their words, but to watch their lips. When they stopped moving their lips I smiled, scowled, looked worried, stupid or whatever the script called for and shoved in my return lines. Thank God, I could understand Tony in the big scenes.

One thing that did impress Miss G mightily was the work of Giuseppe Rotunno, the cinematographer. "Rene," she cried, "Giuseppe is the greatest. I've been photographed by the best in the business–Freddie Young, Jack Cardiff, Norbert Brodine and dozens of others–and Giuseppe is right up in their class. He is the one who got permission from the Spanish authorities to film all of Goya's masterpieces in the Prado. He and his set designers put all the color into *The Naked Maja*. It won't win any Oscars for its performers, but Giuseppe should get one for his photography. Baby, when we are free of MGM we will try and get Giuseppe for our first movie."

Miss G mused for a few seconds. "I guess you could conclude, Rene, that we tampered with the history of poor old Francisco in quite a significant way. There we were playing two romantic young lovers. Agreed, the Duchess was certainly Goya's patron and certainly posed in the nude for him, but they were definitely never young lovers. There's Goya trying to fight a corrupt Court, a hypocritical Church, and the Spanish Inquisition always threatening to torture him. I am being slowly poisoned by priests in black robes. Naturally there is a good old movie ending as I am lying in Goya's arms whispering my closing line, 'Look for me in every Spanish face.' Considering the fact that every Spanish face has been looking at me in the nude for God knows how long, seems a bit difficult to understand."

24 ON THE BEACH WITH THE TENNIS CHAMP

Both Miss G and I read the novel *On the Beach* by the British author Nevil Shute and wept. Producer Stanley Kramer read the book, bought the film rights and sent the film script to Miss G. We read it and wept again. Gregory Peck read both book and film script and immediately agreed to play the part of U.S. Nuclear Submarine Scorpion Commander Dwight Towers. Stanley's offer of four hundred thousand dollars helped Miss G to make up her mind, but it wasn't the money that committed Miss G to the part of Moira Davidson, the Australian girl who falls in love with Dwight. She had fallen in love with Greg Peck long ago. Only it was a platonic relationship for a change. Moira was a fine part. Miss G induced Stanley to employ Giuseppe Rotunno as the cinematographer, so she knew she was in safe hands.

Why was the book so compelling? It anticipated the appalling disaster everyone feared–a nuclear war and its aftermath. In Nevil Shute's evocative book, a nuclear war between the great powers had broken out two years earlier, and within weeks radiation fallout had obliterated all forms of human and animal life in the northern hemisphere. Now, driven by the spin of the planet and its prevailing winds, the silent, death-carrying clouds were moving at their measured pace to slowly envelope the rest of the globe.

Melbourne, at the southern-most tip of the Australian continent, was expected to last until the end. They would survive for about another seven months. It was in Melbourne and its surrounding countryside that Nevil Shute had set his scene for the terminal days of human existence.

Stanley Kramer had assembled his assorted company there for a different purpose. We all hoped we would make it for a few more years. Nevertheless, there was no doubt that we were all a little awed, even scared, at the terrifying imminence of the movie's theme.

"What would you do if it really happened?" That was one of the first questions I asked Miss G.

"What is there to do?" she countered. "Rush out into the street and start screaming? Before long, you would just run out of screams." She continued her theme.

158

"I love that part in Shute's book about the Pastoral Club in Melbourne. It is now the best club in the world because it is the only club left in the world. This lovely old guy has discovered that there are three thousand bottles of lovely plank, and club members are already beginning to feel sick from radiation exposure. He had better raise his consumption by at least a dozen bottles a week if the supply of port is going to end before the world does." Miss G guffawed at the thought. "I'd certainly have pitched in to help him. I mean that is realistic." If nothing else, Miss G was usually realistic. I often thought that Miss G's entire life was lived as if the world might end the day after tomorrow or that she might run out of lovers before the next weekend.

Miss G insisted I go with her. "Rene," she said, "You can't miss this trip. You are coming to Australia."

"What about Bappie?"

"To hell with Bappie. She's hogged the last two Italian trips. She will get into this one–never fear. But you are coming because I need you."

On the happy flight from L.A. down to Sydney and onto Melbourne, sharing the aircraft with us was a contingent of U.S. tennis players. I can't remember if they were representing the U.S. in the Davis Cup or competing in the Australian Championships. It was possibly both. Miss G and that bunch of bronzed, handsome, healthy young guys sure did get on fine together. She was particularly taken with one cute young tennis player, Henry.

Melbourne was a graceful old city, but its founding fathers had not really established the nightclub or restaurant business. Really, the only places with any life were the pubs, and they closed at five in the afternoon. Even in the expensive restaurants, wine was prohibited on tables after nine in the evening.

Miss G was on edge most of the time, and some of her behavior was erratic. We would go to a restaurant, and halfway through dinner she would get up and leave or decide she had to scour the city to find some happy music. We could eat in the St. James Hotel, but that became a bit of a bore. As we had a perfectly reasonable kitchen between the three of us–Miss G, Bappie, and me– we managed to produce some reasonable meals.

Veronique Peck had been much wiser. She had done her homework before arriving in Australia, declining offers of accommodation in our hotel. She had rented a large Victorian house near the beach, a delightful place to accommodate Greg, herself and their baby daughter. She also knew about Australian food. Their meat, fish, vegetables and fruits were wonderful. All that was needed was a cook. Veronique brought a French chef with her. He could have earned Veronique three Michelin stars. Miss G often dined with them.

Miss G was glad to be back with Gregory Peck. Their last two films together, *The Great Sinner* and *Kilimanjaro*, had not created mile-long queues at the box office. They had not done either of their reputations any harm either. Now they were fast friends.

As Greg always recalled with one of his gorgeous chuckles, "You can't keep the audience's eyes off Ava. There she stands, not a line to say, but radiating that almost unearthly beauty. The rest of us in the cast are tearing up the carpets with our great performances and acting our socks off, but no one is looking at us. They are staring at Ava." Greg loved and cherished Ava like an older brother. Greg, his wife Veronique, and Ava stayed bosom friends until the end of her life.

Despite the meals that Miss G gobbled up with the Pecks, she was a beautifully designed female who could eat like two horses and never get fat. When she came home late at night, around midnight, she would often say, "Rene honey, think you could make me a Spanish omelet?"

Usually I had all the ingredients for a Spanish omelet in the fridge: cooked, chopped potatoes, onions, green peppers, garlic and eggs. I found making it no problem, but on one evening while Miss G was having dinner with the Pecks, Bappie and me were sharing a bottle of Scotch and having a heart-to-heart chat about nothing in particular, when I made the biggest fool of myself I had made in the years I had served Miss G.

Undoubtedly it was the Scotch. Bappie and I went down that bottle real fast. At some point, Bappie said, "Rene, why don't you whip up the ingredients for that Spanish omelet. Ava's bound to want one when she gets in."

It was then that the thought, no doubt motivated by the Scotch, hit me. A rebellion! I said, "Miss G's not going to have a Spanish omelet tonight."

"Why not?" said Bappie with interest.

"Because there isn't anything with which to make a Spanish omelet."

"Yes, there is," protested Bappie. "I did the shopping today. All the makings are out in the kitchen on the window sill."

"I'll go and look." I said. A sly and naughty thought began to surface from my Scotch-clouded brain. I went into the kitchen and saw the groceries on the table. It was then that the urge consumed me. I opened the window. Outside stretched a large, dark, open lot. The point of no return had been reached. I picked up the potatoes one by one and hurled them into the darkness. Onion, garlic, green peppers and a dozen eggs followed. Bappie could see me from the living room. I went back and finished my Scotch.

I said, "You see Bappie, we don't have anything with which to make an omelet."

Bappie raised her eyebrows, but made not the slightest effort to interfere or say, "Stop that!" She just sat there like a brooding hen and finished her glass. Then she stood up and said, "See you later, Rene." Then she went off to bed.

I did the same thing. I got a couple of hours sleep before Miss G came home. My head had cleared so I got up and chatted with her. Then Miss G said that she was off to bed. I thought, 'Thank God, I've gotten away with my damn foolishness.' But I hadn't. At about two in the morning that little girl voice called, "Rene, I'm hungry. How about cooking up the stuff for a Spanish omelet and calling me when you have it ready."

I thought, "Oh, my God, I've betrayed her." I got up and banged about for a couple of minutes and then went to her room and said, "Miss G we can't have a Spanish omelet tonight."

Miss G opened her eyes. "We can't? Why?"

"Because there is nothing with which to make an omelet."

Miss G sat bolt upright. "Nothing to make one with? What has that sister of mine doing? All she has to do is a little shopping! You go down there and get her up and ask her what the hell's going on?"

I knew I was caught in a cross-fire. I trailed back down the stairs with doom in every footstep. Bappie had heard the noise, and as soon as I tapped on the door her voice said, "Rene, don't bring your ass in here. I didn't tell you to throw that stuff out."

I appealed, "What am I going to do?"

The voice was unsympathetic. "You figure it out since you are so smart."

I said, "Bappie, please!" I was desperate.

There was a long pause. Then Bappie said, "Your only hope is to ring the manager next door and maybe he's got the makings."

I said anxiously, "Okay." Then I thought about it and knew the manager wouldn't listen to me. "Will you call him for me?" I asked.

Bappie, bless her, answered, "Yes, I'll call him, but Rene, if you ever pull this trick again, you are on your own, understand?"

She called the young manager and woke him up. He'd been in purgatory for weeks with the goings-on attached to his hotel. Yes, he had potatoes, onions, garlic, green peppers, and eggs. Yes, if I came across, he would give them to me. I hot-footed it across, and if looks could kill, I would have been dead. His face was beet-red. I hurried back, chopped up the stuff, made the omelet and went upstairs to tell Miss G that it was ready. She came down in her dressing gown, sat down at the table and yawned. Then she looked at her omelet, yawned again and said, "Rene, honey, it is just that I am so tired. I guess I am not as hungry as I thought I was."

Bappie and I had a big laugh about it for years afterwards, but we never ever revealed to Miss G what we were laughing about. To maintain her own sometimes fragile security, Miss G needed complete loyalty from her small secure circle of friends. A Spanish omelet doesn't sound like much of a test of loyalty, but I knew that my rebellion, minor and silly though it was, would have bruised that intangible trust.

When *On the Beach* started being filmed, one or two problems emerged immediately. One of them was that Miss G kept fluffing her lines. It was a recurrence which annoyed her intensely because after our personal rehearsals, she was very good with her lines. It infuriated Stanley Kramer even more.

No one could tell him that it was all Stella's fault. Stella was Stanley's wife. Stanley, like most other hard-working movie producers, went to bed very early so that he could be on the set equally early the next morning. But Stella sat around drinking and around midnight as we were climbing into bed, Stella would arrive at our front door prepared to go on drinking and not prepared to go home. She did this regularly.

We liked Stella. We liked drinking, but as we had to get up at five or six and prepare for a hard day's work, we could not do that sort of thing. That is why Miss G was fluffing her lines. She was also yelling, "God Almighty, there is Stanley giving me hell about fluffing my lines, and there's Stella keeping me awake all night. Can't someone say to him, 'If you could keep your wife at home, we might finish the picture?'"

It got a bit tense. Someone got the word to Stella, and the movie was soon finished. The atmosphere during that time between Miss G and Stanley arrived at a point where people were saying Stanley was letting it be known that he would never work with Miss G again. Untrue. Stanley and Miss G became the best of friends. Indeed, he sent her one of the sweetest notes she ever got from a director at the end of a film. Nevertheless, these activities were a bit trying as Miss G's love life was also being disturbed.

As I have already mentioned, Miss G was now having a happy love affair with Henry, the tennis champ. In my mind this raised various problems because there were now two suitors in the vicinity who thought they possessed privileges in Miss G's bed.

Frank still had a habit of showing up at unlikely moments, but he was far away in California. So he wasn't the one I was necessarily worried about. It was Walter Chiari.

Australia had admitted tens of thousands of Italian immigrants since the end of World War II. As Walter Chiari was a star in his own country, he had managed to fix up a tour of his own to coincide with our stay in Melbourne. Walter was an intermittent, if not all that popular, visitor to our apartment. Walter was also very athletic, that is he was pretty good at clambering up drain pipes and popping in through open windows.

These dangers meant that I had to double my surveillance duties and see that escape routes were available in times of crisis. I had to see that windows and doors could be opened at ground level as lovers got very agitated at the thought of a three or four-story jump in the middle of the night.

Walter still cherished dreams of marrying Miss G even though Miss G had never given him the slightest encouragement to support his notions. He was aware, he admitted long after the fact, that he knew Miss G always thought he was hanging on to her coattails in order to promote his own professional standing and he was quite hurt at that assumption.

As I have already made clear, Miss G had shared an intimacy with Walter since the years when *The Barefoot Contessa*, *The Little Hut* and *The Naked Maja* were being made. Walter was handsome, sexy, and great fun. He was always likely to overplay his prowess as an athlete. Miss G always smiled a little ruefully at the memory of visiting Cuba on one occasion and taking Walter to visit Papa Hemingway. She said, "I could see at first glance that Papa didn't like him much and that Papa was a bit feisty. After the first drinks, papa asked him innocently, 'Walter, I understand you are something of an athlete.'"

"'Sure,' said Walter glowing with pride."

"'Boxing?' asked Papa."

"'Sure,' said Walter."

"'I've got some gloves,' said Papa. 'Fancy a little sparring?'"

"Walter was quite eager. He was about middle weight and had dancing feet to keep out of harm's way. Papa was a grouchy, rough-house bruiser. He gave Walter time to flick in a few lefts – that sort of thing—and then stepped in and bam! He stood hard on one of Walter's feet and held him solid. He knocked the hell out of him. I had to call time pretty quickly or I'd have ended up carrying

Walter home on a stretcher."

With Henry's constant presence in Miss G's life, I did mention to her the remote possibility that her current three lovers, Henry, Frank and Walter, might show up at the same time one night, each expecting to share her bed, and we might be treated to a three-way boxing match. Miss G howled into convulsions of laughter at the thought, and I eventually joined in her mirth.

I was not far from wrong. On various occasions in the past, Walter had gained entry when doors and windows were closed. A locked door was no obstacle to Walter. He loved the idea of appearing through a bedroom window, and surprise, surprise, an Italian aria would be heard. Most of the time Miss G accepted these forays with loving kindness, but sometimes you would hear the roar, "Walter, if you don't get out of this bedroom, I'll kill you!" At this point, though, Miss G was totally obsessed with Henry. Walter was moving into the past memory brigade.

I woke one night in my bedroom which was one floor below Miss G's. It was hot, and my window was open. I heard a scratching and heavy breathing and an Italian expletive as the climber impaled himself on some sharp edge. Could it be? Was it Walter? Had he decided to pay a visit? My God, he had!

At the time Miss G and Henry were either sleeping peacefully or polishing their tactics for a forceful attack at the net. I knew I had to get their attention. I ejected out of my bed, grabbed a robe, and raced up the stairs. I tapped with urgency on Miss G's door and hissed. "Miss G…Miss G…Walter's coming up the drainpipe." Later, the idiocy of that warning gave Miss G another cause for laughing hysteria.

Henry knew very little about Miss G's background or relationships, but he certainly must have been aware that he might be playing on someone else's tennis court. Maybe the awful, possible headline flashed through his mind, "Henry loses vital Davis Cup match in three sets. Ava Gardner named as Henry's new doubles partner."

Henry went out through the bedroom door as fast as if he were returning a full stretch match point. He had managed to get his pants on. He had one arm in his shirt and carried his shoes and socks. Some of these lovers have minds as wary as racing drivers, as they never know when they may need a fast getaway.

"Follow me," I hissed. We hurried down the stairs past Bappie's bedroom. Reaching the back door, I unbolted it. He paused long enough to get his clothes on, gave me a quick glint of white teeth, whispered, "Thanks," and was gone into the night.

I went back to bed. I wondered if Miss G had woken up. I even wondered if next morning when she opened her eyes and found Walter she thought, "That's funny, I thought I went to bed with Henry last night?"

25 A MATTER OF LIFE AND CERTAIN DEATH

In *On the Beach,* Gregory Peck, playing Dwight Towers, and Miss G, playing Moira Davidson, dominated the movie. Moira was in her thirties, a little dowdy, her looks diminishing, a little dispirited about her life and covering its emptiness with cynicism and a lot of booze. Stanley Kramer had plainly given Miss G her role believing he was casting from real life.

Nothing worthwhile had come from Moira's few affairs. She had never married. She drank a lot because that assuaged the aches of the past. She went on drinking to counter the inner agonies at the thought she would leave the world with a meaningless past behind her.

Then into her life came Towers, the tall, handsome, good-natured and dedicated U.S. Navy career officer, commander of the nuclear submarine, the *Sawfish.* It had arrived in Australia to link up with the Australian navy.

The *Sawfish* did undertake one last voyage up to the west coast of the USA to investigate a mysterious Morse code signal still being picked up in Melbourne. It was only a random tapping but was worth examining. Perhaps some vestige of human existence still survived. It did not. A radio key was still functioning from a power source, but it was caught in a broken window blind, and when the wind blew a garbled signal was transmitted. No other sign of life was detected, and Commander Towers and his crew made the long, weary, submerged return journey back to Melbourne.

The friendship between Moira and Dwight grew closer and warmer. To Moira it soon became obsessive. She had fallen deeply in love for the first time in her life. What an irony, she thought. What a moment for this to happen. She knew she could not weigh Dwight down with such an emotional burden. Nevertheless, just to be near him, to experience the joy of love, even though it was unrequited, was enough. If perchance before the world ended he might return that love, it would be a fulfillment that would make the coming darkness easier.

It was not to be that simple. Dwight accepted that he felt deep affection for Moira. Being close to her helped to blot out the black reality that lay ahead. Dwight was locked into memories of his past life—his happy marriage to his pretty dark-haired wife, his two kids, a boy aged nine and a daughter six. Dwight was aware, everyone was aware, that for the past two years no living creature had survived in North America. They were all dead.

This other side of Dwight could not, and did not, believe that to be the truth. With absolute certainty he maintained that he was going back to his home, a small town on the coast of Connecticut, carrying presents for them: an emerald necklace for his wife, a fishing rod for the boy and a pogo-pogo jumping stick for his small daughter. Moira even managed to discover one of the old fashioned jumping sticks and had it painted and embellished and gave it to him. Dwight was overjoyed.

Was there any point of Moira trying to tell him that such thoughts were madness? To Dwight the memories and his return to shore memories supported and strengthened him and gave him a purpose. Moira had no such illusions. She knew that even if Dwight made love to her, made her pregnant, there would never be enough months left to bear his child.

She thrust such thoughts away from her mind. She lived for the next moment, the next daybreak. Everyone in the small, shrinking community continued with their work-a-day lives as if tomorrow would come. What else was there to do?

Actress Donna Anderson played the part of Mary Holmes. She was married to the young Australian Navy Lieutenant Commander Peter Holmes, played by Anthony Perkins. Their first child, a baby daughter named Jennifer, has just been born. Mary refuses to believe that this mysterious fallout exists. How could it be, when she has just given birth to their beautiful little Jennifer? Jennifer has to be fed, bathed and loved. Doesn't everyone know that? She will grow up to be a lovely young woman–so there!

Peter Holmes breathes deeply and goes along with this deception, as Moira does with Dwight. What other course is there to follow?

"Yes, darling," agrees Peter. "I will go into town and get the new lawn mower I promised you. Yes, darling, Jennifer will have a Christmas tree when the time comes."

I've always thought that *On the Beach* was one of Miss G's most wonderful parts. She could tear the heart and start the tears. She was never maudlin, never out of character, she never faked. She loved…oh God, she loved. There is a picture of her, wind in her hair and blowing across her face and one strand of her hair caught in her mouth. Her eyes are soft and luminous and her heart breaking. The world is ending. Her part was crucial to the film. Her sexuality was crucial to the film. Her love affair with Dwight should turn into a real love affair, a last confirmation of the human spirit though the human sex act was crucial to the film.

Not everyone agreed with that conception. Stanley Kramer did. Miss G did, and I did, too. The two other most important men close to the film, however, thought that a physical affair would destroy the entire movie. Both Gregory Peck and author Nevil Shute thought that. The British novelist, fairly late in his life, had immigrated to Australia taking his family with him. He was now living in a house not far away from Melbourne. At first he would not even come near us. He had been sent the script and so violently disagreed with its conclusion and its new ending that it was some time before he agreed to talk to us at all.

Kramer's contrasting viewpoint was, "This is a serious picture. It is about the death of the world, and it could be totally downbeat. We have to give our audience romance, sex, and hope."

Peck said, "You are corrupting the story, and you are corrupting my character in the story. The self-denial on a matter of principle is romantic. It is honorable. The audience will respect Moira and Dwight for it. It is easy to have them jump in bed together. It is too easy. The denial of that is more touching. It goes deeper. Their characters are stronger for it."

Nevil Shute hated those last scenes for the same reasons. He thought it was a violation of his book. He didn't hate it on moral grounds. He believed it destroyed the validity of Peck's role as the Commander. It was the one thing the Commander could salvage in the midst of total disaster.

Peck said, "It didn't matter at all in the long run because there would be no more life on earth. The Commander grasped that one thing: he would die being faithful to the wife he loved so much."

Miss G and I couldn't go along with these high-minded, chauvinistic male thoughts, and neither could Stanley Kramer. The Commander's wife and family had been dead for two years. He had paid his proper dues, and his love for them continued. To carry romantic loyalty forever was ridiculous. They were dead, all in the grave, a grave which he himself would soon be entering.

He was now deeply and romantically involved with Moira, at times believing she is his wife. To Dwight, to accept the death of his family and to turn to Moira in her deep hours of need was natural and acceptable. Any other course would be an abdication of common sense.

Moira had taken Dwight's empty life to her heart and filled it again. She had taken him out to meet her mother and father at their farm. As Dwight's duties as the last US executive naval officer left alive dwindled, he enjoyed visiting them. The countryside, the hills and green rolling fields reminded him of his own boyhood and cheered him immensely. He began manual work with Moira's father on a dozen jobs that were necessary before the next Spring arrived, ignoring that for them the next Spring would never come.

The plow was drawn by oxen because there was no fuel left. The slowness of old country habits remained. Values and occupations remained: fishing in the quick running streams, swimming and sailing over a blue ocean, lying back with a pipe in one hand and a drink in the other, slightly worried at Moira's capacity for drinking too much. Their love for each other in all their meetings made him happy.

I think that the end of *On the Beach* was one of the most dramatic in film history. The radiation sickness was spreading to the last inhabited regions of Australia. Doctors and health authorities had already received consignments of poison pills which ensured a speedy death. Many people were using them.

Peter and Mary Holmes got the first symptoms—sickness, lassitude and diarrhea—and they knew they did not have long to live. They decided to die in their own beds with dignity and the knowledge that they will take baby Jennifer with them on their journey into death.

Peter heard that maybe in twenty to thirty years the radioactive fallout would have cleared from earth. The fields would still be green, the hedgerows bright with berries and probably fish would still flash silver in the streams. But no birds would sing, no cocks crow, no dogs bark and Mr. Smith would never return home on the 6:32 again.

Dwight also made up his mind what his course of action will be. As the end nears, he will embark with the last dozen or so of his crew who wish to go with him and sail out past the twelve mile limit. There in the deep Bass Straits he will scuttle his ship, he and his crew with it. Their fuel supply will have ended by then. It is in these last scenes that Guiseppe Rotunno's cinematography was so evocative.

Dwight and Moira became lovers. As a last gesture to each other–a farewell honeymoon–they decided to go out to a small village in a remote fishing area, a beautiful little place. What happened? A noisy group of dedicated fishermen had the same idea and chose the same location for their last reunion. Dwight and Moira were not angry, and they joined in.

It started raining, and Dwight built a fire outside their cabin. Around their own fire the fishermen started to sing that wonderful old Aussie folk tune, *Waltzing Matilda. "Waltzing Matilda, who'll come waltzing Matilda with me?"* It was a song that would never ring in the hills again. Moira and Dwight clung together and were silhouetted against the setting sun. The camera was moving in an entire circle around them. As their lips met, the sun sank into the sea.

Next morning they returned to Melbourne, and Dwight readied the *Sawfish* for its last voyage. Moira drove down to his dock to ask him if she could go out with them on that last journey. Dwight took her in his arms and told her no. He must obey naval codes to the very end.

Moira was determined that at least in spirit she would be with him until the end. She got back into her car and drove out at top speed along deserted roads and through lifeless villages to reach a headland high above the ocean. The long black shape of the submarine Sawfish nosed around the barrier of cliffs. Sitting in her car, Moira watched it change course and head south. Sadly, she waved her hand in a final salute.

"Dwight," she whispered softly. "If you are on your way already, wait for me."

She extracted the poison pill from her handbag and with a gulp of brandy swallowed it.

The scene cut then to a camera attached to the submarine's conning tower. As it started its final dive the sea swirled up and covered the camera lens.

The light in that twilight zone underwater could still be seen. Then, as the sub went deeper, it grew darker and finally reached the final blackness.

After viewing *On the Beach* in a cinema, I found the effect of that black screen chilling. For about ten seconds no diffused light turned up, and no one in the audience moved. We filed out in silence. I was grateful to breathe cool air and know that I was alive.

167

Checking in with Miss G while she enjoys a light moment and a smoke on one of what seemed like an endless number of movie sets in the fifties.

26 SHIPS THAT PASS IN THE NIGHT

After finishing *On the Beach*, we went back to the USA and began our usual migrations between the places we liked—Palm Springs, Lake Tahoe and New York. We gained and lost various friends and acquaintances during this period. In Australia Bappie had fallen in love with Arthur Cole, a nice props man working on the picture. They had married and returned to Hollywood to live in Bappie's house high in the Hollywood hills.

It was also during this time that David Hanna, whom we both liked enormously and who was a good friend as well as a first rate business manager, committed the worst sort of crime as far as Miss G was concerned: disloyalty. He had written and published a book about Miss G without her having the faintest idea of what he was doing.

I remember Miss G saying tartly, "There's David; my secretary; my friend. I trusted him. He worked for me for years. Okay, his book was probably the most correct factually of all of them, but what the hell! In Melbourne, I was paying him a thousand dollars a week. Stanley Kramer's production company was paying him the same salary. He had his own private secretary, and he comes out with a book about me – Jesus Christ!"

You can see what I mean about being disloyal to Miss G even about a Spanish omelet, let alone a book!

Another one to bite the dust was Walter Chiari, but he had been on the skids for some time now. He hadn't endeared himself to Miss G in Australia with part of his music hall act, which was a rather cruel and mocking take-off of Frank Sinatra.

There were worse crimes associated with Walter as far as Miss G was concerned. Some time earlier she said to me, "You know, Rene, why is Walter always showing off? He's always sliding down banisters, taking a run at a polished corridor, and sliding for twenty yards. He's always the life of the party. He can't keep doing that on whiskey. He hardly drinks at all! When I've mentioned my suspicions to his friends, they just look at me as if I'm crazy. 'That? Certainly not! Walter's an athlete. Walter's a great sportsman. Walter keeps himself fit.'"

"You mean drugs?" I said.

"I mean drugs," said Miss G.

One aspect of society that Miss G could not countenance was the drug scene. Her suspicions about Walter were eventually confirmed during one trip when we were crossing by train from New York to L.A. They were sharing a compartment with a bathroom. She saw traces of white powder on the edge of a cabinet.

"Rene," she admitted, "I saw these powder traces, and I knew something wasn't quite right. You know me, the best private eye in the movie business. I'd been suspicious for some time. I brushed it off into a Kleenex and when we reached L.A. I gave it to my doctor. He confirmed what it was. Walter is a cocaine addict!"

Things didn't end right there for them, but I was present at the final banishment of Walter from Miss G's life soon after. We were staying at an apartment in Rome a few months after Australia. Walter had rung up and was taking Miss G out to dinner. Miss G was dressing, and Walter had refused a drink. When I returned from Miss G's bedroom, there was Walter standing at the table shaking this white powder from an envelope into folded scraps of paper and sniffing it up his nose.

Such openness was unbelievable! I was shocked. I went into Miss G's bedroom and told her what I had seen. I couldn't understand Walter. It was so stupid! Miss G went out to talk to him. He was quite unapologetic and countered, "This is great! You must try some." For old time's sake, Miss G went out to dinner with him.

She never saw him again after that.

We particularly enjoyed New York because Frank Sinatra always let us use his suite at the Waldorf Astoria. The love affair between them was still in high gear, and there were daily phone calls. If they couldn't reach each other by phone there was an unending stream of loving cablegrams reinforcing their undying devotion to each other.

Don't get me wrong. I thoroughly approved of Frank, and particularly of his ability to handle Miss G, since I knew how difficult she could be. I often grieved that they couldn't get their act together instead of agonizing about it from three or four thousand miles apart.

It was while we were there in New York that Nunnally Johnson paid her a visit. He was an old friend of Miss G's, a sweet man with a dry sense of humor. Nunnally had been in the show and movie business since they first invented it, which meant long before Miss G and I were born.

I made the martinis, and Nunnally said, "Ava darling, as you now reside in Spain, isn't it about time you made a film there?"

Old friends or not, Miss G's look was suspicious. "Nunnally," she said, "I think you have something on your mind."

"You're right. A great Spanish part in a movie called *The Angel Wore Red.*"

"A what?"

Nunnally took a deep breath. "A cabaret girl." Miss G's roar of laughter could have been heard outside on Park Avenue.

"Nunnally, you old bugger, you mean a whore! Type casting me again, huh? You know I've never worked the streets." She thought about that for a second and added, "Yet."

Nunnally's face tried a smile. "Its location is Spain during its civil war. You are a cabaret girl who falls in love with a priest fleeing from the Fascists."

"Spain!" screeched Miss G. "A prostitute who falls in love with a priest!" Sex between a whore and a man of the cloth!" Her laughter could now have been heard in Grand Central Station.

"You've no hope," she said. "We tried to make *The Naked Maja,* the film about Goya, in Spain. That period was two hundred years ago, and the Spanish authorities threw us out. What chance have you got with a civil war that started the day before yesterday?"

Nunnally nodded his head and was not put out. "We have taken note of that. Other locations have been investigated." His eyebrows fashioned two question marks. "It could be moved to Rome."

"I like Rome," said Miss G. "Who's playing the priest?"

Nunnally's smile was sweet as Devon cream. "We've been talking to Frank Sinatra."

This time Miss G's laughter rattled the pictures on the wall. "Frank in a dog collar, singing Ave Maria! You've got to be kidding!"

Nunnally said, "MGM and I are only at the consultant stage. We think it unlikely that Frank would agree. We have Dirk Bogarde in mind also."

"For you, honey, I'll do it," said Miss G. "That is after I've seen the script and you've talked to Morgan Maree."

Morgan Maree had been Miss G's business manager for some time now, and she loved him dearly.

Miss G had been right. The Spanish authorities said, "Forget it." The Italian film makers were delighted, and Titanus Productions took over.

I was too busy to go with Miss G to Rome for *The Angel Wore Red,* but she kept me informed of what was going on.

Dirk Bogarde accepted the role of the defiant, passionate priest willing to risk his life for his faith. Miss G played the Spanish whore, Soledad, whose only relationship with the cabaret was that she could pick up clients at the bar. Miss G liked the part.

The priest, while fleeing through her village cold and hungry, his pursuers aiming to kill him, meets Soledad. She hides him. She does not understand what he's trying to do, but she recognizes a fellow human, who like herself, is defeated. As the days pass, she begins to realize that for the first time she has met a man who desires not her body, but her soul—a man who is gentle, decent, kind and caring.

In turn, the priest, thrown into close proximity with this blowsy, attractive and vibrant girl, is confused. She has saved his life, and he senses an intimacy that threatens both his piety and his celibacy. If Bogarde, Miss G, and Nunnally Johnson had been allowed to work out the film the way they understood it, it might have been a fine movie. But that wasn't to be.

Much later Dirk Bogarde put the whole thing into perspective in his book, *An Orderly Man*. He wrote that *The Angel Wore Red* was "a perfectly frightful film about a priest and a tart in Spain during the civil war. The film opened, apparently to ten Eskimos in North Alaska, closed the next day and sank without a trace."

He also wrote: "It was a magnificent part for Ava. It could have done for her what 'Two Women' did for Sophia Loren. She really put her heart into it. I think she was anxious to be more selective and make better pictures. She played it without makeup, without a bra, with holes torn in her dress. The word came from Hollywood. They put a corset on her and tidied her up. The life went out of Ava after that."

Miss G had a lot of experience with the box-office motives of MGM and the top Hollywood production companies and was not really dismayed. The film was a financial disaster rarely shown in either the US or Europe.

Sometime after that Miss G got fed up with living out in the country at La Bruja, and we moved into a posh apartment in Madrid at 8 Calle Del Arce. Ex-Argentine dictator Juan Peron lived in the apartment below us. Miss G's was two apartments converted into one, and she commissioned an interior decorator to turn it into something beautiful. He certainly did.

There were two floors. Downstairs was a large living room, a suite with an office, a bedroom and bath, which was my domain. The colors were soft orange, green, red, and brown. All warm colors. In the wide entrance hall was a grand piano. The living room and dining room were gorgeous with lovely paintings that came from God knows where. Drapery was light green with tassels and ropes. The dining table was immense, a pale green antique.

Upstairs the apartment reached all across the house, Miss G's bedroom, dressing room, bath and office. The mirrored bedroom cupboards filled all four walls, and off from that ran a huge bathroom. Everything was decorated in shades of green, off-white and beige. On the roof, we had our own patio where we could sunbathe and enjoy barbeques.

It was from this apartment that we commuted to the location of the only film she ever made in Spain while living there: 55 *Days at Peking*. Sam Bronston induced her to play in it. Sam was living in Spain at the time and famous for the epics he had produced there, especially *El Cid*. But what an astute guy like Sam was doing thinking he could make an epic out of *55 Days at Peking*, we will never know. Who wanted to know what the Boxer rebellion was about, and who cared?

In 1900 a dozen European powers plus Japan and America had been cynically exploiting China in dubious trade deals and financial chicaneries for over a century. Their bloated embassies crowded the walled city of Peking, and their contempt for all things Chinese was offensive. In the past there had been many rebellions against them.

Now the Boxers, an extremist group supported by hundreds of thousands of angry citizens, decided to rise again. They were encouraged by Empress Dowager of China who decreed that all foreigners should be slaughtered. Flora Robson gave a life-like impersonation of the blood-thirsty old bird. The ragtag soldiery attached to the embassies, led by the redoubtable Marine Major, played by Charlton Heston, defended the walled city resolutely.

In some mysterious manner Miss G became the Major's mistress, and it did occur to both Miss G and me that having got her name on the billing, they didn't know what the hell to do with her. Someone said, "For Christ's sake get some sex into the picture! Make her Charlton Heston's mistress." Heston gave her a glare occasionally, but plainly he thought he had more important duties to perform.

The characters were cardboard, the script ridiculous, and the sets second-hand, having been used in a previous Sam Bronston Roman epic that had been produced in Spain. The first director, Nicholas Ray, had a heart attack and had to be replaced. The superb cast members: Charlton Heston, David Niven, Flora Robson, Robert Helpman, John Ireland, Paul Lukas, Leo Genn and Elizabeth Sellars, all wandered around trying to work out how they had managed to get themselves stirred into such an epic stew.

"Fifty-five days!" shrieked Miss G. "It felt like fifty-five years!" She was particularly incensed by the 1500 Chinese extras flown in from the USA because they couldn't find a twentieth of that number in Spain.

Their main job was to riot. In one of their riots they had to charge through the Imperial Palace wrecking everything in their path. They were enthusiastic and didn't know the difference between Ava Gardner, Samuel Bronston or Adam and Eve for that matter. One of their fanatical rushes through the Imperial Palace, with Miss G enjoying one of her few acting opportunities, they found her directly in their path and steam-rolled over her.

Miss G was bruised and not amused. She was also not amused by her dialogue, such as, "Mad Americans inside, mad Boxers outside and mad Russians all over the place."

"As far as I'm concerned, that was what was really wrong with *Fifty-Five Days at Peking,*" she said.

Miss G was granted an early exit from this melodrama when they ran out of "mistress" things for her to do, and she was re-routed to get badly wounded while smuggling vital medical supplies to the beleaguered hospital.

Her description of the end of that ordeal was graphic: "Jesus, Rene," she complained. "I've spoken lots of crazy closing dialogue in my time, but nothing like this. There I was lying in the hospital. I'm full of bullets and apparently suffering from a very rare infection which was about to kill me, and there is the doctor waving a knife over me as if he's about to operate on a piece of sirloin. I think, what is he doing looking for my fatal infection with a knife? So I protest weakly, 'You won't find it with a knife doctor.' He shouts back, 'But you must live!' I don't like that idea, so I gently expire, whispering 'I have lived.' I really should have yelled, 'Let me out of here!'"

Miss G was very pleased to be relieved of acting duties before the relief forces arrived to rescue the Marine Major and the embassy staff from a terrible fate. I think the whole garrison felt the same way as Miss G. We returned to our apartment and hopefully kept Dictator Peron awake all night, stamping out our frustration in noisy flamenco.

173

We returned to Hollywood for Miss G's next movie, *Seven Days in May.* Miss G's part wasn't all that big, but she had an important role helping to unmask the Fascists hidden away in the US high command. We had a few chuckles about the fact that once again she was somebody's mistress.

This time she was the discarded mistress of her old friend Burt Lancaster. He played the leader of the conspirators, the sinister top US Air Force General planning to replace the President with someone from his Fascist allies. This was in order to prevent the President from signing an impending nuclear arms agreement with the Soviet President.

Kirk Douglas played the sharp-eyed senior officer who got wind of the plot. It was a fast- moving contemporary plot given credibility by the eyeball-to-eyeball confrontation between Lancaster and Douglas, with Miss G gently fluttering around to keep the confrontation at fever heat. Naturally, the President of the United States beat all the plotters.

We went back to Madrid after that and stamped even harder on Dictator Peron's ceiling. He complained to the police, and two officers arrived stern-faced at our front door. Miss G invited them in. They were both young and good-looking. Miss G was full of apologies. "So sorry, officers. We are just rehearsing for our next film. Would you care for a small cognac?"

The men recognized her, and when she chose to Miss G could spread charm like warm cream. They left smiling after two cognacs.

Peron had all the characteristics of Mussolini. From his balcony he liked rehearsing speeches he would never make anywhere else. We interrupted him with crowd noises. Two girls shouting can produce a very anti-dictator sound.

I guess you could say we didn't get on and were most objectionable. I guess the Dictator was pleased when Miss G decided to move to London several years later.

27 PUERTO VALLARTA AND MEXICO

The Night of the Iguana was without any doubt the happiest film that Miss G and I ever worked on, and arguably her best-ever movie role. I remember John Huston, with his usual air of baby innocence, said "It's an interesting experience. I have plunked these people down together and they have to live their parts for twenty four hours a day. It's not like getting up in the morning and driving to MGM studios." What John did not say was the difference between them was like the difference between catching a bus and landing on the moon.

John Huston had discovered Puerto Vallarta back in the early fifties, long before anybody else in the movie business did. In those days only one unpaved road connected it from the sea back into the hinterland—a road that was impassable in the rainy season. At that time Puerto Vallarta was a fishing village with a population of under two thousand with the usual collection of not-over-cared for shacks and houses, clustered around a church, and scattered along a beautiful sandy shoreline.

By the time Miss G and I arrived at Puerto Vallarta the predatory package tour trade had found it but hardly exploited it at all, and it was certainly not the boom resort it is today.

In his long career John Huston had often abandoned the static Hollywood studios, believing that, for all the brilliant designers and prop men and technicians, a dimension of reality was always an immense gain. John believed in finding a good story and shooting it against its own authentic background, no matter how far away that location might be or what dangers or discomforts it might entail. For one of his most memorable films he roped in Katharine Hepburn and Humphrey Bogart and transported them to the swamps of Africa for *The African Queen*. For *The Roots of Heaven*, he inveigled Juliette Greco into a similar African environment and left poor Juliette suffering from recurring bouts of malaria for years afterwards.

With movies John reckoned you took your chances and hopefully survived. At times I thought he was as nutty as a fruit cake, but he did have one overriding and excellent idea. He thought that he, in particular, and everyone attached to the production should actually enjoy making a movie. Other Hollywood moguls, producers, directors and distributors went gray or bald, had nervous break downs or heart attacks, and lay awake nights working out costs, percentages, and box office returns. John, like Arthur Hitchcock, simply said it was only a movie.

Even so, John Huston's sense of humor bordered on the macabre. Two or three days before shooting was scheduled to start, we were all asked to attend a small ceremony out at the filming location in Mismaloya, where John would make a brief announcement.

Present on this occasion were Richard Burton, Elizabeth Taylor, Deborah Kerr, Sue Lyon, Miss G and Ray Stark. They sat in chairs around a large conference table. They should have known from the grins on the faces of various technicians nearby that John was up to his tricks.

John arrived, carrying six neat little wooden boxes. Silently and gravely he handed one to each of his stars, plus Ray Stark, the movie's producer. With giggles of anticipation the ladies opened their gifts while Richard and Ray were more wary.

In each box, snug in its velvet lining, lay a small gold-plated derringer revolver. Set beside it in separate slots were five gold-plated bullets. The singular difference between these and other bullets was not only that they were gold-plated, but each of them was inscribed with a single name–the name of a co-star, Liz Taylor, or Ray Stark (no recipient had a bullet with his or her own name). The implications were obvious. If you fell out with any of your fellow artists, you could load up with the bullet bearing his or her name and carry out a ritual execution. John Huston smiled down at everyone, then, without saying a word, turned and left.

There was nothing fake about the revolvers or bullets, except that the powder was removed. A short puzzled silence occurred, and Miss G broke the strained atmosphere with a terse comment, "Why wasn't there a bullet with John Huston's name on it, too? We could have all opened fire on him at the same time."

The gimmick achieved lasting world publicity. Ray Stark, even with his own name inscribed as one of the possible targets, wandered around cooing with pleasure. Ray, medium-sized with blonde hair and blue eyes and a serene attitude that cloaked a shrewd determination, could not believe their luck. Ten million dollars' worth of free publicity even before we have shot a frame of film! Ten million! No doubt John had thought about that too.

The joke did not occupy our attention for long. The physical difficulties of getting to and from our Mismaloya location were far more pressing. It was too far removed from what civilization Puerto Vallarta could offer, so I don't think that John H. ever had any great hopes of getting his major stars to settle down there, idyllic as it was. He had rented various houses in Puerto Vallarta for that purpose. Elizabeth took over a huge red brick, three or four story house a block from the beach with the name of Casa Kimberley. Gossip among the cameramen suggested it was a site well-suited to Richard because that was the name of a local gin. We always considered Richard Burton our expert in matters of booze.

Richard announced that his British version of the boilermaker—two large shots of tequila, one shot of triple-sec, and one shot of fresh lime juice, stirred and poured over finely crushed ice—was a well known remedy for many ailments in those sometimes chilly islands and a life-reviving potion.

Miss G had flown in her Spanish helper and maid, so our household consisted of Juanita, Miss G and me. Deborah and her husband Peter Viertel were near neighbors. Deborah admitted that for the whole of the two months of our stay she dreaded the journeys to Mismayola, except, as she put it in her civilized English manner, "Coming back by sea after a long day's work did provide you a pleasant breath of fresh air."

Miss G, who very often water-skied the whole way and then dove in and swam ashore, adored the whole episode.

"Right, everyone," cried the assistant director that first morning, waving his sheaf of notes in the air. "Each day you'll all be picked up from your houses by jeep transport and taken to the beach of Los Muertos below Puerto Vallarta. That means 'beach of the dead,' but don't worry, boats will be allocated to take you to Mismaloya, and no one will drown."

"We hope" was my thought about that remark because it seemed that death by drowning was a far greater hazard than a gold-plated bullet in the back. Mismaloya lay ten miles west of Puerto Vallarta past a high mountainous coastline indented with pretty beaches. Land transport along that coast had not improved one bit since John Huston's first arrival in the early fifties, and only donkey trails connected Puerto Vallarta to Mismaloya. Although the pleasing sight of those nimble-footed little creatures with their big furry ears and dewy eyes picking their way over rocks and through mud, heavily laden with sacks of supplies, has remained with me to this day, so have the memories of those daily journeys by sea.

There was no harbor at Puerto Vallarta or at Mismaloya, only sandy beaches. Everything had to be transported by boat. Previously Ray Stark and his hard-working crews had done a fantastic job ferrying tons of movie equipment and all the necessities of film life to Mismaloya.

During his early research for *The Night of the Iguana*, John H. had contacted a young Mexican architect enthused by the real estate potential of this beautiful coastline. He was endowed with the foresight that within a few years Puerto Vallarta would emerge as one of Mexico's most popular resorts and that the influx of tourists would turn the sand of Mexico's beaches into pure gold.

The architect agreed to build John's entire film complex, including the main set at Mismayola—the Hotel Costa Verde—with the understanding that it would serve a dual purpose. John H. had imagined a native type location; wattle-walled thatched cottages and minimal furniture. The architect's conception had been that of a country club and apartment-type complex. He went ahead with this idea, raising capital from investors and building apartments with red-tiled roofs, balconies, and large assembly rooms.

Getting wind of the idea, Ray Stark, Seven Arts, and MGM began to look at the costs with diminished enthusiasm, but an agreement was reached. Even though the complex was still unfinished when we arrived, they had built enough for our purposes, and we found the apartments with running water and outdoor verandas or balconies with wide views over the cliffs and ocean much nicer than the trailers normally used as dressing rooms.

Los Muertos Beach was a stretch of golden sand. Behind it facing out to sea was a row of unpretentious bars and restaurants where you could sit under the palms and enjoy a margarita. Nearby was what one might call the only modern hotel in Puerto Vallarta–La Tropicana. Two hundred yards offshore were assembled a small armada that would take us to and from Mismaloya; a variety of small craft, launches, a speedboat, and a trawler. The question was how did you get aboard them? The answer was seamanlike rough-and-ready. You were paddled out by rowboat or dug-out canoe and hoisted or hauled aboard. This required very unladylike maneuvers.

The big trawler carried most of the commuting personnel, but we big shots got what you might call private vessels. Elizabeth and Richard inherited the posh boat named *Taffy*, and, to Miss G's delight, we were assigned the speedboat crewed by a pair of local boys. Our speedboat ran flat out, and nobody loved flat out more than those boat boys. They could reach Mismaloya in fifteen minutes, even when towing Miss G as Neptune's daughter behind us.

The same difficulties of getting ashore or back aboard existed at Mismaloya, only the difficulties were even more pronounced. A rough stone jetty had been constructed under the cliff, but on occasions with a big Pacific swell, small boats, unless handled with considerable skill, could capsize and toss both crew and passengers into the ocean. Ava solved that problem by usually diving overboard and swimming ashore. "Strong as an ox that girl," said Deborah admiringly.

Mismaloya itself was a small cluster of thatched huts sitting at the western end of this beautiful half-moon of golden sand at the side of a silver stream that cut its own path through the sand and into the sea. About fifty Mexican-Indians lived there—friendly, smiling people delighted by everything that went on. Behind, rising steeply from the beach, was a hill with the Hotel Costa Verde perched on top, and from there on everything rose steeply upwards to the vast mountain ranges often hidden in the clouds.

The set designers had done a great job with the Hotel Costa Verde. With wide patios, irregular stone steps, and a heavy tiled roof, it blended into the green vegetation, bougainvillea and swaying palm trees. Tethered in the shade was the large iguana which appeared in the picture. It looked as fierce as a small dragon, but it was really a well-fed and contented creature, totally happy and unaware of its starring role.

Our bar at Mismaloya, one hundred and thirty seven steps up from the beach, should have been preserved for posterity. Only John Huston could have masterminded it. Of course, he knew that besides himself he had many brave boozers to contend with: Richard, Miss G, and Liz occasionally. Even Deborah admitted that in the sultry heat, a glass of cold Mexican beer was very palatable. There were many other members of the cast, plus the cameramen and technicians, not to mention the ever-changing hordes of media men and women who knew a good bar when they saw one. This was an exceptional bar because all the drinks were free. Deborah observed Richard's drinking and, even for Richard, he was at it a bit hard. She said the only other film star she had worked with who could match him was Bob Mitchum.

Miss G always swore that you had to pass through the bar to reach the set. My observation told me that after climbing all those steps, Miss G went through the bar to have a quick one for revival purposes before reaching the set. Many people felt that way.

Besides the bar, there was a dining hall with kitchen equipped to feed one hundred and fifty people at a single sitting, as well as a big hall for dances or parties, plus the usual cutting and editing rooms.

In a nutshell, Mismaloya was a paradise of serenity and peace, a vast contrast to life back in Puerto Vallarta. Activity filled the air for practically twenty-four hours out of every day. There was animal noise—honking donkeys, squealing pigs, clucking chickens, barking dogs. Human noise—old wooden carts groaning, heavy lorries grinding, motor scooters with unfurled mufflers, radio sets and disc players turned up to hysteria pitch. Endless celebrations with fireworks and fire-crackers caused you to think another revolution must have broken out. And, of course, at the rhythmic heart of any Mexican gathering there were the strident trumpets of the benevolent mariachi troubadours. When rushes (that's footage of scenes from the previous day) were shown in the small Puerto Vallarta cinema to invited audiences, I'm inclined to think the entire population of the town saw some parts of the film, according to the cheers and roars of laughter aroused at the sight of local characters used in crowd scenes.

Only one sound really got to me—the confounded cockerels. Instead of crowing like well-bred roosters heralding the break of day, these lunatic fowl worked on some abysmal cycle of their own and screeched whenever they felt like it.

There were compensations. Night came, and it got cooler, the air balmier, the cicadas shrill, but romantically authentic with the sky clear and star-filled. You got used to the noise in the daytime, almost learned to love it, but the nights were beautiful. It was such a change from one's normal mode of life as to be almost unbelievable.

The history of events that got us to this terrain was quite interesting. Miss G's first encounter with John Huston could not be called propitious. In fact, it was calamitous. The two of them met in the early forties, between Miss G's divorce from Mickey Rooney and her marriage to Artie Shaw. A young married couple, friends of Miss G's, included her in an invitation to have dinner with John over the mountains at his ranch in the San Fernando Valley. They commiserated that poor John was so lonely out there all by himself. John H. was a great host. Solid drinks were served before dinner, during dinner and after dinner. Everybody got sloshed. So much so that in the laughing small hours, it was decided for everyone's safety they would spend the night there and drive back to Los Angeles the next morning.

In her allotted bedroom, Miss G had just removed her shoes prior to undressing when, surprise, surprise, the door opened and John slid through. From the smirk on that long priestly face, it was clear that he had not entered to say prayers. Clearly he expected female consolation to cure his lonely blues.

Miss G decided she was not part of that scenario. With a quick sidestep, Miss G was out through the door and running. On bare feet she was one hell of a good runner. John H. was no slouch, and he pounded after her. Seeing them in the moonlight after two hectic and evasive circuits through the trees and shrubs must have seemed a strange phantasmagoria. Miss G was not amused. Only one avenue of escape was left. Fully clothed, she dove into the swimming pool. John skidded to a halt on the brink, regained his balance, roared with laughter and went off to fix himself another drink.

Miss G, dripping and furious, grabbed a towel, banged on the doors and hauled her friends out of bed, screaming, "Back to Hollywood, now!" Miss G in full torrent of rage was splendid. Dawn was breaking as they crossed the mountains with the young couple still murmuring explanations about poor John being so lonely.

"Poor John," Miss G shrieked between yells of laughter at the recollection. Three days later John up and married Evelyn Keyes.

Odd thing though, you'd never have guessed in the years that followed that not only would John become one of the most important influences in Miss G's life but one of her greatest friends. However, at the time, she could have killed the old goat.

In his autobiography John admits, "I had met Ava when Tony Veiller and I were working on the script of Hemingway's *The Killers*. As I watched her on the set I was intrigued. I sensed a basic fundamental thing about her, an earthiness bordering on the roughneck, even though she was at pains to conceal it. Sometime later, I met her again and tried to make a conquest. I was completely unsuccessful. No midnight swims, no weekends, no Huston."

It was sixteen years before they met again. We were living in Madrid. The phone rang, I picked it up, and a voice with the lilt of the Irish—after all, John H. had been master of the hunt in Galway and changed his passport from American to Irish citizen during that period—said,

"This is John Huston. Could I have a word perhaps with Ava Gardner?"

I turned to Miss G and said, "John Huston."

She said, "God Almighty!" We were not doing much at the time, and I think she had adored John from the moment she met him. She had forgiven his first mistake of assuming that pretty divorced ladies were legitimate prey, of not knowing that southern ladies needed to be courted. Miss G picked up the phone and said "Hello, Mr. Huston."

With his usual adroitness John made no mention of their first meeting. "Ava darling", he said in a voice that could charm the birds off the trees and the fish out of the stream, "I'm a stranger in these parts, but I've got my producer friend Ray Stark here with me, and we've got hold of a Tennessee Williams play with a part that might interest you. We wondered if you might like to join us for dinner and a few drinks, and perhaps we could knock the town about a bit. We're staying at the Hilton." She agreed.

Suspicions disappeared. Miss G was always a pushover for a few drinks and a night on anybody's town. Besides, since that first encounter John had made some very fine films with some great actors.

During that week-long entrapment in Madrid John H. courted Miss G with dinners, wine and flamenco shows at Miss G's favorite night spots. John, pleading old age, left the party around midnight, giving the usual advice for the two youngsters to go on enjoying themselves. Miss G had every intention of doing that, and Ray Stark did his best to entertain her until dawn broke.

John H came out of it looking fresh as a daisy, having Miss G under contract for eight weeks' work in Mexico for a fee of four hundred thousand dollars. Poor Ray, after endless hangovers and little or no sleep, was ashen and hollow-eyed but still tried to look as if it had all been worthwhile. Miss G, as usual, never went to bed much before dawn and then slept from dawn until about three in the afternoon, so she looked radiant. The long journey into *The Night of the Iguana* had begun.

The essential plot of the movie was summed up by someone in a special edition of *Life* magazine in on December 20, 1963: "Sue Lyon as the teenager lusts after him; Deborah Kerr as a tender artist saves him; and Ava, as the triumphant slattern, gets him." The him being poor persecuted Richard Burton, playing the part of an Episcopalian priest dismissed from his post for drunkenness and sexual involvement with teenage girls. One could testify that Richard had been training for this part all his life.

Abandoned, haunted by his sins, brought close to madness by his religious mania and reduced to near beachcomber status, The Reverend Shannon has finally landed a job as tourist guide to a busload of spinster-eyed schoolmarms from Blowing Rock, Texas—a group of ladies from the Bible Belt with vigilante consciences. If Shannon does succumb to the temptations of strong drink or virgin girls he will certainly be reported, lose his job and sink forever into despair and obscurity. Can he be saved? With pretty, nubile, teenaged Sue Lyon, a passenger who singles out Shannon as her potential seducer, it seems unlikely.

Sue is also chaperoned by her mother's friend, the hatchet-faced, lesbian-inclined Grayson Hall, who is watching Shannon like a suspicious wife and waiting to pounce. Desperate for breathing space, Shannon instructs the bus driver to make for Puerto Vallarta. Nearby on the coast is a rather run-down hotel owned by an old girlfriend, Maxine Faulk (Miss G).

Also staying there is Hannah Jelkes (Deborah Kerr), a romantic, wandering artist, doing good for the whole world and caring for her ninety-seven year old grandfather, a poet (Cyril Devanti, who in real life was actually getting on towards that age). He and Hannah have been offered temporary accommodations by the indulgent Maxine to give them the chance of selling some of Hannah's sketches to local tourists. Hannah spots Shannon and decides he needs her help to save his soul.

As the bus pulls up on the road under the terrace of the Hotel Costa Verde, Maxine is standing there, looking down. Attired in a loose, low-cut Mexican dress, she is strong, sexy, blowsy and alluring, the essential Miss G, in fact. As the bus passengers disembark, she spots Shannon and screams delightedly, "Shannon! Hah! My spies told me that you were back under the border…that you went through last week with a busload of women—a whole busload of females, all females, Hah!"

You know instinctively that in the past there must have been other rewarding encounters between the two. You also know that, while Shannon may have found temporary sanctuary, he is now the only human with male credentials available in a den of predatory lionesses.

28 THE CHACALA BUS AND TENNESSEE WILLIAMS

The Chacala Indians who live in small palape roofed villages along the coastline west of Puerto Vallarta can not believe what they were seeing. A bus— a real, huge, single-decker bus with driver and passengers—was driving across the waves about half a mile offshore.

They shouted to their wives. The children screamed with excitement. They crossed themselves. It was fortunate that in their religion miracles were believable phenomena.

"That bloody bus," said Clarence Eurist, Unit Manager of *The Night of the Iguana*, "drove me to the point of insanity." Clarence was a reasonable, quiet, philosophical man who rarely expressed any deep feelings. We were sitting outside the Mismaloya bar on top of our hill experiencing the warm sunshine, the blue sky, and the sea below beyond a slope of palm trees, a shimmering surface stretching to a distant horizon. Miss G had finished her stint before the cameras for the day. I don't remember which page in the script we had reached, but it had all gone smoothly. We were sipping margaritas, and Clarence just happened to be passing by and stopped for a chat. The subject of the bus surfaced. Miss G stirred the crushed ice left at the bottom of her margarita glass with a delicate forefinger.

"I thought you and John got along in complete harmony," she responded.

"Oh, we do," confirmed Clarence, "and we're of long standing, but sometimes I feel that John's search for perfect authenticity touches perfect lunacy."

I had almost finished my margarita. I said, "But what's perfection got to do with a bus?"

"You've seen the bus?" questioned Clarence forlornly, as Miss G held aloft a long, lovely sunburned arm at the brown-faced Mexican face peering from the doorway. The face grinned and disappeared.

Miss G said, "Everybody's seen the bus. Old, dirty, battered, and what the hell it's got 'Blake's Tours' painted on its side for, I'll never know." Clarence released another of his long reflective sighs. "Authenticity," he said.

We both knew all about the broiling heat inside the bus when the first interior shots were filmed in a Puerto Vallarta back street. "Christ!" Richard said, "All the schoolmarms and I nearly died of heat exhaustion."

Clarence nodded this time with some exasperation. "You know we could have bought a similar bus in Los Angeles, sawed it in half, shipped it down here, welded it together again, and got a vehicle at half the cost and half the number of perspiring man-hours that damn bus gave us." The waiter arrived with three fresh margaritas, which cheered me up considerably. Clarence didn't look any happier.

"I don't quite follow this conversation," said Miss G. "What about a bus?"

"It couldn't be just a bus. It had to be a Mexican bus. It had to look, feel, smell and behave like a real Mexican bus. It had to be a Mexican bus that had struggled over Mexican roads, bounced in Mexican potholes, been marooned in Mexican streams, and towed out of Mexican mud."

The sun was beginning to tilt down towards the sea. Early cicadas were turning up for the evening concert. The second margarita was making all of us feel happier now. As Miss G's interest in the bus seemed to be evaporating and I felt that poor Clarence needed a little backing in his story, I said, "So what did you do?"

"John and I traveled the length and breadth of Mexico for what seemed like three years, but was actually three weeks, looking for John's perfect old bus. We examined big buses, fat buses, thin buses, two-tier buses, and then, at last we arrived in Tepozotlan."

Miss G regained a little interest and asked if he could spell that. "No," said Clarence. Tepozotlan is a small, hot, neglected little town somewhere in Mexico. There was John's outrageous little vehicle just moving away from a stop where it had been unloading passengers. "That's it," cried John, starting to chase it, but I held him back by the sleeve, pointing out that an exact replica bus was just pulling into view. There were, in fact, five of them in service. Five dusty, battered little buses with worn upholstery and torn seats toiling through Tepozotlan at elderly speeds and bringing relief to Mexican feet."

"You managed to buy one?" I asked.

"The manager of the bus company was very suspicious of our motives. He was a sweet little man with a big black moustache hiding his worried face. What did these two funny-looking Americanos want trying to deprive him of one fifth of the town's transport?"

"We want to buy her or hire her," said John.

"I am regretful, but no," replied the manager. "She is a link—very vital—in our passenger service. We could lose one fifth of our fares."

"If you estimate the amount of fares you would lose, and add the cost of gas, oil, tires, and servicing you would need, we will double that amount and pay you a fee on top of that. After roughly two months we will return her as good as new."

The manager looked even more worried and said, "Well, I shall have to consider...."

"Besides," John went on, "We shall be using your bus in a film that will be seen all over the world. When she comes back, she will be the most famous bus in all of Mexico. You could even raise our fares to travel in her." Miss G figured that cinched the deal.

Clarence paused to allow more gloomy reflections to register on his face. "So there we were in romantic old Tepotzotlan, a million miles from anywhere, with John now back on other work, leaving me to figure out how to transport a battered old bus that could scarcely cough its way down the main street, let alone cross the mountain ranges and rivers and terrible roads before we reached Puerto Vallarta."

"You made it," I said, trying to resurrect a spirit of victory.

"Sure, with pushers and pullers and tractors and sweat and blood, sweat and tears. So we shot the scenes we needed in Puerto Vallarta town as per script. Then we built a huge pontoon and anchored it offshore, and then we pushed out movable wooden tracks and manhandled her aboard. Then we took the launch and tied a rope to the pontoon, gave everybody who wanted one a bus ride over the sea, headed for Mismaloya and unloaded her the same way. The local Indians didn't know if they were mad or we were mad."

Miss G said, "If you'd hit a storm you'd have been bus-wrecked."

"Sometimes, Ava, I wish we had been. Then we wouldn't have to return the bloody thing back to Tepozotlan."

Miss G smiled. "Then John would have fished her up by submarine and got her back somehow. He'd given his word."

"That was what I was afraid of," said Clarence gloomily.

As production on *The Night of the Iguana* churned along, to everybody's surprise—and I know it had nothing to do with the threat of those gold-plated bullets—e veryone in our confined tropical community got on very well. Despite the heat and humidity, the tropical storms, the mosquitoes, the creepy-crawlies, the night-flying insects that bashed into naked electric light bulbs with the fury of Kamikaze suicide pilots, the lavatories that wouldn't work, the fact that there was only one telephone linking us to the outside world—the one in the Puerto Vallarta post office which opened and closed at mysterious times, and the line was awful—we all got used to such minor irritations.

There were a few minor puzzlements relating to the film script, though, such as Huston's insistence on having all hands on deck whether they were filming or not. Miss G said to Deborah, "Honey, do you know what the old bugger intends to do?"

Deborah smiled sweetly and said, "Ava, darling. I think you are referring to the fact that we shall be shooting the film in chronological order, like a stage play. Not a bad idea. You know where you are."

"I don't start until page forty. When do you start?"

"Not until page eight," replied Deborah, and both girls spurted with laughter.

"God Almighty," cried Ava, "and the whole script is only 140 pages long. Shall we ask the old darling if we can go off to New York for the first month and go shopping?"

They did not make that request. The "old darling" was having none of that sort of hanky-panky. Everyone stayed put.

"Gives you all a chance to soak up the atmosphere of the place, to understand your characters, gives you something to build on," said Mr. Huston firmly.

No doubt at all that John H. was the man in charge. He stalked around the set of the Hotel Costa Verde in a dark Mexican shirt, loose, large-pocketed safari-jacket and white slacks. He was tall, thin, stooped, with a creased brown face, prominent off-white teeth, a shock of gray hair, and a cigarette never far from tobacco-stained fingers. He never raised his voice, never lost his temper, but cosseted, cajoled, soothed and sympathized and got it done his way.

A new threat then arrived—playwright Tennessee Williams—who was determined to change Huston's way, and unfortunately it seemed his main target was Miss G. Tennessee had been enticed down from New York by John Huston, for John would never think of making changes in the work of such a creative artist as Tennessee Williams without consultation. Well, not often he wouldn't.

Williams arrived, sporting a clipped piratical black beard, carrying his portable typewriter. At his heels danced his cute, small, black poodle named "Gigi," whose entire experience of life so far had consisted of New York pavements, and she decided this Mexican life was paradise. She even got around to paying a courtesy call on the iguana. Tennessee's boyfriend, Freddy, also arrived, but he wasn't half as much at home.

From the moment we first met Tennessee, Miss G and I decided that not only was he a playwright genius, but also a really nice guy, even though most of the time he was quite certain he was right. At his first press conference with scores of happy journalists transcribing every word he spoke for posterity and continuing to do so during the rest of the time we were in Puerto Vallarta, both John and Tennessee were available and spoke their minds at the drop of a hat. I'm not sure about Tennessee, but John knew all about the value of publicity, especially if there's a bit of conflict in it.

Tennessee said, "I did not offer to do the screenplay of *Iguana* for a number of reasons. I did the screenplays for *The Glass Menagerie*, *A Streetcar Named Desire*, *The Rose Tattoo*, and *Baby Doll*, but now I am fifty-two years old, and turning plays into screenplays is not all that creative, and I can't squander any more years."

He smiled indulgently and went on saying that he would sooner let someone else handle the screenplay of *The Night of the Iguana*, particularly if it was someone he respected. He respected John Huston and Anthony Veiller very much. He then added a flavor of lemon juice caution to his praise. He said, "However, I do care what happens to my plays on the screen. That's why I am here now. I care very much."

Tennessee did not waste a moment fraternizing with the lay-abouts in Puerto Vallarta, or even spend much time with our small group of *Iguana* actors and actresses. He occupied a small apartment in the newly constructed complex at Mismaloya, and his typewriter could be heard tapping like a woodpecker at 6:30 every morning. Not that Tennessee was stand-offish. He served his time in the bar and treated it as a general recreation center. He talked to everybody. He believed in his play and knew there were strong differences between himself and John about various screenplay changes.

John H's contention was that Tennessee had conceived the character of Maxine—the blowsy, over-the-hill, but grateful for scraps, fifty-year-old lady as played by Bette Davis in the Broadway production—as an act of love. Towards the end of the play he had rebelled against his own creation and tried to shade her into something she was not—a sort of she-devil, a devourer of men who would in the end toss out Shannon as soon as he bored her. Tennessee thought John had changed Maxine from the word go. That was the essence of the disagreement. Our wonderful Pacific setting provided a spectacular backdrop for their arguments.

In those mountainous regions of western Mexico with cliffs as a rocky barrier against the immense high-roller drive of the Pacific Ocean, tropical storms were commonplace. They arrived with tropical suddenness. On this occasion the sun was setting. There was no breeze, but abruptly the palm fronds began to rustle, to shiver and make soft sounds almost as if they were human. Dark clouds began to scurry in from the mountain tops. It got much darker. Flashes of lightning cut vivid zigzags across a sky now purple-black. Then bang, bang, bang—thunder crashed round our ears in a quite terrifying bombardment. You felt that the lightning bolts were aimed directly at you. The driving wind caught the palms, and torrential rain came cascading down. Coconuts thudded to earth. Doors slammed shut like rifle shots. Window shutters banged backwards and forwards as if they'd taken on a life of their own. Canvas coverings were ripped off or blown sky high. Hired help, technicians, every able-bodied citizen rushed around, soaked to the skin but exhilarated, trying to tie everything down or prop everything shut. For a few brief minutes a cannonade of thunderous rain closed out the world.

The generators went out and with them the lights. The generators lived private lives of their own, often deciding to quit functioning for twelve or twenty-four hours at a time. The lack of electric illumination made the bar much more cozy, a refuge against nature and its storms. Candles were lit and oil lamps brought in. At the bar demands for more beer, more margaritas, more everything increased and were met. The bar was always crowded, more so if bad weather or a storm like this prevented the usual boat exodus back to Puerto Vallarta. At the moment it was full of actors, stars, character players, walk-ons, technicians, prop men, secretaries, script girls, newsmen, and associated free loaders, all noisy and happy. The thunder soon trailed away, its anger diminishing, but the continuing flashes of distant lightning still dug into faraway valleys to show it where to hit next.

That evening, John H. and Tennessee Williams were sitting at one table with Gabriel Figueroa, our brilliant Mexican cameraman. Listening in were two or three others, including me. Miss G, who was fiddling around in her apartment dressing room, had sent me ahead to get our favorite barman to prepare her usual, authentic, Richard Burton boilermaker. John H. never cared who overheard his conversation. In fact, I think he positively liked it. It publicized his points of view. John knew I was listening in, using me as a sort of unofficial communication channel to Miss G.

Tennessee said, "John, I admit that the film script is better constructed than the play ever was, but there are some things in it that I don't like at all."

He paused, and John blew a stream of smoke out of one side of his mouth, the eyes in the lean face never moving, the right arm, hand curled around his drink, resting on the table. Occasionally he swapped cigarette and drink by carefully balancing drink on the edge of the table, taking swigs, and then reversing the process. He listened. John H. was a good listener.

"John," said Tennessee, "you know I was never thrilled when Ava was cast in the first place. I know she's great for the box office. I know that, but I've always said she's too beautiful to play Maxine. Maxine's brazen, blowsy, a slovenly tart that uses sex and booze as life support systems, the way Bette Davis played it on Broadway. She has to play a beaten-up old dame thankful for anything she can get."

I could have butted in there to tell Tennessee that Miss G was polishing up her performance as only a really committed actress could. Miss G never could stand or wish to understand method acting. Hers was a purely natural performance. I decided the time was not right, and it was not my place.

Tennessee had already heard about our other freshening up activity. "I understand that Ava's just spent a lot of time at these beauty spas. I've already met Ava. She is great. I love her." A touch of exasperation had entered his voice as he went on, "but if she comes out of this film looking beautiful, the whole point of her part will be lost."

I could have intervened with another valid point here, but I didn't. Before we started any film Miss G, aided by my gentle persuasion that if she didn't get up I was going to start singing, went into strict training. No booze, no sex, no cigarettes, no late nights; only health and strength. She was to be a clean-living, home-loving girl. She arrived at the studio or on location nervous as a kitten, but as fit as an Olympic athlete, and ten times more beautiful. Of course, what ninety-nine percent of movie directors wanted from her all through her movie life was a beautiful, sexy, sinful lady. Miss G may have been great as Lady Macbeth or Florence Nightingale or Eleanor Roosevelt, but no one wanted her to play those roles.

Now Tennessee Williams wanted her to play dowdy. Sure she could do it, but it would be a special sort of dowdy—Ava Gardner dowdy. Tennessee had other objections as he went on without any conviction. "I believe she can do it, but it will be a battle getting it out of her. I want her to work with a real southern accent. She's picked up a phony accent in Hollywood. That's no good."

I've got to say, I've always admired Mr. Huston's self-control. He was just as famous as Tennessee and far more worldly in a director's province. Most directors would have hit Tennessee over the head with a baseball bat. John did not take the slightest umbrage. He knew Tennessee understood the complexities of both their crafts but that power lay in the hands of the director to blur or obliterate the original conception. And contractually John retained that power. Tennessee also knew John was fair. If Tennessee made his point convincingly, and if it made sense, John would accept it.

John exchanged the position of drink and cigarette for the fifth time which meant that his glass was empty. He made his recognizable wave of fingers towards the bar, and a waiter hurried over to refresh everybody's drinks.

"Tennessee," he said slowly, "Ava Gardner is a Tar Heel from North Carolina. As you know, that means someone who sticks to his position in the battle line. They put shoes on her and took her to Hollywood, but basically she hasn't changed a bit. She's still a Tar Heel at heart. She's very happy picking up her North Carolina accent again. She is much happier than she was with that MGM crap. I cast Ava because I know her, not because of any performance she has given. I can tell you, Tennessee, Ava can belt it out, as well as belt it down, given the chance. You'll see. You'll see a very fine actress at work." Tennessee looked slightly distressed.

"John, you have poured syrup over her. She's got to be unsweetened and brought back to earth. She must reflect the world, and the world is hard. To be successful, the play must remain a tragedy, a tragedy. Make Ava sweet and loving, hang on a happy ending, and you will destroy the whole thing."

29 THE DELIGHTS OF MISMALOYA

One morning about midway through filming Miss G began the day shrieking blue murder, "Lies, lies! Rene, have you seen these headlines?" She brandished a Mexican newspaper, "Lies, rubbish!"

Oh God, I thought. The story's broken. Our scandal is revealed. The Mexicans are insulted. My Spanish was terrible, but by the size of those black headlines, I could guess they said something awful, like "Famous Actress Ava Gardner Shares Love Nest with Two Beach Bums" or perhaps "Shameless Behavior by Hollywood Film Star."

"They are saying," yelled Miss G, "that Emilio Fernandez and I are engaged to be married!"

Relief overwhelmed me, and I said, "Is that all?"

"Is that all?" shrieked Miss G, "I hardly know the bum."

She was right. We scarcely knew Senor Emilio, although we had heard about some of his exploits, especially about the first time he met Elizabeth Taylor. The love affair between Elizabeth and Richard Burton had ignited when they first worked together in the movie *Cleopatra* and had achieved headlines in every part of the world. The news that a plane carrying the lovers was about to arrive at Mexico City's airport caused huge crowds to assemble there. First into the aircraft as the steps were placed into position, shrugging off all attempts at interference, raced this huge, black-mustached Mexican in Poncho Villa sombrero with silver-cased revolvers dangling from either holster. He glared along the aisle until he spotted Elizabeth sitting next to Richard. He then rushed towards her, seized her by the arm and tried to tug her from her seat to go with him.

There was complete pandemonium! Was this a revolution or an attempted kidnapping? Not bothering to consider either possibility, Richard tried to thump him and missed. Elizabeth screamed, and passengers froze in their seats. Officials arrived, and peace was restored.

Apparently Emilio was an associate director on *The Night of the Iguana* who had been appointed by John Huston to escort Liz Taylor safely through the crowds. Emilio, as usual, had adopted a direct approach. Richard threatened to

190

kill him if he ever approached Liz again. Liz smiled and said she understood the mistake. John admitted that, indeed, Emilio was an old friend of his. He had hired him to satisfy the Mexican law which specified that a certain number of nationals must be employed on any film made in Mexico.

"Emilio's weakness," said John affably, "is his tendency to shoot people he doesn't like."

As far as we were concerned, Emilio's only duties consisted of being seen occasionally on the set, much more often in the bar, and always giving the eye to any attractive female who appeared in his vision. That included Miss G, so we always steered clear of him. We also harbored serious suspicions that it was Emilio himself who had started the marriage rumors rolling.

The world's press picked up the story with alacrity. Cables arrived from Hollywood, New York, Sydney, Paris, London, and from anywhere and everywhere seeking to discover the identity of this mysterious Emilio Fernandez who had captured Ava Gardner's lonely heart. Emilio became a national treasure. Pressed for action by an enraged Miss G, MGM's press departments issued loud and vehement denials. These quieted the foreign press, but the delighted Mexican papers wouldn't let go, and even when they did, it was with a final flurry of national pride.

"Jesus Christ, Rene," Miss G squealed, "they've slanted their stories to indicate that bloody Senor Emilio Fernandez changed his mind about marrying me." Oh well, it gave us something to laugh about.

Not all the Mexican press, however, were obsessed with such trivia. From the time we arrived some of the more left-wing papers had been smoldering about the decadence of the aliens who came to Puerto Vallarta to indulge themselves in drink, drugs, and a lay-about life. Now the finger pointed directly at us: Puerto Vallarta people are being criminally despoiled of their land, their beaches, and their way of life. Children of ten to fifteen are being introduced to sex, drink, drugs, vice, and carnal bestiality by gangsters, nymphomaniacs, and heroin-sniffing blonds.

I must say, I thought that was a bit harsh if it referred to our hard-working group of movie makers. I didn't think for a second that Miss G was despoiling the lives of her boat boys. They all seemed to be having a very good time together.

I will admit that we all seemed to drink far too much. Miss G, I know, thoroughly approved of Richard Burton's cry, "Who's ever heard of a movie being made without a bar? A bar is ethnic to movies, part of our culture." That statement was probably invented during one of Richard's night sessions when, ignoring Liz's most tender appeals, he refused to leave the bar at all.

"Back to Puerto Vallarta, no!" he would roar. "Should I risk breaking my bloody neck going down those steps? No! Risk falling overboard in the dark? No! There's good company here. Good conversation, plenty of bedrooms to fall into a few yards away, and no distance to get on the set next morning."

Miss G adored Richard and normally would have accepted his advice, but she had her boat boys always ready to ferry us home.

During our time in Mexico, Miss G was pleased about the friendship she struck up with Deborah and Peter Viertel. The friendship between us and John Huston we took for granted, and we all gave him credit for his astute cunning in lumping us together in these intimate relationships. Miss G had always shied away from mixing very much with the rest of the cast in her movies outside studio hours, but now for the first time since I had known her, I actually heard her discussing the trade of acting, the penalties of fame and the excitement of anticipation about working each day. Usually she brushed those aspects aside. It was just a job like any other.

Miss G had known Peter Viertel in her early Hollywood years. They had played tennis together, dined together and were good, but never intimate, friends. Like Miss G, Peter loved swimming and snorkeling, but he'd never tried waterskiing. Miss G introduced him to the sport, and often they would cut white swathes across the blue water of Los Muertos Beach together. Occasionally all shifted back to their house for drinks and a little chat. It was always a nice time.

Our friendship with Richard and Liz was of a different character. Liz and Miss G were old friends, but the addition of Richard to Liz's life created a new dynamic. There was a serenity attached to Deborah and Peter but an air of conflict within the Liz and Richard household. Liz had been married three times before she met Richard, and he had been married only once to Sybil. One had to admire John Huston's skill in casting people with real problems into counterparts in the movie with fictional problems. Miss G was in the clear, having arrived in Puerto Vallarta footloose and fancy free. As I've hinted before, the boat boys, provided by John, were always waiting for her slightest command or a little "flirt", as she called it, to embellish her characterization. Richard, however, had arrived loaded down with guilt and inner conflict, perfectly typecast to assume the Reverend Shannon's fictional sins of flesh, drink and the devil. Indeed, he was able to enlarge his portrayal with his own virile Welshness, and a dark, brooding, melancholic quality the Welsh call "hiraeth."

Liz on the surface seemed quite untroubled by events and was, as usual, ravishingly beautiful. She was immensely attached to and protective of Richard, even when he talked belligerently about their private affairs in public—even making jokes about their chances of getting married. Elizabeth had brought her six-year-old daughter to Puerto Vallarta. She was a lovely little girl with incredibly turquoise blue eyes, dark lashes, and an air of innocence like her mother's. Not that I am saying that Liz's eyes in those days were all that innocent, and in the diminutive bikinis she wore (a different one every day, I swear), she was gloriously provocative.

Miss G, with her usual candor about such matters, later said of Liz's allure: "I've known Liz for ages, through Mickey in the first place because he worked with her when she was in her teens in National Velvet. I knew her when her little breasts started sprouting. I remember they swelled very quickly, and she didn't do anything to push them down either. I don't blame her. She had a tiny waist like I did. We used to compare sizes. I was twenty-three when I made *The Great Sinner* with Gregory Peck, and Irene designed a special corset that we pulled into nineteen inches, but that was a bit tough, so I guess I must have been a regular twenty-one inches at the time. I had a thirty-four cup and hips to match—not bad. Liz was about the same."

Without a part in the film, Liz was able to plan a leisurely routine. She caught the launch *Taffy* every day at noon and arrived in Mismaloya in time for lunch. She was quite happy to chat with any newsman about her present and future plans, and they were around for the entire two months. Even when Michael Wilding, her second husband and father of her first two children, turned up as an agent for the firm that represented Richard Burton, she was not the slightest bit fazed. Liz always managed to keep her previous husbands in perspective, knowing that earlier love affairs were not nearly as intriguing as present ones.

Never before had I seen Miss G go overboard about the sheer magnetism and talent of any actor as she did with Richard Burton. Oh yes, she recognized him as a sexpot all right with that shock of black hair, those electric blue eyes, that raddled complexion, that powerful muscular figure, and that resonant, lucid, evocative voice. Miss G adored every note.

Miss G knew Richard was not for her, though. She had her own inviolable set of rules and ethics about such things. Never steal a best friend's husband or boyfriend. That was Rule One. Rule Two was that there were always more than enough males around anyway. Even so, after she had spent close to eighteen years in the movie business playing opposite a whole bunch of talented gentlemen, Richard blew in against her with the force and freshness of a Pacific Ocean hurricane. I think it also had something to do with John Huston's original premise. You were there in Mexico in an old run-down hotel called Costa Verde. It was all real and believable, and certainly Richard Burton as the drunken old sot Reverend Shannon was both real and believable.

Born in the valleys of Wales, son of a Jenkins coal miner, part of a brood of seven young Jenkinses, from childhood Richard was bright, boisterous, and determined. As a schoolboy, his talents were recognized by Philip Burton, a gentle, gifted Welshman and BBC radio producer. With father Jenkins' agreement he adopted Richard, took him into his own home, and changed not only his name, but his entire life. Richard won a scholarship to Oxford University and never looked back. As an orator, he was matchless. His memory was astonishing. Out would pour Shakespeare, the Bible, or a dozen poets from the Elizabethan era to Dylan Thomas, for whom he had a great respect. Yet there was nothing conceited about Richard's performances. He was modest and appreciative of anyone who cared to join in. He had a wonderful bouncing sense of humor always on tap.

"He's such an original," Miss G exclaimed about him. "He is such a god-damned assertive, aggressive, certain-he-is-right male chauvinist Welshman. When he talks, the world listens, and the bugger never stops talking." Miss G's voice was rising with excitement. "When we are rehearsing, he draws me out in a way I've never experienced before. He makes the dialogue sound so natural that I answer instinctively, and then discover that it is the dialogue. What about that then?"

Often Miss G was Richard's friendly American target, but she could take care of herself. I think it had something to do with the love-hate conflict in their parts as Shannon and Maxine that they carried forward into their off-camera sessions.

"Now Ava, me old darling," started Richard in a fake Irish accent on a particular night in the bar, "I bet you've never heard Irish singing or a Welsh choir belting it out in your whole life. I mean what do they know about singing in the soft green undergrowths of North Carolina?"

"More than you will ever know," answered Miss G, sweetly.

"In the Welsh coal mines, lass, the miners are winched up the shaft harmonizing in Welsh hymns loud enough to knock down the Houses of Parliament. Do those simple farmers growing their cotton and tobacco crops go to work with a song on their lips? The Welsh valleys are stuffed with tin-roofed chapels that thunder with the rage of hymns and the denunciation of sin."

"Honey," Miss G replied in the molasses-sweet North Carolina accent she was using for her part as Maxine, "let me tell you, Wales isn't the only place where the preacher men sound off. When I was a little girl growing up, everyone was too busy to take me to Sunday school, so my little black friend Elsa Mae, about eight, same age as me, we'd sneak out to the Black Holy Roller church nearby. Baby, you sure did get good singing and good preaching there. We were all sinners doomed to flaming hell. That used to frighten the shit out of Elsa Mae and me, but we clutched hands and decided we wouldn't steal any more watermelons from other people's fields, and I think it influenced me into trying to have a good time as long as I could before I was consigned to the flames. And talking about great hymn singing, you ever heard of Mahalia Jackson?"

Richard threw his hands up as if he'd been struck by a divine revelation– half Burton, half the Reverend Shannon–"Ava, my darling, now we've reached common ground. Who has not heard of the great Mahalia?" And heaven's above, there was no way of stopping or upstaging this man because he's off singing in full voice, "Joy to the world, the Lord is come, let us rejoice and sing."

And by golly, within a few seconds the song was taken up by the whole bar. They knew the tune if they didn't know the words. They were on their feet, some banging their glasses on the table, and Richard was conducting an uproarious sing-along. It was fun, really fun. I've never known a film crew and a horde of totally different people have such a good time together in such an unlikely place. Remember, I'm talking with hindsight. If you can recognize happiness when it's happening, you are doubly fortunate. Let me tell you that both Miss G and I knew that we were very happy on so many of those evenings.

30 MISS G AND THE BEACH BOYS

The days were long and sunny, beginning with dawns revealing opalescent seas and pale pink skies and ending with blood-red sunsets. The Pacific Ocean was always the boundary for our western horizons, and at night the moon shimmered on its surface.

There were rains and storms during which John Huston retreated to the bar with his film crew and played endless games of gin rummy while everyone enjoyed bottomless margaritas. This scenario brought serenity to our existence there—a timelessness in a peaceful Mexican lifestyle. We were all absorbed by the pace and progress of the film, and every day we counted the advancing of pages we had achieved. To me one thing was close to unbelievable. Miss G was, for the first time in her film career, actually enjoying being on a set when she wasn't working. She enjoyed watching other members of the cast doing their scenes.

In early October we were down on Mismaloya Beach watching Grayson Hall's marvelous characterization of Sue's demented chaperone. There she was standing in the shallows bawling hysterically out to sea. Out at sea was the Reverend Shannon, neck deep in the waves enjoying playful antics with bikini-clad Sue as she squealed with joy.

"Come back, come back," Grayson was yelling. "I command you to come back. Leave that man alone. You are in my charge. Your mother will never forgive you. Come back immediately." Tennessee Williams sure could invent challenging situations.

Making *The Night of the Iguana*, said John sometime later, was a serene experience, but he also indicated his gratitude for Tennessee Williams' near genius ability to improvise. John remembered the time he was having difficulty with one particular scene. On the scripted page it read well and was full of conflict and drama. However, acted out, it was dull. It simply did not work.

The scene opened with Richard sitting at a chiffonier before a mirror in his Hotel Costa Verde room, shaving. At his elbow stood a half empty bottle of Scotch which he had been doing his best to empty. Without any tap on the door, sexy Sue in mini skirt and mini everything else tripped in, determined, it immediately became clear, upon her own seduction. Richard spun around, stood up to defend his virtue, and in his haste knocked the bottle of whisky to the floor where it shattered into pieces. He then tried to fend her off, to make her aware that such an event would mean immediate exposure and ruin for him. But it just did not work. John then turned to Tennessee for help.

Tennessee pondered and then rewrote the scene. In his new version Sue bounced in and Richard knocked the bottle to the floor, covering it with broken glass. Agitated and barefooted, Richard advanced towards her with hands outstretched to keep her away, never noticing that his feet were cut and bleeding. Sue sees this and begins to laugh. In a second she slips off her own shoes and joins him in this painful sort of love-play. The scene was startling and dramatic, and it worked.

Later, still in October, Richard and Miss G were shooting the hammock scene. Richard was lounging in the hammock, and Maxine, feeling he had been scruffy for too long, decided to give him a shave. Richard, tolerant with drink, genially agreed. After he was smothered with lather the phone rang. Richard yelled, "Ill tear that bloody thing off the wall!"

Miss G's shouted reply should have come out as, "In a pig's eye, you won't," but instinct won as she shouted, "In a pig's ass, you won't." Loud laughter came from the crew–though, of course, it required a retake.

I thought there was only one scene in the entire movie when Miss G tried to duck out of her part as the cheerful, sexy, blowsy hussy, and I guessed why. But before I go into it, I would like to make it clear that the two boat boys (Ricki was the name of one of them) had no part in the movie whatsoever. There were also two beach boys in the movie with whom Miss G was presumed to be enjoying sex and who sent her crazy with their insistent maraca shaking rhythms. They were two young and gifted Mexican actors, Fidelmar Duran and Roberto Leyva. Their dramatic scene together was played in the moonlight with Miss G waist deep in the swirling sea, as the two beach boys shook their maracas while circling around her like predatory animals. I guess it was pure guilty conscience when she pretended to be quite huffed, and a little shocked. "John, honey," she protested to Mr. H, "don't you think this scene is a bit over the top?"

John, who knew every little detail of what was going on in his production, looked innocent and said softly, "Yes, but you can do it, girl, yes you can." To make sure she couldn't escape, he joined them in the waves, directing the scene like old Father Neptune.

Finally it came to one of the big scenes in the picture—the iguana's big dramatic moment of being set free. Richard, in a symbolic gesture, suggested that he too was freeing himself from the bondage of guilt and releasing himself from Sue's nubile body. With Deborah's efforts to save him for God and Maxine's boozy entrapment causing him to feel ensnared, he decided to cut the iguana free. The happy lizard was then supposed to scuttle away into the jungle, but like hell he was. With no rope collar holding him, he turned up scaly eyes implying he wanted to know what was for supper. Even a gentle prod with Richard's foot would not budge him. The animal actually needed a jolt from an electric prod, a mild shock instrument invented by one of our technicians to stir him on his way. Even then he only moved at a very slow pace back to his native habitat. It was the slowest dramatic exit I've ever witnessed.

During the filming Miss G and I experienced a problem completely unrelated to the film. We were visited by Miss G's brother-in-law Larry Tarr. He just came to have a good time for a bit. Miss G and I loved Larry very much, but occasionally our love would dwindle. This was one of those dwindling occasions.

Larry, mixing in film circles at a high or low level, inevitably thrust out a firm hand and loudly introduced himself as "Larry Tarr, the man who launched Ava Gardner into the movies." This, regrettably, was absolutely true.

The saga began in North Carolina when Beatrice (Bappie) Gardner, Miss G's older sister by twenty years, got married to a very handsome young guy named William. As a tiny tot Miss G adored him. He played games with her, and she loved every minute of it. Handsome William, as a husband, possessed one unfortunate trait. He simply could not be faithful. After he had half a dozen consecutive affairs, Bappie finally got fed up and announced that she was going to divorce him.

The reaction from the large Gardner family was one of horror. Divorce in a tiny town like Smithfield, North Carolina, was unheard of. Did she not realize that there had never been a divorce in the Gardner family—ever? With calm pragmatism, Bappie retorted that there was going to be one now. She forsook William, home, and relatives and set off to seek her fortune in Richmond and later New York.

In New York she met Larry Tarr. Larry took an instant shine to her. Larry's father had five sons and owned a string of photographic shops and studios. When he died he left one to each son. Larry inherited the one standing on the corner of 45th and Fifth Avenue. With fast talk and sweet promises, he married Bappie, and they lived above the shop. Young Ava, now in her middle teens and lovely, was allowed to visit during her school holidays, and Larry, recognizing a really beautiful girl when he saw one, immediately began taking pictures of her. One of these was exhibited in his showcase window on Fifth Avenue.

The picture was spotted by a young passer-by named Barney Duhan who held an errand boy's job in MGM's New York office. Barney tended to upgrade that lowly position into that of MGM talent-scout when the need arose. It often arose because Barney had a healthy desire to date young and pretty girls, and certainly the girl in the showcase photo was that. His problem was how to get her phone number and start his routing. He tried a little deception in Tarr's Photographic Shop.

Bappie happened to be filling in for Larry's usual receptionist, and she listened to Barney's "innocent speech" with deep suspicion. Phone numbers were not handed out to strange young men. Was he a talent scout for MGM and did he have identification, she asked, as he looked far too young for such a post.

Barney knew he had lost this one, and he made a swift exit. Bappie reported the incident later that day when Larry returned. Immediately all of

Larry's entrepreneurial skills emerged. Within seconds he was on the phone to MGM's office, and brushing aside defensive secretaries he was put through to one of the top executives. Yes, they were interested in finding new talent. They were prepared to look at photographs if he brought them around. They looked at Larry's photos and were indeed interested. However, it took a few weeks to retrieve Ava from Mama's clutches and to get permission for her to take a film test. As they say, the "rest is history". With Bappie as chaperone, Ava was transported to Hollywood and became a starlet.

Larry was a part of our lives, and Miss G knew all about him. With some affection, Miss G informed me of Larry's service overseas in World War II. "As far as I could work out," she said, "he was AWOL for half the time and behind bars for the other half. I don't think the Nazi panzer divisions felt threatened by Larry."

Nevertheless, we loved Larry. Born and bred in New York, he was short and dark-haired, with no claims to good looks. In a crowd he would just disappear as crowd wallpaper. He was dapper. That's the word for Larry— dapper. Sharp as a needle, he was convinced to the point of lunacy that life had to be embraced, enjoyed, and fulfilled for twenty-four hours a day. In any part of the planet he was prepared to start a party, which one felt might go on forever or at least until Larry dropped. We were at that point now.

We were in Puerto Vallarta's only building that passed as a nightclub, and it was booming with the beat of drums, trumpets, guitars, and loud voices. Larry had just fallen off a table where he had been performing a Spanish dance he had tried long ago with us in Andalusia but never mastered. Ricki and friend picked him up, dusted him off, and poured more margaritas into him. Off he went between the tables, a plastic flower between his teeth, gyrating and hopping and making a complete fool of himself. Larry was always the life and soul of the party. Miss G and I exchanged resigned glances.

Larry was now fashioning a line of conga dancers to lead through the tables and then out into the night. Knowing Larry, I said I hoped he knew what he was doing. Miss G responded that Larry never knew what he was doing. We gave another mutual sigh and gave up.

I believe Larry was drunk from the moment he set foot on Mexican soil. Sticking firmly to the Dean Martin philosophy, 'if you don't want a hangover, stay drunk', he got himself into all sorts of trouble in every bar in Puerto Vallarta. On several occasions with the luck of a veteran acrobat, he managed to ship himself to Mismaloya without falling overboard. There he caused maximum turbulence but was treated with affection by several of the crew who could recall his adventures when he visited the locations of Miss G's other movies.

The police gave him the benefit of every possible doubt on a variety of occasions, but on one particular night when he became over pugnacious they popped him into the local jail. That was serious.

We were told that even a short sojourn in a Mexican jail is not a pleasant experience. Being confronted by a local judge was not a hilarious occasion and, knowing Larry's ability to play merry jokes and his astounding disrespect for the law in general, we decided such contempt might get him a sentence of from one to five years!

Miss G had a heart-to-heart with John H., and judicious enticements to the local judiciary were made behind the scenes. Larry was extricated from the jailhouse, steered to the airport, given a one-way ticket to New York and firmly pushed aboard the plane.

No doubt he would meet us again in some far off corner of the globe. After all, he had given the world Ava Gardner. That must not be forgotten.

Despite that slight hiccup in Miss G's personal life, the script pages ticked steadily away, but then in November two events occurred—one that was very close to us and the other a tragedy for the whole world.

Our hill at Mismaloya was decorated with apartments and cottages, and some of the apartments had second floor balconies. Assistant Director Tom Shaw and his side kick Terry were sitting out on their balcony when, without warning, it collapsed, and they plunged downwards in a cascade of concrete rubble. Terry wasn't badly hurt and returned to work two or three days later, suffering only aches and bruises, but Tom Shaw received serious back injuries. He was taken away by stretcher from Mismaloya and then flown to Mexico City and on to Los Angeles for hospital treatment.

The accident left us all depressed and a little fearful when it was revealed that the builders had used sand from the beach to mix with cement—its salty content making it quite unsuitable for that purpose. Those with balconies that looked down on the rocks at the edge of the sea took deep breaths and did not venture out on them again. Of course, any hope of the complex functioning in the future as a country club and holiday center was ruled out, and it was soon completely abandoned.

This distressing incident was insignificant compared with the news of President Kennedy's assassination. It struck into the hearts of Miss G and me with particular poignancy. On several occasions the handsome, shock-headed young senator from the east coast had sat chatting in our small apartment when he called to take Miss G out to dinner, and each visit was a fond memory.

November 30th was scheduled as the last day of shooting, but, as usual, there were a few retakes to be done. Nevertheless, the end of the movie party went ahead as planned. It was held in the Mismaloya bar with spill-over into the canteen and dance hall, and two hundred townspeople were invited. Everyone dressed in their best, especially the ladies, but the wafts of expensive perfume were almost obliterated by the drench of citronella oil keeping the mosquitoes at bay.

Miss G wore an outrageously expensive harem-type outfit designed by Pucci, while Liz wore a simple white jersey top with skin-tight white slacks. Her skin glowed, and only the huge diamond brooch pinned to her jersey could compete. A lot of drinks passed down a lot of thirsty throats. At one point, John H. stood up to say a few words, but only a few people managed to hear them.

"In this strange movie business," he said, "we come together and make moving shadows on film, and when we disperse, the shadows are all that are left of our close association. If the shadows are good, our trip together was worthwhile."

Then he gave one of his wolf-snarl grins and added how glad he was that none of the six owners of the derringers had felt the need to shoot off a couple of slugs at anyone in particular. The audience roared when he ended, "If this movie had been Cleopatra, it would have been a massacre." The sun was well above the horizon before the last guests began to tread wearily down the steps and take the boats. There were tears, kisses, hugs, and vows of eternal friendship. Everyone was unanimous in their feeling that, though at times it had been difficult, more often than not it had been glorious and certainly unlike any movie-making experience they ever had or were likely to have in the future.

The next morning John H. passed me in high good humor with no semblance of a hangover. "How's Ava getting on with the boys?" I did a quick second take. It was the first time the old buzzard had indicated that he had any idea of what might be going on with Miss G, Ricki and friend. I decided truth was best. I replied that Ricki definitely was the one in favor.

"I thought so," said John H., still pausing. "I hope she doesn't want to take him back to Europe with her."

I stared at his departing back. I felt a chill. My God, I hadn't even considered it. At lunchtime, I said to Miss G, "I've got the tickets for the return flight to Mexico City. We leave Thursday morning, okay?" One of those winsome, innocent smiles spread across Miss G's lips, and I realized that John H. was on the right track.

"Change the tickets to Friday. I have got one or two other things to do." Another chill crept down my spine. Most of the star players and important technicians would have left by Thursday.

On Friday we boarded the aircraft. Miss G was ahead of me, but as I peered round her shoulder, along the aisle, I could see Ricki sitting in the outside of three seats there. Ricki was still in his open necked shirt, old slacks, and I'd bet my last dollar he was still wearing those damn thong sandals. Miss G had given him money to buy a ticket.

He stood up as Miss G reached him and allowed her through to the window seat. He moved in to sit next to her, but I laid a quick arm on his, gave him the "excuse me" smile and pushed past to occupy the center seat. For Miss G the farewell party had never really ended, and at this moment she was still on a drip feed of margaritas – margaritas that would inevitably be replenished by the attentive cabin staff. For one of the few times in the past weeks I ducked the drinks, for, if Miss G was more than a bit misty about our collective responsibilities, one of us had to be sane and sober. I reset my face into a fixed smile to meet the questioning looks some of the people we knew were giving us.

We reached Mexico City, and a hired car whisked us to our hotel. All of those arrangements had been taken care of. Ricki stood next to us at the desk with a broad smile on his face, as happy as Larry. He had never flown in an aircraft before or seen a city as large as Mexico's capital. And as I surmised, he was still wearing those bloody thong sandals. I never could work out why those damned things caused me such inner rage.

Without batting an eyelash, Miss G, adopting the touch of grandeur she assumed when she was half-pissed, instructed the desk clerk to find Ricki a room on our floor.

Up in our suite, with Ricki safe and sound in his, Miss G said, "Oh, Rene, I hear Dorothy Dandridge is doing her great nightclub act at that neat restaurant we know. Why don't you give them a ring and book a table for three—we'll give Ricki a treat."

"Miss G," I said firmly, "It's a swanky joint. He can't go there in an old white shirt and slacks and that, that"—I tried to keep the scream out of my voice—"pair of thong sandals."

"Guess you're right," answered Miss G. "Why don't you take him out to the shops and buy him slacks, shirt, shoes, anything he needs. He'll look real chic for the party."

I extracted Ricki from his room, and he followed me to a nearby shopping mall. I equipped him with the necessary clothes, and then we found our way to a shoe store. The young man who served us was pleasant and spoke good English but naturally chatted to Ricki in Spanish. What he thought about a black girl buying a pair of expensive shoes for someone who was plainly from the sands of some Pacific resort didn't seem to have crossed his mind, as he said cheerfully, "He tells me this is the first pair of shoes he has ever owned in his life."

I offered what I hoped was an enigmatic smile and said, "Figures."

Back in the hotel, Ricki took his new clothes and shoes up to his room, and as I passed the desk the young clerk, who was talking on the phone, waved to catch my attention and beckoned me across. When I reached him, he placed his hand over the receiver and said with a smile, "Miss Jordan, can I take it that you are Miss Gardner's slave?"

"Her what?" I asked.

"Her slave. I have a young lady on the phone asking if I have seen Miss Gardner's slave. Her English is not good." I knew who it was. It had to be Juanita, our Spanish cook. "She does not think there is any difference between 'maid' and 'slave!'"

I gave him a smile, "At this moment, I think she might be right."

Juanita wanted details of when and how she was being returned to her own country. She was reassured. That was okay, but nothing else was okay.

The visit to the nightclub passed without too much hassle. It was very crowded. No one really noticed that Ricki couldn't bear wearing shoes and carried them in his hand. What was a little more worrisome was the amount of alcohol Miss G was consuming. I knew from past experience that soon she would recognize her own danger signals—she was pretty good at that. She'd recognize that the days were blurred, the hands were shaking slightly, and she'd need a drink before she got out of bed. Then she would quit, totally. She would snap out of it as she would snap off an electric switch, and she would run for cover to a hideaway, a health center or a rented house in Palm Springs. There would be absolutely no booze for weeks or even months.

Sure enough, next morning she asked that I book us into that wonderful health spa we used when we first arrived in Mexico. "What is it? Thirty miles or so outside the city?"

I felt a wave of relief and said, "Only an hour by car." So she had finally recovered her senses? No, she hadn't.

"Book a room for Ricki, so he can come too."

The wave of relief turned icy cold. A vision of those faces flashed across my mind—the faces of the women who inhabited that place. Those blue-rinsed banker's wives, those titled heiresses, those dictators' mistresses, those pop star celebrities, those terry clothed, wrapped and cream-encrusted ladies all flashed before me.

"Miss G, I can't do that."

"Why not?" she asked.

"If you remember, men are not allowed in. I, as your maid, slept in the motel a short distance away and visited you only if required."

"We'll take Ricki," said Miss G, ignoring reality.

I knew there was not the slightest chance of Ricki gaining admittance to this exclusive female establishment. They were all immensely wealthy and all resolutely female. They were all enraptured by the whirlpools, mud baths, the warm swims, the wax treatments, the gentle pummel and massage, the muesli-yogurt and mint tea existences, and the outrageous prices that ensured peace, privacy, and temporary oblivion. Men were objects who inhabited other planets, captains of industry who signed the necessary checks.

Miss G drained her margarita and glanced to see if there was any more in the pitcher, and there was. "I'll only need one bag, Rene, honey."

I filled her glass and said, "Miss G, I'm not coming."

"Not coming?" Miss G looked puzzled.

"No, Miss G, I will stay here and wait for your return. I don't think you will be gone for long." Miss G sipped her margarita and looked disinterested.

"Suit yourself," she said, dismissing the subject.

I went to pack her bag. I arranged the car with the desk and saw them off with my second-hand, fixed smile.

Next morning just before lunch, the phone rang, and the desk clerk informed me that Miss Gardner had returned. I went down to the foyer to meet the two of them. There she was, Ricki beside her, still carrying his shoes in his hand and not looking very happy.

My heart bled for Miss G. She was white-faced, deathly tired, and still hazy from drink. God, I knew her so well. I knew she was ashamed of herself, and I knew she was ashamed of being ashamed. She had been humiliated, and she knew it was her own fault. No doubt Miss G had been told in very polite terms—for the Mexicans are invariably polite and understanding—that young men carrying their shoes in their hands cannot become part of any recuperative health program.

We all went in the elevator, and as soon as I opened the door of our suite, Miss G went straight through to her bedroom and closed the door. She did not say a word. The "experience" had finally fizzled out. I paused in front of Ricki and said, "Ricki, it's all over. Go back to your room and collect whatever things you have there. I am going to arrange with the travel agent at the desk to get you a ticket back to Puerto Vallarta, give you some money, and arrange a car to take you to the airport."

Ricki nodded and smiled. He knew his time was up. It would not have surprised me if I had been told that Ricki didn't know who Ava Gardner really was. To him she could have been just one of those 'film people,' one of those generous, pretty, amiable, heavy-drinking older ladies needing his solicitude. After all, there would be a succession of those lovelies available on those Puerto Vallarta beaches in the future.

Miss G woke around noon the next day. I said, "Miss G, we are packed, and I have two departure times direct to New York and then on to Madrid. Three o'clock or six o'clock."

"I think we'll take the first," Miss G said.

Ricki was never mentioned. Not a word of explanation, justification, or commiseration was exchanged between Miss G and me, either then or in the future. It was just one of those experiences. There were a lot of those types of experiences waiting in the future.

31 "IN THE BEGINNING..."

At least a month before we had finished *The Night of the Iguana* and were still enjoying Puerto Vallarta, John Huston was outlining his plans for his next epic production, *The Bible.*

As usual, we were sitting at the bar on top of the hill at Mismaloya. The sun was making up its mind about its dive into the sea, and a pale moon high above the palm trees was trying to get off to an early start. Ice clinked in our glasses. A happy day's shooting lay behind us.

Huston explained, "It's the biggest film deal I've ever undertaken. Dino de Laurentiis wants me to do *The Bible*, a twenty million dollar production. It's to be shot in Egypt and Italy."

Miss G looked at him over the rim of her glass and said, "You gonna do it?"

Huston dodged the question. "I told Dino it would take a lifetime. Dino laughed and said, 'God only took six days to make the world. John, you've got a little more time.'"

Miss G took the glass away from her lips and asked in disbelief, "You are playing God?"

Huston's voice was playful. "Can you think of anyone better? It's only a voice-over." He paused and went on, "Ava, I've already done a lot of work. I had trouble casting Noah. First, I tried Charlie Chaplin. He couldn't appear in any film but his own. Next, I tried Alec Guinness. He had engagements years ahead. So, as I loved animals and Noah had to handle them, I decided I'd better do it."

"God and Noah and animals?" said Miss G, her suspicions rising. "Animals?"

"You know, Ava, the animals went into the Ark two by two: lions, tigers, giraffes, antelopes...."

"Won't they eat each other?" I asked.

"Not if we're careful," Huston said. "The casting is a bit difficult. I've got Peter O'Toole to play the Lord's messenger, the angel specially sent down from heaven. There will be three angels, and O'Toole's playing all three."

"Jesus! All three?" said Miss G.

"That's what O'Toole said. So I asked him if he'd ever seen an angel."

"I would have thought he'd seen dozens," said Miss G.

"Ava, O'Toole said his upbringing had prevented that. So I said, Peter, all angels must look alike. He asked if he'd get three salaries, and I said no, but he said he'd take the job anyway."

"This is not a comedy is it?" asked Miss G, swallowing what was left of her margarita.

"Quite the opposite. Dead serious."

Huston's serpent eyes retreated to slits as the long smile spread across his face. "Got a great part for you, Ava darling. Sarah, wife of Abraham and Mother of Nations."

Miss G's voice rose an octave. "Mother of Nations! John, be sensible. How old was Sarah?"

"Ninety when she bore her first child by Abraham," Huston replied.

"Ninety!" screeched Miss G. "And all that Biblical language? No way, honey!"

Huston smiled in my direction. "Rene will love to feed you your voice cues when you're talking to Abraham."

"Abraham who?" demanded Miss G.

"Abraham, George C. Scott."

"Never met him," said Miss G.

I knew she would take the part.

After *The Night of the Iguana* was finished, Miss G attended the premier in New York City, which got very good notices. For the next few months we spent time surveying civilization with the help of our four favorite hotels: The Savoy in London, the L'Hotel in Paris, the Hilton in Madrid and the Grand in Rome. We also spent time out in our Madrid apartment plaguing Ex-Dictator Peron. We suffered no hardship.

Miss G's attendance at health spas was frequent, and not a drop of alcohol passed our lips in all that time. As a result, we tripped through the doors of the Grand Hotel in Rome with Miss G looking exquisite—absolutely beautiful. The cast of *The Bible* was assembled there: George C. Scott, Peter O'Toole, Richard Harris, Stephen Boyd, Franco Nero, and many others, and naturally the director, John Huston.

Huston had already completed the opening sequences of the movie faithfully following the direction laid down in that magical opening sentence of the Bible: *"In the beginning God created the heaven and the earth."* For this awesome task he had entrusted photographer Ernest Hass, who specialized in photographing the outdoors. Huston had sent him to tour the world and to film active volcanoes, roaring waterfalls, towering mountains, immense ocean waves and other awe-inspiring natural phenomenon. Blended together, they formed a fantastic opening, lasting three minutes. Considering the overall cost per minute, they certainly should have been fantastic.

Then came the creation of man and woman in the Garden of Eden.

"That wasn't too hard," Huston said. "The female and male models haven't changed all that much. The serpent that tempted Eve was difficult, really difficult. Unlike Noah's Ark, where with a lot of training and a little film trickery we were able to show the animals trooping into Noah's Ark two by two, snakes didn't seem to care much for acting. We solved the problem by getting a sinuous male dancer dressed in a skin-tight snake-like costume and a snake head with glittering eyes. He came slithering through the branches to tempt Eve with the forbidden fruit."

With his huge physique, tough, hardened, craggy face and deep-set eyes, George C. Scott was made for the part of Abraham. I mean, how can you visualize what those immense, tyrannical, patriarchal, founding fathers of Genesis looked like? Read Genesis and you'll get some idea: *"The Lord said, I am the Lord God of Abraham, thy father, and the God of Isaac; the land whereon thou liest, to thee will I give thee, and to thy seed. And thy seed shall spread abroad to the west and to the east and to the north and the south, and in thy seed shall all the families of the families of the earth be blessed...."*

Yes, Huston certainly knew what he was doing when he cast Scott. The fact that George C. Scott was a formidable actor, a towering personality whose magnetic performances in many films will be admired for years to come is indisputable. The fact that he scared the holy hoots out of Miss G and me is also indisputable.

What was disputable? Was it all or partly Miss G's fault? John Huston thought that it was Miss G's fault.

"George fell in love with Ava," Huston said. "He was insanely jealous, extremely demanding of Ava's time and attention. And he became violent when they were not forthcoming."

But that wasn't until later. That first night in the Grand Hotel Miss G was invited up to Huston's suite to meet George C. Scott, and they got on very well. They went out to dinner that night and almost every night after that. And during the first week in Rome, Miss G was certainly intrigued and attracted by Scott's masculinity and his intelligence, charm and wit. They had lots to talk about, especially about their dual roles in the film. By the time the first week was over and we had started filming and Miss G had become a very good friend of Scott's, my first suspicions were aroused.

The first words ever spoken to me on the set by the great actor were, "Rene, have you got an aspirin?" I got him one from the props man and he said, "Thank you."

I began to notice that Scott drank a lot of vodka. I knew Miss G always had a bottle stored somewhere, and it seemed to me that Scott did the same thing.

Then came the evening in the Grand Hotel when Miss G said, "I'm just going up to George's room for a drink. I'll be back in twenty minutes or so."

I knew she wasn't going out to dinner with him. She wasn't dressed for that sort of occasion. If they had decided to go to dinner, she would have rung me. I waited and waited for her to return. Two hours passed. Then three, then four, and I thought, "Where the hell is she?"

Then I consoled myself with the thought that she must be chatting about the movie with John Huston and George in Huston's suite. There was no harm in ringing and finding out. Huston answered and sounded a bit strange and asked, "Did Ava tell you where she was going?"

"Yes, to see George C. Scott," I answered.

There was a long pause. "Rene," Huston said, "I'd go up there and give a little knock."

So I did. I tapped on the door and found it was open. I peered inside. There was Miss G sagged across the cushions on the settee as if she were asleep. There was no sign of Scott. I went across and shook her and said, "Honey, wake up. Are you all right?"

She opened her eyes and straightened up. "I guess so," she said in a puzzled voice. "George and I had a few vodkas. I must have fallen asleep."

There was an empty bottle and glasses on the table. We talked about what might have happened when we got back to our suite, but she couldn't remember anything so we let it slide.

A week later the same thing happened. This time Mr. Scott came down to our apartment, and I left them alone drinking while I went out shopping. I got back three hours later. This time Miss G was lying on the floor. There was no sign of Scott.

I got her to her feet, and she said, "Rene, how the hell did I end up on the floor? Something very strange is going on."

I said, "Miss G, it sure is."

I had heard about the brutality drunken men could inflict on women. I knew that a man could use the hand to chop an opponent into insensibility. I was pretty sure that this was happening to Miss G.

I also guessed that Miss G was probably trying to match Scott drink for drink. She was confident in her ability to survive. Miss G used drink to make her feel good and stay happy. Scott's reaction to an overload of vodka was totally different. I could already see that Miss G was trying to cover up for him.

When I was helping her dress, I would notice bruises and say, "Listen girl, where did you get this mark?" She had alabaster white skin that bruised easily. She'd brush my question aside with a slightly apologetic smile and go on the defensive.

There were also other things which weren't quite right. Miss G also said, "For Christ sake Rene, never mention Frank Sinatra's name—ever. George goes crazy with jealousy."

I could remember the time when Frank also lost his cool if Howard Hughes' name came up in conversation. It's funny how situations repeat themselves.

John Huston used to stroke his chin and look at me oddly during these first weeks, but the only advice he gave me was, "Rene, I think you should keep a closer eye on Ava when George is around."

I knew that as far as Huston was concerned, there was a lot riding on this enormously expensive movie. Vast amounts of money had already been spent, and more was going to be spent in the future.

When the first shots of *The Bible* were completed, we moved about sixty miles east of Rome into the Abruzzi Mountains and booked into a delightful hotel in the town of Avezzano. George C. Scott and Miss G were now going out to dinner practically every night. It was always Scott who insisted she join him.

"Rene, he is drinking a hell of a lot every night, and he gets angry, very angry," Miss G told me. "Now he's jealous not only of Frank, but of all my friends."

Because of our close relationship, I didn't tell her that Scott was even angry with me. His voice when talking about me was always mocking and unpleasant. "Oh, Rene, Rene..." It gave me the creeps.

In the peace and quiet of the Abruzzi Mountains, Miss G began to tell me about her affair with Scott. Yes, she had been very attracted to him from the very first. When he began to plague her with the idea of marriage, she even began to think that it might be a possibility.

Miss G followed the dictum that if she felt strongly enough about a man she would go to bed with him. She had done that, thus establishing a strong human bondage, and I do mean "bondage."

She was still deluding herself into thinking that somehow it might all work out. When sober, Scott was a wonderful guy—thoughtful, caring, and totally apologetic for his drinking bouts that led to violence. Perhaps she decided he could change. Perhaps she thought she could influence him.

I thought this was a major mistake. Like so many other women who had found themselves in a similar plight, she was enmeshed in a situation from which she could not extricate herself. I began to worry about the days ahead. I began to worry very much. We had work to do!

Work in this case was just that: work. Don't think that film-making with John Huston was always wine and roses. Huston was a realist. He liked to film in realistic settings. I shall never forget the day we were filming on the top of some mountain in the Abruzzis. The weather, like all mountain weather, had been lousy: sun, wind, rain, clouds...the lot. For most of the time Miss G and I had been seeking shelter from the elements. It was getting late. The weather did not look like it was improving. John Huston and his film crew were camped out about fifty yards higher than us on the mountainside. Doing their usual thing, they were playing cards waiting for the weather to change.

Huston's crew was a splendid collection of film technicians. The director had collected them like glorious old and young treasures through the years. They all adored him. He adored them. They made for a happy fast-moving film team.

Miss G was fed up. "Rene, it's ridiculous," she said. "There isn't going to be any more sun. We're stuck up on this mountain top. I want to go back to the hotel and have a drink. You go up there and ask that old bugger, John Huston, if he's going to film again today or not."

Feeling the same way as Miss G, and doing my duty, I said, "Good idea. I'll go and check."

I had gone half way up the mountain when the thought struck me like an axe in the back of my neck. There I was, Miss G's maid, a frail black girl. I was about as important in film production circles as dust in the wind. I was going to march up to one of the finest film makers in the business who, by the way, was surrounded by his outlaw gang, and demand to know why we shouldn't stop work.

"Holy Jesus!" There they sat at their portable table on their portable chairs. About eight of them. Their noses were glued to their cards held about four inches from their eyeballs. This was serious stuff. These guys had been doing this for twenty years. It was a man's world. Dollars were at stake. Who the hell cared about movie making? Huston looked like one of the rabble.

I stood there. Nobody cared. Then Huston caught sight of me out of the corner of his eye. Without turning his head or removing the cigarette from his mouth, he said, "Hi, Rene." No point in beating about the bush. I took a deep breath and said bravely, "Mister Huston? Miss G wants to know whether or not we are going to work some more today."

Nobody looked up at me. The cards still kept slapping down on the table. They sounded like tombstones falling on my corpse. Then suddenly Huston, with a broad smile on his face, turned and looked at me and said, "Now Rene, that is a very interesting question. Tell you what we do. You decide whether we shoot any more today or whether we go home."

The guffaws were loud. "Your decision, Rene. We will accept it."

Again I took a deep breath. "Well, Mister Huston, Miss G says she's cold. She wants to go home. I'm cold. I want to go home."

"Right," said Huston. He looked at his gang. "Hear that fellas? We are through for the day."

And we were. I went back and said, "Miss G, don't ever send me on a trip like that again. It was terrifying." I told her what had happened. She laughed all the way home.

She was not laughing three or four nights later.

Over the years Miss G and I had perfected our party-starting equipment. Why go out hunting for a party when you can carry all the makings with you? Our portable record player, with about eighty records and our drinks, constituted our party-starting equipment.

Miss G had gone out to dinner with George C. Scott, and a few of the crew and cast had congregated in our suite to do a little partying. It was getting close to midnight. That was our deadline because we all had to get up and go to work the next morning. Most people had drifted away. Twinkletoes O'Toole and I and a couple of others were still on our feet, but about ready to give up. I was certainly ready. Usually Miss G arrived back after dining with Scott much earlier than this, and I was worried.

I had reason to worry. The door opened, and there was Miss G. She had a black eye, and her face was puffy. She was in a terrible state. She had been beaten up.

"Good God!," exclaimed Peter O'Toole. "What's happened?"

Miss G did not intend to tell anyone. O'Toole was caring, but he soon knew it was better if I took over.

While I was bathing Miss G's eye and trying to calm her down, she explained what had occurred. Their dinner at a small restaurant in town had been reasonably successful. They arrived back at the hotel, and Scott had suggested a nightcap.

Then he really began to drink. He started shouting. He started hitting. Next morning our makeup man, DeRossi, almost went mad. "Your face!" he yelled. "Who did this to you?"

Later, John Huston took me to one side and said, "It's up to Ava. She could pull away if she wants to. You protect yourself, Rene. It's up to Ava."

We all let it slide.

I understood Huston's dilemma. He had to distance himself from events. He had wanted someone titanic to play Abraham. He had wanted someone imbued with the rage of angels. He had wanted someone with a heart of steel and an almost demonic compulsion to found a nation. He got him in George C. Scott.

Huston even admitted, "When George has downed a few vodkas, he is an even greater actor." Huston always thought that the scene in which Abraham faced God, imploring him and bargaining with him in order to try and save the city of Sodom and its people from destruction, was perhaps the most powerful scene in the whole movie. The anger of Abraham and of George C. Scott never abated.

A few nights later Miss G and I came down to dinner in the hotel restaurant a little later than usual. We chose a table for two and sat down. Across from us was Scott at a table with Huston, and Scott was boozed out of his mind. He saw us, and his entire attitude changed. He kicked a chair out of the way, stood up so violently that his own table fell over, and then he strode across to us.

John Huston was no slouch when it came to action. He leapt up on George C. Scott's back, winding his legs around his waist and clamping both his arms around his head. Scott couldn't see. He wrenched around like a blind man. Other guys rushed to help.

Huston yelled, "Rene, get Ava out of here! Now! Get her out!"

I got her out, but there was more to come. There was a time when Abraham stripped off all his Biblical robes and stormed off the set in his underclothes.

Then there was the time Miss G said to me, "John Huston's asked you to do him a big favor."

"What's that?," I asked innocently.

"George has been smashing his way around town. He's in prison."

"Figures," I said.

"John wants us to go downtown and get him out. George is Abraham. Abraham is the Bible. No Abraham, no movie!"

We drove down to the prison. I took one look at it and screeched, "Miss G, that ain't no prison! There are no bars at the windows. It's a loony bin!"

"Gotta go and try," said Miss G.

She entered and then came out a little white-faced. "You're right, Rene," she said. "It's not a prison—just a sort of holding place for visitors who go nuts. George will be back on the set this afternoon."

Then came the incident that might have created a lot of trouble for the film, since Miss G's presence in the film was as necessary as Abraham's. Miss G had been with Scott when she slipped on a rug, fell heavily and broke her shoulder. I didn't believe a word of it, but she stuck to her story. She was in a great deal of pain. Only Huston, DeRossie, the makeup man, the doctor who was called, and I knew about it.

She walked around for four weeks in a football cast that the doctor had plastered around her shoulder. She was in pain all the time. With her covered up in biblical robes, you would never have guessed she was encased in plaster. No one could ever accuse Miss G of not being a real trooper when working on a film.

We asked around to find a harness to replace the plaster cast. Someone knew a doctor in Madrid who had treated a great number of injured football players for broken shoulders. Huston changed his shooting schedule, and Miss G and I snuck off to Madrid. The doctor cut the cast off and bandaged her like a mummy. She was bandaged like that until the end of filming.

For me the finale of our troubles climaxed when we were back in Rome. Frank Sinatra had been making a film in Italy which coincided with *The Bible*. He had been busy, and we had been busy. He had certainly heard about our troubles. Being Frank, he had rented a beautiful villa outside Rome and flew by helicopter back and forth to his various locations. He always called Ava "Angel," and one day he rang us at the Grand and said, "Angel, why don't you and Rene come and stay out here at this villa? My gang's here, but there's plenty of room. I'm leaving in a few days, but you could stay on until your movie is finished."

We dodged his offer for two reasons. First, we knew that Barbara Marx, widow of Zeppo Marx, one of the famous Marx Brothers comedy team, was one of Frank's assistants and was with his party. Miss G had introduced the two at a tennis tournament years before, and now she sensed they had developed a relationship. Secondly, as Miss G wisely remarked, "If George C. Scott finds out we are staying with Frank, he will really go off his head." He had done that several times already.

When Sinatra left Italy he rang us again, repeating the invitation, "Angel, come and stay here. There's a big pool, and it's all paid for and there's a car."

This time we accepted with alacrity, telling only John Huston where we were. It was great! A glorious pool, beautiful rooms, terraces and endless drinks. We settled down to enjoy the splendor, racing in by car when we were needed on the set.

One night we had sat up pretty late drinking and chatting by the pool. Miss G decided to go to bed, and I said that I'd finish my drink, clean up and lock up. Rags stayed with me to keep me company.

It must have been around midnight when the iron gate leading into the pool area suddenly clanged open. I turned my head, and, oh my God! George C. Scott was bashing through, drunk out of his mind. He was a raving maniac as far as I could see. He saw me and strode forward shouting, "Where is she? Where is she?"

I didn't stop to answer or argue. I fled. The only escape route was around the pool, and I took it. In an absolute panic of terror my mind said, "If this man catches me, he will kill me!"

Then a lunatic fringe entered the situation. Rags thought this was a game, a happy chase around the pool. He was at my heels barking and having fun. I was now running fast and George C. Scott was chasing me. How many circuits of the pool I made, I'll never know. Probably two or three. The circumference of the pool was my only defense.

Then I suddenly remembered the small storeroom just off the pool that the caretaker, who lived on the premises, had shown me. He kept all the tinned goods there. I turned the corner, ducked inside and closed the door. Rags missed this action and raced on, barking as if the game was still on.

By then Miss G had heard the commotion and foolishly came out onto her terrace, which was one story up and overlooking the pool. I heard her say, "George?" and of course he raced around and up the steps to get at her. They went inside.

I thought, "Oh God, what now?" They were quiet for a while.

Then he started smashing up both Miss G and the room. The fact that he thought the place was Sinatra's helped his enthusiasm. I knew the procedure by now. He started hitting and punching his victim, and she wouldn't resist. If he knocked her down, she'd stay down and pretend she was unconscious.

To resist him was to risk getting more of a beating. God knows why she stood it. But Scott had made one mistake. He had wakened the caretaker, and the caretaker woke the two big guys Sinatra had left for just such a situation. They were quick to come to Miss G's rescue. Scott was escorted off the premises and taken back to where he'd come from.

Next morning Miss G was sore and confused. As there were only a few days of our film schedule left, we decided to return to the Grand Hotel. We heard that Scott had created so much disturbance in the hotel that the management insisted that he pack up and leave. He found accommodation in a third rate hotel about a mile from the Grand. I remember the entire incident vividly.

After various troubled phone calls between Scott and Miss G, she decided to move over to his hotel and join him. I couldn't believe it. I was Miss G's maid. Rags and I were her companions and protectors. Was it our duty to move over with her? It was, and we did.

Miss G couldn't really explain her reasons. She knew it was crazy, but she was driven by an awful compulsion. These days the truth about abused women and wife batterers is out in the open and better understood. Miss G was behaving in a well-known pattern of abused women. Scott's sequence of abuse was dangerous. It would start with a drunken rage, a quarrel, the beating, and then there would be remorse the next morning. And of course, there was a declaration of undying love and the blackmail of what he would do if she left him. Women believe this sort of junk.

Often it is because they believe that they have nowhere else to go, no one else to turn to, have no money or decide the devil they know is better than the future alone. So they stay. Often they are killed because of that mistake.

One aspect was different about George C. Scott's rages, and that was his insistence that Miss G marry him. The fact that he was already married to actress Colleen Dewhurst didn't seem to matter. As Miss G remarked, "When

I'm flat on my back and he's hitting me in the face shouting, 'You are going to marry me! You are going to marry me!' it's not the sort of marriage proposal a girl enjoys."

I tried to stay in the crummy hotel. I just couldn't. I was simply too scared. For two nights I had listened to Scott being awful to Miss G, and that was it. The third morning, I spoke up, "Miss G, listen. I'm taking your clothes, the baggage, and Rags back to the Grand. I'm afraid of this man, and I'm not going to take any more chances. You can stay here or you can come with me."

Miss G's hesitation lasted only a fraction of a second. She said, "I'm coming with you."

We went back to the Grand. Miss G arranged for a friend to fly to Rome to pick up Rags and take him on to New York, which would be our eventual destination. The film was wrapped up. We had our small farewell parties with John Huston and Peter O'Toole and the rest of our friends and took a flight to London. We did not see George C. Scott. As the plane lifted off from Rome airport, I thought, "Thank God that is the last we will see of him!"

I should have known better. I should have known that Miss G, at root, was deeply, basically and unalterably female. She had given her mind, her heart and her body to this man. She could not forsake him. God help us, she could not forsake him.

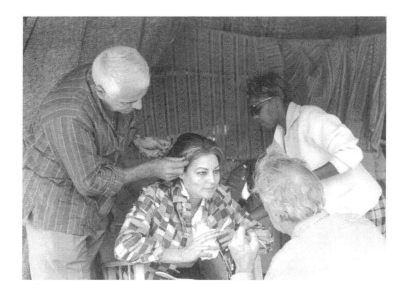

A make-up artist works his magic as John Huston and I try to comfort and counsel a battered and bewildered Miss G during the filming of The Bible*.*

32 DISASTER

The taxi took us into the center of London, and the talkative cabbie filled us in with all the news: weather, sports, possibilities of war, great theatrical productions, and an update on the royal family. We cruised down the Strand and turned into the Savoy Hotel courtyard. It was raining.

As we marched in Miss G said, "Thank God we're back. I'm beginning to think that I could live here."

"It's raining," I said.

"Good," said Miss G. "I like rain."

I had known for some time that Miss G was thinking of quitting Spain and moving to London. First, she could speak the language. Second, the Londoners left her alone. If they recognized her on the street or in a restaurant they might smile and nudge a companion, but very few would come up asking for an autograph or ask her how Frank Sinatra was getting on. Her privacy meant a lot.

We also loved the Savoy, with a room on the river and a sweeping view of the Thames outside the bustle and noise of theatre land. There were restaurants up every side street, theatres and cinemas in every direction, cheerful cabbies, understanding bobbies, a lower climate of violence, and pubs in which people would argue cheerfully and sociably.

We were back in a civilized world! We went shopping at Harrods, Peter Jones, and all the little shops we knew about from our frequent visits to London. We lunched and dined in our favorite restaurants. We had one lunch at Rules, that old and well-loved restaurant off the Strand. We sat at a corner table upstairs, where on the wall above our heads a picture of the bearded King Edward VII stared with a saucy eye at an opposite picture of one of his most favorite British subjects—the gorgeous actress Lily Langtry. Little did we know that in the future Miss G would play Langtry in another John Huston movie, *The Life and Times of Judge Roy Bean.*

We visited various friends, among them writer Robert Ruark and his wife Jenny. When Miss G was in Spain making *Pandora and the Flying Dutchman,* Bob and Jenny lived in Tossa de Mar on the Costa Brava where the film was shot. They became very good friends.

Before Bob started his career as a best-selling novelist he had worked for the Hearst group of newspapers. Bob said they operated two lists—the Angel List and the Poop List. Bing Crosby and General Eisenhower and other favorites were on the first list. Frank Sinatra and some others were on the second list, and nothing commendable about them was ever printed.

Four days after we arrived in London, the phone rang and Miss G answered. Her face changed, and she said doubtfully, "Well…" and went on listening. Finally, she said, "Well…okay…about six." She replaced the receiver.

I asked, "George C. Scott?" and then thought it just could not be. It just cannot start all over again.

"He's sober," Miss G said. "He hasn't had a drink for days. He wants to apologize and make up for all the trouble. He has tickets for *Othello*. I've said I'll go."

"He's staying here, in this hotel?" I asked.

"It's all right, Rene," Miss G said. "This is London. This is the Savoy. He will behave. He's promised. I've got to give him a chance."

Miss G had a suite with a lounge and a bedroom. I had a room directly across the corridor from her. I went back to my room. I had no desire to see George C. Scott. I thought, of all plays, *Othello*! That dramatic wife-killer! The actor would soon be speaking those infamous lines: "Get me some poison Iago, this night. I'll not expostulate with her, lest her body and beauty un-provide my mind again: this night, Iago." And that rat Iago would reply, "Do it not with poison; strangle her in her bed. Even the bed she hath contaminated."

Othello would respond, "Good, good, the justice of it pleases, very good."

Yeah, real good! Strong stuff to mix with a quart of vodka. I waited up. I couldn't bother with dinner. I thought, "Miss G, what is the matter with you? Are you out of your mind?"

I heard them come in. No doubt Miss G had been drinking also, to ease the pain. Then the noise, his shouts and the banging started. I thought, my God, the hotel must hear this. It went on for maybe half an hour. Then there was silence. I guessed he had run out of vodka or gone to the bathroom. I had to take a chance. I left my door open, ran across the corridor and turned the knob quietly. No sound. I peered in. Miss G was standing by a table. Scott was in the bathroom.

"Miss G…Miss G," I whispered. "Quick. Quick."

She turned, saw me and ran. We closed the door behind us, shot across to my room and locked the door. Miss G was shaking. She sat down on the bed.

I asked, "Has he finished the bottle?"

She nodded. "Yes. What shall we do?"

"He'll be furious when he sees you have gone," I answered. "Then he will go foraging for another bottle. That will take him twenty minutes. As soon as he has left, I'm going to ring down to the desk and ask them to move us to another suite."

I was right. He was furious. We heard him muttering as he opened her bedroom door and slammed it behind him. We heard his heavy tread moving toward the elevator. I was on the phone before he had even pressed the button. The desk was very helpful. I was passed on to a senior guy. I think they scented trouble. Good hotels have noses for trouble.

"You would like to move to another suite, Madame? Yes, Madame. At once, Madame. If Mister Scott asks any questions, we shall not answer them."

The Savoy was magnificent. Within five minutes they had moved us to another floor, bag and baggage, meaning the load of suitcases that Fontana had specially made for Miss G. Ten minutes later we were relaxed. That night we enjoyed a good night's sleep. Next morning we discussed what we should do.

I advised, "We should ring TWA now and make reservations on the first plane that's leaving for New York."

Miss G said, "Rene, I can't do that. I have appointments."

"Cancel them!" I urged.

"I can't, Rene. George will never find us here. We'll slip in and out like ghosts."

Miss G kept her appointments, and by late afternoon we were back in our suite. About half an hour later the door burst open. It was always terrifying. Scott never turned a door handle; he just hit the door with his full weight and, if that didn't do it, smashed it in with his foot.

Our second suite had a bedroom, lounge and bathroom with a transom window that opened onto the corridor. How useful that window would later prove to be. Scott advanced, sneering, "Ah, Rene...ah, Rene's here!"

Rene wasn't there for another second. I dodged through the door and crossed to my bedroom with the speed of light. I sat on the bed wondering what to do and found myself trembling. I never figured out how he found us. Maybe he bribed a servant, but I always had a notion that Miss G might have told him. I simply could not work out her tolerance for that man.

I listened to the usual shouting and arguing. A couple of hours passed, and the row was still going on. Then I heard him leave and knew he had finished one bottle of vodka and had gone to get another. He had sort of "rest periods" between bottles.

As soon as he had gone I dashed to Miss G. She was dazed—almost a willing victim, I thought. I went to the bathroom and got a wet a towel and held it to her head.

"Miss G, we have got to get out of here!," I said. "He's dangerous. We have got to run!"

By now I had spent five or six minutes trying to get Miss G together, and I figured I had about twenty minutes before Scott returned. Scott, as I realized later, had only slipped out to his room to pick up a second bottle of vodka. Now he was at the door with the new bottle in his hand and an unpleasant look on his face.

"Rene interfering again....uh?," he snarled. He advanced, placed the full bottle on the table, and took the empty bottle and smashed it against the side of the table. It shattered, leaving jagged edges. I have had some frightening moments in my life, but that was certainly the worst. It may have been only a melodramatic trick, but I wasn't waiting to find out.

I was thin and agile, and George C. Scott was slow and heavy. I was around that table and out through the door like lightening. I heard the door slam behind me and the key turn in the lock. Now, I really didn't know what to do. This was the Savoy Hotel in London, England. How could a small, unimportant black girl rush screaming down the corridor yelling, "George C. Scott is murdering Ava Gardner with a broken bottle!"

I stood out in the corridor, brain dead. Then I saw the transom window of the bathroom. If I could get through that, I might be able to do something. But what? I'd be trapped. I wasn't built to be James Bond. How was I going to get through that damned slit anyway?

A young man in a uniform was passing by. He looked like a bellboy. I grabbed his arm. "I've got to get through there," I said as I pointed up. "Have you got a box or stool I can stand on?"

He might have said, "What the hell do you want to do that for?" Not in the Savoy. "Certainly, Madame," he said politely. "There's a broom cupboard just along here. Let me see what we can find." He reappeared with a fairly stout box. It could have been an orange crate for all I knew. I didn't ask for a leg up, and so he passed along the corridor and out of my life. I guess the guests at the Savoy were always asking for orange crates to use to climb through transom windows.

It wasn't too hard for me to leverage myself up, balance on my stomach and swing my legs through. I wiggled down to stand on the edge of the bathtub. No sounds came from the bedroom. I held my breath and opened the bathroom door a crack. If I made a mistake now, I was in real trouble. Luck was with me. I glimpsed Scott's back. He was looking out the window at the River Thames. He held a glass of vodka in his hand. Miss G was turned towards me. She looked mystified as a brown arm appeared out from the bathroom door with a small brown finger beckoning.

Miss G was a bright woman. I heard her say, "I'm going to the bathroom."

She was beside me in a second. We locked the door. I pointed up at the transom. Miss G was quick and agile as a gazelle. I flushed the toilet to give credibility to her exit and to cover any noise. She dropped down into the corridor and I joined her there. No words were spoken. We joined hands and fled towards the sign that read EXIT. We went down those stairs at record speed, pushed open a fire door, and we were out in London's lovely evening air.

A left turn, left again, and we were among the scurrying pedestrians. Big red buses were passing, shoppers with noses against brightly lit windows, taxis discharging passengers. Freedom never looked so sweet!

To my surprise, I was still holding my purse. All those acrobatics with a purse in one hand! A woman's life and heart lie in her handbag!

We walked down the Strand toward Trafalgar Square and turned into a crowded pub for a drink. I pushed through to the bar to get double scotches. Miss G sipped hers, and I said, "No hurry. It will take him twenty minutes to kick the bathroom door down."

Miss G said, "Let's go to Susie's. She will put us up." Susie was a friend of Miss G's, a nice American girl. We got a taxi and went there. She was pleased to see us. We drank a lot that night, just to get over the shock.

Next morning, hung over, I rang the hotel and said, "This is Miss Jordan, Miss Ava Gardner's maid. There was a bit of a rumpus last night. Could you tell me if it's safe to come and get our luggage?"

In that sweet Savoy fashion the man at the desk said, "Quite safe, Madame. The gentleman in question was arrested last night. He is now at the Bow Street police station. I understand he will be brought up this morning or afternoon on a charge of being drunk and disorderly."

I thought, "Jesus! Disorderly?" In England for a drunk and disorderly charge you can usually get away with a five pound fine. We had to get out of London fast!

We rang TWA and made reservations to leave that afternoon for New York. When we paid the bill at the Savoy, we had one last, sad surprise. The manager said gently, "I'm afraid, Miss Gardner, that it will no longer be possible for us to accept reservations from you in the future. The recent occurrences have put the lives of too many of our clients in danger."

Back in the New York Regency hotel we felt safe. That was a mistake. The sad saga of George C. Scott's infatuation continued endlessly.

A week later our hotel room door was kicked open. Scott had arrived. Once again the same old round-about of recantations, apologies, outrages, screaming rows, and beatings started. Never a sound emerged from Miss G. Then impending disaster came. He had talked her into going up to his house in Connecticut. I protested loudly.

"Miss G, you are mad! He will never leave you alone! He might kill you!"

"Rene, he has promised not to drink," she replied. "He is fine if he doesn't drink. We will get along. I'll just go with him. Everything will be all right."

I knew I was beaten. I pleaded, "Miss G, if you are in real trouble, just ring me. Say anything; anything at all and I'll understand. Just please, please ring me."

I sat by the phone like a bomb disposal officer waiting for it to go off. It did the next afternoon. I knew by her voice that it was bad. "Rene," she said, "could you give me that recipe for fried chicken with dumplings?"

Jesus! Fried chicken with dumplings? I made some silly reply and put down the receiver. Miss G and her sister Bappie had been raised on Southern fried chicken—not with dumplings! She was in deep trouble!

I had one hope to fall back on. I had read in the newspaper that Frank Sinatra was in New York staying in his suite in the Waldorf Astoria. I got through to him.

"Mister Sinatra," I said, "I think Miss G is in bad trouble, and I don't know what to do." I told him all about it. I didn't have Miss G's phone number or address in Connecticut. Frank just said quietly, "Don't worry, Rene. I'll take care of it."

Later that evening Miss G was back in the Regency Hotel. She didn't want to talk about what had happened. I guess two big guys knocked on the front door and told Mr. Scott to say goodbye to Miss G.

We left New York and took refuge at the Main Chance health spa in Arizona. Miss G needed to rest, dry out and regain her health. She had the Mamie Eisenhower suite, as usual, and Rags and I holed up at our usual motel. It was the only one in the vicinity. I rented a car.

A few days later I overheard her on the phone. Again she was talking to George C. Scott. I always knew that by the tone of her voice. Soothing, softening.

"He's driving across the country to Main Chance," she said.

"Miss G," I pleaded urgently, "Let's go!"

"I can't go Rene," she said. "I haven't finished my treatment here."

That was rubbish! "Miss G, I'm not staying," I said. "I'm packing your things and putting them in the back of the car. I'll leave you one bag. Rags and I are going to L.A. We'll wait for you at the Beverly Hills Hotel in our usual bungalow. I'll leave a ticket at the airport for you if you want to get away in a hurry, but I am going."

I spent my last night in that motel feeling like a hunted fugitive. Scott was bound to check into the motel when he arrived, since there was no other around. Next morning, I was up very early. I took my suitcase, with Rags trotting beside me, and headed for the front door. I was half way towards the car when I heard his voice shout, "Rene!"

I ran and hit the car like a rocket. Rags jumped in beside me. A cloud of dust across the desert marked our route to L.A.

Miss G survived for three nights. Then Bappie called me and said, "Rene, I'm going out to the airport to pick her up. That fool has finally had enough. I'll bring her back to the bungalow."

Oh my God, I could have wept when I saw her! Her head was swelling. Her face was bruised and puffy. The bungalow had a lounge, two bedrooms and a little kitchen. Bappie went back home to her husband, and I cooked Miss G supper of lamb chops. She was tired but ate them up.

I washed the dishes and went to my room thinking that at least we would get a decent night's sleep at last.

It was unbelievable! There was a great crash as George C. Scott burst through the door with anger in his voice. Miss G protested, "Now George," be reasonable. "Now George, just sit down and talk, and I'll get you a drink."

Then there was the usual smack as he hit her and the beating started. I got out through the side door and sped for the nearest telephone. I was scared out of my mind. God, when was this ever going to end?

I shrieked at Bappie, "He's back! He's back! For Christ's sake get a doctor! Get someone! Get help! He's going to kill her!"

"Okay, okay!," Bappie yelled back. "I'll get someone. I'll get everybody!" She banged down the receiver.

I hurried back to the bungalow and went in through my side door. The terrible noises from the next room had stopped. I sat there wondering what I should do. Fifteen minutes later Miss G's own doctor arrived. I heard him knock, open the door and go in. More silence. Then Bappie and her husband arrived and two more guys. I peered in.

George was sitting there with his head in his hands. Miss G's face was a mess. Bappie was erupting with rage, and George just continued to sit there with his head in his hands.

He was a great actor, a man of high intelligence, a marvelous talent full of warmth and wit and integrity, but this was a role he could not handle.

God, the intensity of his obsession! John Huston had identified it as "insanely in love." Scott had tracked Miss G from Rome to London to New York to Arizona to Beverly Hills. He had roared across the desert and over the Sierra Madre Mountains to smash into our bungalow. He was exhausted, unshaven, defeated, the victim of his own raging madness. I guess Miss G knew that more than anyone else. She pitied him, understood him and tried to assuage the hurt even though she was hurting herself. Maybe he was a victim as much as Miss G.

He just sat there with his head in his hands.

We never saw George C. Scott again.

33 THE EMPRESS OF AUSTRIA-HUNGARY

The critics were flattering about Miss G's performance two years later in *Mayerling* as Empress of the mighty Austrian-Hungarian Empire that ruled a vast chunk of central Europe in the nineteenth century. The movie is still shown on television, its colors slightly faded, which is sad, because Miss G's costumes were among the most beautiful she ever wore in her long film career. She looked absolutely lovely.

One reviewer wrote, "Ava Gardner rises gracefully and touchingly to the challenge portraying Elizabeth as an accomplished and neglected woman who shrinks from her public role, but wishes to be closer to her son than their separate lives permit."

Howard Thompson, the distinguished *New York Times* critic, observed, "The surprise of the picture is Ava Gardner as the enigmatic Empress of Austria. With an uncertain smile and husky voice this beautiful lady is the most beguiling character in the movie. She movingly underplays her few scenes."

According to Sydney Guilaroff and me, however, it's a marvel that Miss G ever got around to playing some of her scenes at all. When offered the part by MGM in their remake of a 1936 movie, Miss G commented, "Well, at least they're promoting me from whoredom to royalty. It makes a change."

Miss G had now finally made up her mind to move from Madrid to London. There had been good years. She had enjoyed Spain and all the friends she had made, and we left our Madrid apartment with many regrets. But it was time for a change. London offered greater possibilities. While Miss G never for a moment thought of giving up her American citizenship, for the rest of her life London would be her permanent home.

We had a firm base in London and could scoot around as we pleased. Our first scoot was across to Paris to the Studios De Boulogne where the film was being made and where Miss G was to be fitted for her beautiful wardrobe of elegant gowns. No one in the film world was better equipped to display them than Ava Gardner.

We stayed at Miss G's favorite super-luxury hotel, named with true French realism—some might call it snobbism—L'Hotel. We also met Omar

222

Sharif, Miss G's co-star. Sharif immediately captivated us with his sense of humor, his charm, his immense knowledge about practically everything, and the fact that he was completely on Miss G's wave length. Both of their philosophies coincided in the belief that acting in the movies was only a way of making a living.

Sharif knew Paris intimately. He proceeded to show us corners of the city we did not know existed. For many years he had a black valet who operated in much the same way as I operated for Miss G. He was one of the family. Often as a foursome Sharif would whisk us off to some restaurant where the cuisine was more important than the clientele or their social standing. Sharif loved Russian restaurants with a passion. That was a bit unusual, since he was Egyptian.

I shall never forget those marvelous meals, with whispering violins in the background, which invariably began with chilled caviar and iced vodka, followed by vintage champagne. Those were the sort of "starters" that impress themselves on your memory.

In those days, on the brink of the seventies, our foursome of two blacks and two whites might have caused a few eyebrows to rise and a few mustaches to bristle in Georgia or Mississippi, but the sophisticated Parisians merely smiled amicably and paid far more attention to their superb three-star food than to us. Sharif got really sentimental in that atmosphere, but he was always the perfect gentleman. No hanky-panky.

Before *Mayerling* started shooting Sydney Guilaroff arrived from Hollywood. Sydney was our oldest and dearest friend. Sydney was tall, very handsome with a distinguished air, and he always wore a white tie. He was a serious sort of man until you got to know him. He was, without any doubt, one of the great hairdressers of this century.

Sydney was an important figure at MGM before Miss G arrived in Hollywood. He had started out as a hairdresser in New York where Joan Crawford was one of his clients. She thought so highly of his creations that she insisted he go out to Hollywood and style her hair in all her movies. There he remained as hairdresser for Miss Crawford as well as for the great Greta Garbo, Norma Shearer and a continuing sequence of favorite MGM stars.

At first Sydney was cold-shouldered by the diehard studio unions. Louis B. Mayer was conservative, but he recognized talent when he saw it. That recognition plus a chorus of praise from a succession of glamorous beauties convinced everyone that Sydney had to be retained. Mayer made Sydney an executive. The unions could not harass executives. Sydney was the executive in charge of MGM's Hairdressing Division.

From the beginning of movies, studios had been filming hundreds of historical stories—stories of ancient Egypt, Roman and Anglo-Saxon stories, portraying every tribe, dynasty, monarchy or revolution known to mankind. Scenic background had to be manufactured, costumes designed and hairstyles created. Who knew what Cleopatra's hair looked like when she went for a boat ride down the Nile with Mark Anthony or what Marie Antoinette's hair looked like when she went off to the guillotine? Sydney did!

Even though he hadn't had a ringside seat at the time, Sydney understood that hairstyles had to look authentic but also be acceptable to the modern eye and not a subject for laughter or derision. He studied ancient sculptures, mosaics, friezes and artifacts all over the world. He scrutinized time-worn manuscripts and observed cave paintings, sketches, cartoons and old masters. He then adapted and absorbed what he saw into the hairstyles he created. Sydney was an unsung genius, and as time went on he did much more than just create hairstyles.

A hairdresser is on the set usually before anybody else and works more hours than anybody. He also has duties which carry him onto a set during the actual shooting. The position, coloring, shading of a star's hairstyle is of paramount importance to her appearance. A wrong light, a piece of scenery behind her head, a dozen tiny mistakes can make a vast difference to her beauty and a dramatic impact on her performance. Sydney set out to make certain that his hairstyles and his ladies did not suffer through such neglect.

During those years on the sets of many of MGM's most expensive and prestigious productions, Sydney learned more about film art than many directors or technicians. But Miss G didn't know the man or who he was to become when she first met with him at the start of her career. As she recalled, that meeting was catastrophic. As a new girl Miss G found herself on a call sheet and was expected to be in that salon shortly after daybreak. She entered shyly, sat in a chair and to diminish her nervousness began to chew gum. Not only did she chew gum, she cracked gum! Sydney heard the sound and almost exploded. Nothing so vulgar had ever occurred in his temple dedicated to his art. He discovered the culprit and towered above her while Miss G tried to disappear inside the upholstery. Sydney forgave her.

That was the beginning of a deep and abiding friendship that developed between them in the months and years ahead. When I began to work for Miss G, I was included in that friendship. Indeed, in all those years at MGM, beginning with and continuing through practically all her pictures, Sydney and I were the guardians of our dear, lovely, dingbat lady. Wherever Ava Gardner was, no matter what part of the world, no matter how desperate or unhappy she felt, all she had to do was ring Sydney, and he would arrive to bring advice and aid.

Never did we have more need of aid than during the shooting of *Mayerling*. In those weeks Sydney and I exchanged more panic signals than Admiral Yamamoto at the Battle of Midway.

Film stars tend to chronicle their careers through their successes or failures. Success in Hollywood terms means record takings at the box office. Failure is no clatter of cash registers. Miss G's mind never worked like that. First, she thought of every film she made as a job, work to be done. When it was over she asked herself if we had fun. If so, then it was a success.

The Bible, even though it was directed by our true and dear friend, John Huston, would rank at pit-bottom and *The Night of the Iguana* as sky-high. *Mayerling* also entered our sky-high rating, even though it was a box office disaster. Even Sydney and I had a hard time preventing the Empress of Austria-Hungary from falling on her ass on occasion.

Miss G loved filming in Paris. We had a lovely, warm, sympathetic, friendly director, Terrence Young, and the cast including James Mason, Catherine Deneuve, Omar Sharif, Genevieve Page and James Robertson Justice, who was a lovely, fruity real life replica of His royal Highness King Edward VII.

The script was based on a true story. At the end of the last century, Crown Prince Rudolph, played by Omar Sharif, heir to the Austrian Hungarian throne, fell in love with a commoner, Maria Vetsera, played by Catherine Deneuve, even though he was married to Princess Stephanie of Belgium. It was a tragic love story that ended in a suicide pact between the two lovers in a hunting lodge in the forest of Mayerling.

As usual, the true story was enhanced and embroidered with fictional incidents such as intrigues at court, plots to free Hungary from Austrian rule, and fierce confrontations between father and son. Emperor Franz Josef, played by James Mason, was a stern, martial figure. Miss G, cast as the Empress Elizabeth, was only ten years older than Omar Sharif who was cast as her son. Miss G had some difficulty in acting as a mature, consoling and helpful advisor to her son. In some of their film scenes it was suggested that Mama and Rudolf were so consoling to each other that they might well have been having an affair.

Well, they were not! Miss G pulled off her role well and, as I've already mentioned, with a bit of help from Sydney Guilaroff and me.

I loved the film. All the main characters were splendid, and the film rose to a climax which was moving and tragic.

At the start of the film Miss G arrived in her usual splendid condition—fit, slender, alcohol-free and set to fire on all cylinders. Then we met Omar Sharif, our happy Parisian excursions started, and we began to drink a little more, to eat a little more, and to exercise a little less.

One of my prime duties before any film started shooting was to do a "dry run." That did not mean reading the script and playing the other parts to Miss G's cues. It meant me journeying out to the studio and giving it a hard look. Where was our dressing room? Did it have a couch and a toilet? Did it have a refrigerator? How far was it to the sets? Did we have to cross open territory, or were we under shelter? Finally and most importantly, where could I hide the bottles of booze in case Miss G needed a swift pick-up?

As already mentioned, Miss G would start out as a figure of perfection. Then slowly the drinking would increase, and halfway through the film Sydney and I had to watch her acting performances closely. Three quarters of the way through the film we were usually on red alert. And from that moment on we had to be ready to step in with evasive action.

Sydney and I surveyed Miss G from different vantage points. He would be prowling around, stepping in between every shot or every time the director would call a halt to adjust her hairstyle and whisper encouragement or advice into her ear.

I would be standing much closer to her to offer a quick drink if necessary, but trying to keep the size down by adding more water or ginger ale. When Miss G's dramatic ability got close to the danger level, Sydney would come swinging across with our code sentence. "Rene! The curls are flying!" That meant that

Miss G would probably be smiling when she shouldn't be smiling or frowning when she shouldn't be frowning or when, in a scene with her son Rudolph, her husky vowels began to sound as if she was inviting him to her bedroom instead of giving him a lecture on the state of the Austrian economy.

I don't think the situation was hidden from anybody, including the director. Everybody loved Miss G and understood her little idiosyncrasies. Since her performance as seen in the rushes was quite superb, nobody really minded or complained. But as far as Sydney and I were concerned, there had to be a limit to this. Proper excuses had to be made. "She didn't sleep at all well last night. She's been feeling off color the last couple of days." And tactful hints: "I do hope they wind this up pretty soon. She's so tired." Or as a last resort: "I wonder if we could call a halt so that the doctor could give her a B-12 vitamin shot? She needs the stimulation."

Miss G was normally blissfully unaware of our intervention, and at the end of the shooting day her rhapsodic smile would be followed by, "Well, now we can all have a little drink."

Another problem was the matter of Miss G's weight. If she had ample opportunity to exercise as she did while filming *The Night of the Iguana,* when she used to water ski from Puerto Vallarta to Mismaloya, she never put on an ounce. But in *Mayerling,* Paris was full of temptation. If a movie buff studies the slender lines of Miss G's face in the first shots and compares them with the rounded happiness of her face in the closing scenes, he will discover quite a difference.

Miss G's eating hours were always incredibly unconventional—a habit I had caved in to early in our relationship. It was not unusual for us to be stuffing ourselves with roast pork or chicken and sopping up alcohol in the splendor of our L'Hotel bedroom in the small hours of the morning.

Miss G hated eating or drinking alone. Having me eating and drinking with her and talking over the triumphs or problems of the day made her happy. And most of the time Miss G was a load of fun with a few drinks in her. As they say, "If you can't beat 'em, join 'em." It was always a pleasure to join Miss G.

34 HANGING JUDGE ROY BEAN

After *Mayerling,* we returned to London, and Miss G settled down in her Mayfair apartment and began to enjoy life. For Miss G, London had everything: theatres, cinemas, restaurants, scores of Spanish restaurants, lots of flamenco and easy access from London airports to all parts of Europe and the world. As I've mentioned before, Miss G even liked the weather.

"Sure, it rains in England." She said blithely, "I like rain. London rain is not a slashing torrent that wipes you out. It's fine rain. Thin rain. Nourishing rain. It gives me tranquility. I can grow."

"Gee," I thought, "she should tell the tourist board that one."

We had been traveling backwards and forwards between Europe and the States for years and for so long that I thought I could apply for a job as an airline hostess. That thought had led to the idea that had been formulating in my head for a long time. Miss G's protestations that she wasn't a film actress and couldn't care less if she ever made another film were understandable and true. She had enough money to settle down comfortably, and it was now obvious to me that she was embedding herself in London and intending to do just that.

I like England, but it wasn't my country. All my family were in the States. And something else had cropped up in my life – a man. I had met him on one of our numerous journeys to California. He had a good job, a great sense of humor, and he wanted to marry me. I wasn't sure if marriage appealed to me. I explained all this to Miss G.

"Rene, honey," she said. "Give it a go. I've had my share of marriages, and if I ever got married again it would only be a re-marriage." She grinned, and I knew who she meant. Frank Sinatra and Miss G were never out of touch.

She went on, "I'll miss you, honey, but if it doesn't work out, you can always come back. If and when I do another movie, you can come with me." She paused and smiled again. "But when you're running at fifty like me, who the hell wants you as a movie actress anymore? I'll probably just retire as the Empress of Austria-Hungary."

I knew she wouldn't, but I didn't argue. I went back and got married. Church, guests, families, the lot. I tried to settle down. I knew we weren't going to start our fried chicken dinners with iced vodka, chilled caviar and vintage champagne, but what the hell. I could survive on fried chicken alone. He was a decent guy. We went to the same church. I probably drank more than he did, and we got on in bed. We were looking at a bright future as we headed towards the sunset.

We didn't get there. It didn't work out.

No point in going into the why and wherefore. It was a mutual parting. Then before I even had time to work out what the future held for me–boom! My sister Tressie and I were driving at a sedate pace along a narrow road when around the corner came a large car at full speed and hit us head-on. I woke up in the hospital in great pain with a smashed face and two broken legs. It was a miracle I wasn't killed. Tressie was hurt, but not so badly.

For me it seemed life had ended. For weeks and months I couldn't walk and couldn't speak because my jaw had to be reconstructed.

Miss G didn't even know about the accident. For a time I think she thought I was still crazy in love. A couple of people tried to get in touch with her through agents, but the agents couldn't have cared less and didn't pass on the information. Then the first letter I could write reached her.

Miss G's cable back was immediate. "Rene, baby, just got your letter and I am sick about my little sister's Capricorn luck. If there is anything you need, let the office know. I will contact them immediately. Will be in New York next week–Waldorf. Please telephone me there. Keep your new little chin up. Love you very much. Love to Tressie."

Not long after that we were on the phone, she yelling, "Okay, you can't walk. I can. Therefore, I'll come over and see you."

Nurse Ava Gardner arrived and took charge. "Now, we've got to get you fit. We are both going to Main Chance to get you in shape. I've got to get in shape, too. We've got work to do."

"What work?" I asked.

"Roddy McDowall's movie. He's crazy about *Tam Lin.*"

Roddy McDowall was one of Miss G's oldest friends. He had been in films for years, starting off as a British child actor. His latest movie was *Planet of the Apes*. Roddy had been a smash hit as the leading ape-man. He had long harbored ambitions of becoming a director and after directing various features, he had put *Tam Lin* together as movie package. The fact that Miss G agreed to play the lead may have helped him get backing.

At that moment, however, I was in the dark. "Who's *Tam Lin*?" I asked. "Sounds like Roddy's new girlfriend."

Miss G hooted. "No, baby, no. Tam Lin is a handsome young man entranced by the Queen of the Fairies."

"Fairies!" I exclaimed. "Fairies?"

"Rene, stop worrying," Miss G said, and she explained, "Real fairies, story book fairies. The story of Tam Lin and the wicked Queen who seduces him comes from the legends of Celtic folklore. It is an old Scottish fairy tale. Robert Burns knew all about it and recreated the story in one of his ballads."

"Not Walt Disney and not like *Snow White and the Seven Dwarfs*?" I asked.

"No, and not like *Cinderella, Jack and the Beanstalk* or *Old Mother Hubbard*," Miss G said. "Serious stuff; real evil stuff. In the original legend, the Queen of the Fairies is a wicked old slut who has a passion for young men half her age. As the Queen, she lures them to her bed and makes sure they live a life of ease and luxury. When she tires of one, she chunks him out. If they tire of her and decide to opt out, baby, they are in deep trouble. They get the chop."

"I don't think this fairy story would put many little children to sleep," I said.

"Rene, Scottish kids were tougher in the old days. Anyway, for film purposes the legend has been modernized. It is a bit like those *Dolce Vita* movies the Italians used to make. Society doomed by decadence, sexual orgies, immorality, lack of belief, anarchism—you name it, they do it."

Scotland was breathtakingly beautiful. Even when it rained, or the mist blew in from the sea, it was beautiful. The girls were beautiful, too. Even the film critics were rather endearing about the whole thing.

One critic said, "Miss Gardner's screen image develops from her penchant for underacting and her touching quality of doomed vulnerability. She is slightly ridiculous here as a demonic den-mother to a retinue of pubescent sybarites who look like a freaked out cast for a Pepsi commercial."

And another said, "Ava wears her years well…her skin is still flawless, her dark eyes so intensely fierce that the screen smolders, her still graceful figure costumed to perfection could lead men to their doom for desire. You simply forget how poor the basic story is when Ava is on screen. When she switches on that voice and walks around in those Balmain clothes as magnificent as a black widow spider, you realize Ava Gardner is the creature we have almost forgotten exists—a star!"

The trouble was that practically nobody saw *Tam Lin.* First of all, the film company ran out of money—no fault of Roddy's—and had to find an extra injection of cash to complete the music dubbing. Then no one wanted to distribute it.

Afterwards Miss G said to anybody who asked, "I saw it, and it's a damn good little picture. I care terribly what happens to the film, not so much for me but for Roddy. He is just starting to make a career for himself as a director, and this is so important to him."

Miss G was being loyal as usual to all her friends. I don't think she even got paid her fifty thousand dollars' salary. The film company just went broke. Even when the film was salvaged later by American International Pictures, it attracted only minor headlines.

We were all reunited a few months later when John Huston began work on *The Life and Times of Judge Roy Bean.* Both Miss G and Roddy McDowall were in the cast.

Without doubt, John Huston could have charmed birds from trees, fish from streams, or Ava Gardner from whatever bar she was in without any difficulty whatsoever.

There is also no doubt that as Miss G grew more experienced in her trade as an actress she began to question and interfere with the dialogue she was given. And that became perfectly evident during the filming of *The Life and Times of Judge Roy Bean*. She didn't like it *this* way. Why couldn't she say it *that* way? John Huston stopped such feuding at the source. He would rehearse her line by line and word by word and by the time he had finished, he would have her fixed in a loving strait jacket of obedience.

35 THE BLUE BIRD

You come out of London's Hyde Park on the south side, not far from the Albert Hall, and Ennismore Gardens stretches down into the serene, gray-stone, upper-crust regions of Knightsbridge. The road itself runs down a slight hill and comes to a dead end, although there are other roads crossing it. Cobblestone footpaths lead through to the green area surrounding the huge Catholic Church. Beyond that lies the Old Compton Road, and Harrods is about four hundred yards away to the left.

It is an area of Georgian and Victorian splendor. The noble facades of housing are three or four stories high with portico entrances and lattice iron-work balconies. It is a posh area, a pleasant area with small parks protected by locked gates to which only residents possess keys. High trees lend a rare distinction. For most of two centuries, the houses have been inhabited by the "haves" and the "have nots," the haves keeping their horses and carriages stabled in the rear mews and the 'have nots' cooking the food and keeping the fires going in the basements. Its history was televised imperishably in the TV series *Upstairs–Downstairs.* Now most of the grand houses have been divided floor by floor into apartments.

Not satisfied any longer by her flat in Mayfair, Miss G and I had been apartment hunting for quite a while in the early seventies. Armed with estate agents' prospectus, we had seen a lot of London before we stumbled on Ennismore Gardens. On this expedition it had been raining quite heavily, and we had paused at a lot of pubs to keep up our spirits. We were in fact a bit sloshed when we arrived at the house in Ennismore Gardens.

We pressed the bell, and although there was an elevator, we walked up to the second story. The lady who opened the door was charming and immediately offered us a drink, possibly with an intuition that another might complete the sale. We accepted and then made the tour. Miss G was rapturous and did not haggle.

"I'll buy it now," she said.

We moved in within a very short time, and Miss G would live there for the rest of her life. We had a lovely time furnishing it.

After scouring London show rooms and bringing in pieces of the Spanish furniture she liked, we went off to Paris, Madrid, and Lisbon and got a whole load of stuff ferried back to Ennismore Gardens. The big living room ran right through from front to back, the long front windows opening onto the balconies, giving her Welsh Corgi dog Morgan a chance to test his lungs (by then, Rags had sadly departed this world).

Miss G had boxes to grow her flowers. There were many bedrooms and an excellent kitchen. The décor owed a great deal to the Orient, and we were not worried at all by which part of the Orient the ornamentation came from. There were screens and vases and big chests. There was a fireplace and a comfortable chair on either side. It was very cozy. In fact, I had a hard job tearing Miss G away to go off and be a film star again, but she went.

The place was Hollywood. The film was *Earthquake*, an epic about what would happen to L.A. if such a thing ever happened. The film was directed by her old friend Mark Robson, with Charlton Heston co-starring.

Earthquake turned out to be a monster money-spinner and was later to be among the top twenty movies in all-time rental records. Why? Not because of the love interest, but because everybody loves a great disaster, especially if they are not in it. And especially if the disaster is shown as graphically as those designed by Frank Brendel, the special effects man. He won an Oscar for them. Six lane highways were torn up and ripped apart by cataclysmic subterranean forces. Great canyons opened in the earth, with railway locomotives, cars, apartment blocks and human beings falling into them. Skyscrapers tilted over and crumbled into rubble. Electric pylons rent apart and electrocuted everybody in sight. Water mains burst, and dams sent roaring torrents through the ruined city.

They had even invented a new large screen effect called "Sensurround," which did everything but hit the moviegoer on the head with a block of falling masonry or drown him in the floods, while watching poor old Charlton Heston and poor Miss G clinging in each others' arms and ending by being swept down a sewer pipe to certain death.

Several movie critics seemed to enjoy drawing parallels between this occurrence and the careers of both Charlton Heston and Ava Gardner. Both, they maintained, had been major stars during the same period. Both were studio-groomed film stars; both had maintained their screen star popularity for a great number of years, and now they were slipping down the sewer together.

Miss G was not sure if any of this was complimentary. She had vivid memories of that swept-away incident. "Jesus!" she exclaimed. "I said I didn't need a stunt girl, so Mark Robson let me do it, but it was tough. I had to let myself be carried away by this raging torrent, and baby, it came as close to reality as anything I have ever known. I had to sink under as if I had been drowned and then, out of camera shot, swim underwater for about twenty yards to the dock."

Strangely enough, serious critics gave more attention to Miss G in *Earthquake* than in many of the far better films she had made. Perhaps they found it hard to do a dramatic think-piece on earthquake special effects. Several wondered how Miss G, now fifty-two, had been so popular so long. *The New Yorker* magazine, not noted for focusing much attention on Hollywood film stars, came close to the truth about Miss G: "She has a dreamy hurt quality, a generously modeled mouth, and faraway eyes. Maybe what turned people on was that her sensuality was developed, but her personality wasn't. She was a beautiful rootless stray, somehow incomplete, but never ordinary, and just about impossible to dislike since she was utterly without affectation. To Universal, she is just one more old star to beef up a picture's star power, and so she is cast as a tiresome bitch whose husband (Charlton Heston) is fed up with her. She looks blowsy and beat-out and that could be fun if she was allowed to be blowzily good-natured like her heroine in *Mogambo*, but the script here harks back to those old movies in which a husband is justified in leaving his wife only if she is a jealous schemer who made his life hell."

After *Earthquake* another dilemma entered our lives, and on the emotional Richter scale it was much more destructive. I can't say I was surprised. We were in Rome, and the telephone lines between Rome and Los Angeles for the last three weeks had been buzzing with conversations between Frank Sinatra and Miss G.

She opened the subject to me. "Rene, you know as well as I do that if I'm ever going to marry again it will be with Frank. If I don't marry Frank, I'll be alone for the rest of my life, because nobody else interests me."

I said, "Miss G, when it comes to second-time-around, it's usually with a different fella."

"Not with me, honey," she said emphatically. "It's Frank or no one."

"Is that what Frank wants?" I asked.

"He says he does. As you know, he has been on the phone for weeks saying he loves me, and why don't I go back and we start all over again. We're older and wiser now."

I didn't think they were wiser, but it was not my business to make smart remarks. So I just asked, "By starting all over you mean getting married?"

"Yes, get married."

"But what about Barbara?" I asked. Barbara Marx had been Frank's secretary, and they had had a close personal relationship for a long time now.

There was a long pause after my question, and then Miss G said, "Frank says that if I'm sincere in my intention to go back and marry him, he will tell Barbara what we're going to do. I've made up my mind. I'm going back. I'm going to marry Frank. And you and I are going to Fontana to get them to make me a trousseau now!"

She did not sound like a woman who was totally happy about the whole thing. The trousseau plan sounded more like some sort of gesture of defiance.

We went to Fontana. They were really happy to see us. We wanted daytime dresses, evening dresses, cocktail dresses, sports clothes, casual outfits. Gee, we were good for business! Negligees, peignoirs, we bought them all. They were delivered to the Grand Hotel.

I had an uneasy feeling. Miss G was still glued to the phone, but she didn't tell Frank about the trousseau. I took that as a bad omen. I got the impression that Frank was saying, "Angel, come across here and we'll get married. Yes, of course, I'll talk to Barbara, but if you don't want to come back, I'll marry Barbara."

I suppose it was that last sentence that stuck in Miss G's mind. Barbara had been around a long time, and she was plainly in love with Frank. Now Frank was giving Miss G not so much an ultimatum, but an option. It worried her. Supposing they got married and their usual riots resumed? It wasn't fair to Barbara. It wasn't fair to anyone.

I remember that final decisive telephone conversation between them. She put down the phone and said, "Rene, let's both sit down." We sat down, and she gave a long sigh. "It's over," she said. "I told Frank he should marry Barbara. It's better for all of us."

Frank did marry Barbara. From Miss G there were no tears. There was a depression that lifted quite quickly, and she and Frank remained friends for the rest of their lives.

To help herself get over it Miss G decided we would go to Hawaii for a holiday. Normally we would have tooted off to Cuba, which we adored, but we couldn't go to Havana because the Government had barred such travel. The sun and the sea made a pleasant change. Afterward we went back to London, where Paul Mills had a film script he wanted Miss G to read with actor Dirk Bogarde.

This was in the period of the Cold War when CIA, spy thrillers, and dirty work over and under the Iron Curtain were in vogue. *Permission To Kill* was to be shot in the mountainous area of Austria. This sounded like a good idea, but it was so damn cold it turned out to be a bad idea. At least Freddie Young's magnificent photography added significantly to the film.

The real trouble was it lacked credibility. *The Spy Who Came in From the Cold* worked well. *Permission To Kill* was loaded with unlikely characters. Dirk Bogarde was an unlikely British agent belonging to some mythical British secret service and never comfortable in the role. Bekim Fehmiu, another ex-mistress role for Miss G, was chief of an equally unlikely Communist National Liberation Party who wanted to re-defect back behind the Curtain. Then there was a British Foreign Office homosexual traitor, with Timothy Dalton in that part. Stir the pot with blackmail, unscrupulous reporters, poor Mr. Bekim Fehmiu getting himself blown up in a railway station, and guns banging and shooting all over the place.

Thank goodness no bullet had Miss G's name on it, so we were able to return to Ennismore Gardens and get warm.

The next film, *The Blue Bird,* was equally ill-fated. George Cukor, hero of *Bhowani Junction* and one of our favorite people for years, was directing it.

The Blue Bird was a fairy tale, a fantasy appealing to children from age six to ninety-six. Two little children from a humble peasant home set in some far-off idyllic background decide to leave their cottage, and in a "dream-trip" set off in search of the Bluebird of Happiness. It was a fantasy journey in which they experience the highs and lows of human existence. To achieve this Cukor enlisted the acting ability of an assortment of talented artists. Elizabeth Taylor had four parts, Mother, Witch, Light, and Eternal Love; Jane Fonda was Night;

Miss G was Luxury; Cicely Tyson was Cat; Robert Morley was Father Time; and Harry Andrews was Oak. There were many other parts identified as Bread, Sugar, Milk, Fire, Sick Girl and Fat Laughter.

The movie industry had tried to get the story off the ground twice before. In 1918 Paramount made it as a silent movie. In 1939 Darryl Zanuck directed a version with child mega-star Shirley Temple in the lead. No excitement followed either production.

This version, co-produced between USA and the USSR, was set in Leningrad and was the source of one of George Cukor's well-worn jokes, but it is still funny and possibly true. Cukor and his assembled team of cameramen and technicians marched into the huge Soviet studio, and Cukor made his first little speech: "I am proud to be here working in the very same studio where in 1925 Eisenstein made his great film, the immortal *Battleship Potemkin.*"

The Soviet co-producer piped up equally proudly, "And with the very same equipment!"

As the weeks passed, however, Miss G and I became more interested in survival than in the success of the USA/USSR co-production. The atmosphere in Leningrad generally was one of deep suspicion. The faces of the Russian people on the streets, and of those with whom we worked, were grim and depressed. No one smiled. The Soviet technicians were in no hurry to do anything. If they could waste time, they wasted it. Food was dreadful. At the canteen we queued up for everything and hoped we got something on a plate before the grub ran out. At the hotel we surrendered our passports and hoped that they hadn't been lost in the KGB archives. Getting up to our bedroom was like trying to find a vacant cell in Alcatraz.

At the foot of the elevator sat a hefty, boot-faced Soviet heroine with x-ray eyes. We were guilty before we put a foot inside. On our floor sat another lady the size of a Japanese Sumo wrestler, jangling her keys like a wardress and handing over our room key as if she were surrendering her long-past virginity.

The room was drab. The plumbing was uncertain. The steam heat was always a problem.

I had now become catering officer for both Miss G and Miss Elizabeth Taylor. Thank God, they both loved fried chicken. I had brought with me in my baggage, with a prescience obviously endowed by some long-past great-grandmother, a large black iron frying pan. Can you imagine a frying pan in one's personal luggage? Even Soviet customs couldn't think that was a bomb. It was invaluable.

I rarely went to the studios. I didn't have time. My duties took me to the marketplace. I guess it was one of those favored marketplaces reserved for high officials and visiting foreigners. It was still abysmal. You queued for everything. Always you were faced with three long queues. Each would take half an hour. Hopefully you would join the first, hoping it was the chicken, fish or meat line.

You couldn't handle or choose anything. You just pointed and, plunk, it was wrapped, and a hand stretched out for the rubles. Then on to the next queue—maybe potatoes, cabbage or vegetables—and the third perhaps milk, butter, margarine or cooking oil. Then back to the fortress hotel and up to our bedroom where in the bathroom we had an electric cooking ring. I cooked the meal. The girls brought home the vodka. We had a lot of laughs complaining about everything. The local joke concerned actress Jane Fonda, who was thought to have communist sympathies. How could she stand it here where she had no one to convert to communism? Her husband at the time also provided us with a bit of laughing gossip. He stayed out late one night and returned after lock-up hour with all hotel doors bolted. Angrily he began banging and shouting. He spent the night in the hotel jail. Every hotel had one.

George Cukor was the only intelligent guy when it came to forethought. He had weekly food parcels mailed to him from Fortnum and Masons and Selfridges in London.

Occasionally we were invited to the limited feasts. Even George was under considerable strain the entire time. To start with, the film was under-funded. Miss G was so fond of Cukor that she agreed to play her part for nothing, which I thought was pretty decent of her.

I was surprised when, toward the end of the picture, Miss G came in one night very upset. Apparently Cukor, who everyone knew could be very nasty indeed if he felt like it, had turned on her and berated her at his very nastiest. She couldn't understand it. They did not speak for the rest of the film and left Russia without saying goodbye to each other, their long friendship apparently over.

The whole experience attached to *The Blue Bird* seemed doomed. It was almost impossible to get out and see the sights. On one occasion Miss G was determined to visit some special square she had heard about. In conspiratorial tones she communicated this to me.

"Rene, I am going off by myself. Nipping out. Finding a taxi. Getting him to drive me to the square. Having a quick look around, then catching a taxi back."

She returned defeated. "Can you believe it, Rene? The taxi took me to the square. I got out, walked about three yards when another car pulled up beside me with a door thrown open. It was our car, the one that takes me to the set every day! Same driver with the sour face. 'Miss Gardner, get in the car,' he ordered. I said, 'But I just want to have a look around this square.' This time it's a real angry KGB order. 'Do as I say Miss Gardner!' I think he would have dragged me in if I hadn't obeyed."

We were all glad to be back home after that. I was glad when Miss G and I were watching a television film one night in Ennismore Gardens—a funny film with Katharine Hepburn and Spencer Tracy directed by George Cukor.

We screamed with laughter, and Miss G said, "I don't care if George and I have fallen out, I'm sending him a telegram of congratulations." She did, ending with, "They don't make 'em like that anymore."

His return telegram read: "Ava, they don't make 'em like you anymore."

I was so pleased they were friends again.

A nice dinner in a London restaurant with Ava, her brother Jack Gardner, his wife Rose, and a reporter whose name I can't remember, sometime in the seventies.

36 SETTLING DOWN

Miss G was now firmly settled in London and not really interested in making any more films at all. It was only after her business manager pointed out that, despite reasonable assets, middle-aged ladies have to work occasionally if they wish to maintain their lifestyle that Miss G took the hint and was open to offers.

One among the bunch of films Miss G made in the seventies was *The Cassandra Crossing.* I was with her in every movie or television film she made in the seventies and eighties, indeed everything she did until the end of her life. In between times I was spending a lot of time in Sacramento trying to build up a hairdressing business I had started.

I think Miss G summed up her part in *The Cassandra Crossing* very well: "I'm a middle- aged, very rich lady with a young lover who is a heroin addict and a drug smuggler, a real nice type. I'm also married to an important, ruthless arms-manufacturer who makes millions out of killing people. However, I don't love either of them. In this role, I'm not an emotional woman. I'm a realist. I just play with men. I don't take life or other human beings seriously."

Miss G then gave one of her big grins and added, "Makes a nice change. In real life, it's always been the other way around, men taking me for a ride."

The film was made in the Cinecitta Studios in Rome. They had built this really beautiful mock-up of the luxurious express train there. And, as Miss G was to spend weeks with Sophia Loren, Ingrid Thulin, Richard Harris, Lee Strasberg, Burt Lancaster, and Lionel Stander, it was nice to be able to lounge in first class carriages, have a drink and chat with old friends without having a camera peering at you.

Sophia Loren's husband Carlo Ponti was producing the picture, and even though the drama aboard an express train had been done time and time again, this one was quite original. A trans-European express was hurtling through Europe and about to pass through Iron Curtain countries when a passenger fell ill with a deadly and contagious virulent bacillus. Naturally there was a medical genius aboard who was able to identify such mysterious diseases, even if he can't do anything about it. It now becomes very awkward when lots of people become very sick and start to croak. Mainly nasties died, not many of the goodies, and certainly not one of the major characters. Certainly no one in their right mind would want to kill off Ava Gardner or Sophia Loren before we have had a good look at them.

The tension was heightened when the train was shunted off into quarantine in a very suspicious area of Poland, and all sorts of troubles began. All got over their difficulties and ended up happily ever after. I mean, what are films made for?

Miss G's continual chant was, "Thank God for directors, cameramen, and writers!" These were the props she relied on. Still, she almost dropped dead when a couple years later she was cast as a television reporter and had to talk directly to the camera in *City on Fire*.

"Rene," she yelled, "as a movie actress you never, never, never look at a camera. Now I've got to stare one in the face. In a movie, people say something to you, and you answer them. That's called dialogue. Now I've got to go on yakking about all the disasters that happen in the city of Montreal without a cue line to answer. I'll never do it!"

I replied, "Miss G, you know you will."

And she did.

First of all, she settled down with lots of dialogue with her co-stars Shelley Winters and Henry Fonda. She was delighted with her first frontal attacks on a camera. "They were wonderful," she said. "They just prop up what you've got to say on a card below the camera, and you just read it." She began to laugh. "Trouble was, I'd forgotten my glasses, so I had to learn the bloody lines after all."

That movie, *City on Fire,* and two others she made around the same time, *The Sentinel* and *Priest of Love*, were the last of what you might call "cinema movies" that Miss G made before the television people got hold of her. In February 1980 she appeared in *Harem*, an ABC Special Sunday presentation, together with her old friend from *Mayerling,* Omar Sharif, and Sarah Miles. Maybe it attracted a large audience. The only magazine ad I ever saw showed Sharif resting on an oriental rug with a nubile harem girl in close proximity and half a dozen others waiting their turn in the background.

In July 1980 *The Smithfield Herald* in North Carolina featured a photograph of Smithfield's Mayor Kenneth B. Baker wearing an Ava Gardner tee-shirt and signing his proclamation that August 2nd be declared "Ava Gardner Day." This was to honor the 45 movies she had made, and the fact that she had been born and spent her childhood years in the nearby rural Grabtown and Brogden communities, and was therefore a local heroine. Miss G sent a letter of thanks, along with her regrets that she could not be present for her special day. She also sent all the home-folks her love.

In 1983 she flew back to Hollywood for the television recording of John Huston's Life Achievement Award presentation by the American Film Institute. Miss G began referring to herself as a comfortably well-off old lady who does a film now and then but is really far happier simply walking her dog.

She was pushed off that comfortable perch in 1985 when CBS-TV wanted a big name in its nighttime TV soap opera, *Knott's Landing,* to compete with stars Joan Collins and Linda Evans on other primetime soaps.

Why not?" Miss G said. "Everybody is watching *Dallas* or *Dynasty,* so if I don't do it now I never will." So off we went to the CBS studios in Los Angeles for a three-month stint. At $50,000 a program, her business manager had brokered a good deal.

At first she was scared out of her wits. "Rene, you know how much I rely on a director, sticking to his coattails, getting to know him. Jesus! Here they use a different director for every episode!"

Her television part was Ruth Galveston, wife of billionaire Paul Galveston whom she married on his deathbed, thus inheriting his dough. She was a hard, ambitious woman, and *Knott's Landing* producer Larry Kasha was not only surprised, he was enthralled. "She's just wonderful," he said. "I can't get over it. She's professional, knows her lines, is very respectful, and very prepared. I love her. She is nothing like the star thing you always hear about. She really is an actress."

I could have told young Larry that Miss G had been behaving like that through all her film career.

She was still nervous. "Christ!" she said, "In one of those episodes, I forgot every line I was supposed to say. No one's going to offer me another job after this, I promise you. I look like hell among those babies."

She was talking rubbish. She looked great among "those babies." What's more, those babies both loved and respected her, and CBS was very interested in expanding her part and keeping her on in the series. They too had caught onto the idea that, unlike old soldiers who just "fade away," a great star like Miss G just keeps on getting better and better.

Figures of a million dollars for Miss G to continue with the series were now making headlines. But Miss G had made up her mind. Seven episodes of *Knott's Landing* were enough. She missed London, and she missed her dog, Morgan. Besides, she had already been penciled in for another monster television film.

I have a pretty good idea that when NBC started running the Biblical tele-film *A.D.* in March 1986, twelve hours of it spanning five consecutive nights of glorious color, a lot of people changed channels.

Miss G played Agrippina, ambitious mother of the crazy Nero and seducer of Emperor Claudius, but as everybody in the five-part series was either slaughtered, raped, whipped, crucified, or annihilated in some manner, seduction seemed only one of the more civilized sins.

It covered the decades after Jesus' death but introduced events with Old Testament history, then chunks of the Gospel according to St. Luke delivered practically verbatim, and rumbled on through a string of loony Roman Emperors.

It employed thirty-three famous actors and 350 others with additional speaking parts. To film it Producer Vincenzo Laabella rented a section of Tunisian desert to erect his magnificent fake palaces. It cost 25 million dollars. It was an epic. A big, dumb, colorful epic. As one critic observed, much of its dialogue seemed like unfathomable Shakespeare. No one really cared. No one had the stamina to care. But it will probably be repeated at Easter for years to come.

Miss G and everybody involved with *A.D.* enjoyed it, and everybody got paid.

After *Knott's Landing* and *A.D.*, Miss G was seen by television producers as a considerable asset. She avoided most offers, but she agreed to play in the four-hour television movie of William Faulkner's *The Long Hot Summer*. Her business agent had first sounded Miss G out about the movie. "They want you to play Jason Robards' mistress," he said.

"Mistress!" yelled Miss G. "Mistress! I'm old enough to be a motherly old wife by now."

"Mistress," her agent repeated firmly. "One hundred and sixty thousand dollars."

"I'd be anybody's mistress for that," said Miss G.

It was a lie. Miss G only did what she wanted to do, and the money could go hang. She was intrigued with the idea of playing with these two young television upstarts, Don Johnson of *Miami Vice* fame and Cybill Shepherd of *Moonlighting.* And especially with one of her favorite stars, Jason Robards.

But Miss G also did it because not only did she like Faulkner and the cast, but she especially liked the young director Stuart Cooper, who had spent three years arranging and directing *A.D .* and with whom she got along so well. Cooper also adored Miss G and lectured reporters about her peerless qualities: "You know this old saying that some people have this affair with the camera lens and some people don't. Well, Ava has it. I've never seen an actress throw dialogue away the way she does. She says the line and says it with the right inflexion and absolute accuracy. She says it and gets rid of it. Then she plays between the lines. She plays the subtext."

I could have informed young Cooper that at the age of sixty-two Miss G had served a very long apprenticeship, but I guess he knew that already. He went on: "It's there in her eyes and that's what the camera picks up. Her walk; I've never seen an actress walk across a set the way Ava does. I mean she has a magical walk. Where she gets it, I don't know, but no one I've ever seen can move so gracefully from A to B and with this kind of erotic quality."

That young Cooper! He was a real sharp perceiver.

Still, the world had changed. Before production began Miss G said, "Rene, remember how we used to look at those actors and producers and say, "But they are so old! How times alter. Now we look and say, 'Jesus, they are just kids!' About time we thought of quitting."

We did quit, but not in the way Miss G had imagined.

We started off filming *A Long Hot Summer* in Thibodaux, Louisiana, about eighty miles southwest of New Orleans. It was Cajun and Bayou country, swamp country, big wide black rivers, mosquitoes breeding, millions of nameless bugs trying to grab a bite. Alligators with noses above the water waiting for a bigger bite. Country dotted with those romantic plantation mansions. White pillars like in *Gone With the Wind.* Feathery moss hanging from the trees. Accents like thick cream.

When we arrived we found they had already been filming and were behind schedule, so we were marooned with nothing to do in a motel for a few days. Miss G made valiant attempts to stay healthy. There was a pool, and she swam a lot, walked and played tennis. She found the climate and the humidity very trying. A lot of bugs bit her. In fact, she always swore she caught some disease down there, but no one will ever know whether that was true or false.

Miss G did what was required of her, and then the unit moved north to Marshall, Texas, which is only about twelve miles across the border from Louisiana. More location and filming, and I had a feeling that Miss G was suffering.

Stuart Cooper was pushed hard by his shooting schedule. His Hollywood producers had promised him eight weeks shooting and then screwed him down to thirty seven days. He was not pleased at all when one of them told him, "It's only television. It doesn't matter."

Cooper reported hotly, "I told the producer, I don't care if it's only going to be shown on a two-inch postage stamp. It's going to be the best!"

At the end of the film he was still enthusiastic about Miss G. "She had so little to do in *A Long Hot Summer*," he said. "I wish the part had been bigger, something that she could really get her teeth into, because when you have someone like Ava Gardner around, you want to let her go, let her paint. The stuff we are talking about is so intangible. There is a diamond there. It is special. It can't be taught, and you can't learn it. You either have it or you don't." He could have been writing Miss G's epitaph.

Miss G had "it" all right. She was born with it. Her performances on the screen were exactly the same as they were in real life. As she always said, she could not act, she could only be herself.

In the closing stages of the film Miss G began to crack up. "Rene, I have got to get out of this or I'm going crackers. I'm feeling terrible."

I said, "Miss G, there is only a couple more weeks to go."

"Rene, I can't stand it here. I want to go home. I want out of this part. Do you think Stuart will understand?"

"Sure he will, but he won't be able to do anything about it. It won't be his decision. It will be the producers back in Hollywood."

This was the very first time that Miss G had ever tried to pull out of a job. I couldn't understand it, but she was dead serious. "Anyone can play this part," she said. "Anybody can fill in."

I did not like to remind her that she had already played a lot of the part and nobody could fill in. I said, "Why don't you ring the agent? See if he can do anything."

She did and came back with this report: "They won't budge. He says why don't I try and talk to them myself." She did. When she put down the phone, she turned to me, her expression hopeless. She had been told, "Miss Gardner, I'm very sorry. We are not buying your talent; we're buying your name. At this point in the film to replace you would be very expensive and very difficult."

I said, "Let's ask Stuart if he can speed your part up."

He did, and we were out of there within a week and back in Hollywood. Miss G said she was still feeling "off." She flew back to London. I went back to my hairdressing salon in Sacramento. It was more than two weeks before she rang me. That was strange, since she often was on the phone damn near every day.

"Are you all right, Rene?" she asked.

"Sure, aren't you?"

"Well, I am now, but Jesus, I've been sick as a dog. No, twice as sick as a dog."

"What happened?" I asked.

Miss G explained, "I had hardly got back to the flat when I woke up in the middle of the night with a thick horrible rash that you wouldn't believe. Long red streaks and welts all over my body from head to toe. Can you believe? From head to toe, some of them the size of my finger! My face was swollen. I looked a wreck. I called Carmen (she was Miss G's new maid) and she didn't know what it was. Poor thing, why should she? I was itching, itching all over, in my hair, on the bottom of my feet, all over. God, it was awful! So I called the doctor. Yeah, in the middle of the night. They do that sort of thing in England. He rushed around because I told him I was certainly dying of some terrible disease. I almost screamed at him, saying, 'I thought a kidney stone was the worst pain I could have, but this worse."

"What did he do?" I asked.

"You know doctors," Miss G said. "They have seen it all. He just gave me one of those doctor smiles and said, 'Didn't you know that making you itch is one of the oldest tortures in the world?' I said, "No, I don't know, and what are you going to do about my itch? He gave me morphine. Thank God, I expected I would become an addict, but I didn't and slowly the damn thing went away."

It was the start of Miss G's recurrent illnesses. She never made much of them. She would get a cold. She had a touch of the flu. I'd start the telephone conversation saying, "Miss G, you sound great today."

She would say, "Rene, you should know it's just my Oscar award-winning voice. I feel lousy."

I said, "Miss G, when you feel all that bad, why don't you come back here to consult your own doctor?"

"I think they are all the same," she said. "Maybe a bit cheaper over here. Maybe when I'm on the verge of dying, I will come back."

"Miss G, don't say such things," I said. I didn't like the sound of it at all. She didn't ring for quite a while after that. Then she did.

"Rene, it all started with that flu. In London, everybody got the flu. I got the flu, but you know me. Walking ad for health and strength. I would go to bed. I'd get over it. I'd go swimming, walking, and racing with Morgan, and then back in bed. And the doctor's started me on antibiotics. As far as I can see, nobody knows what's in them, or what they are suppose to do, but they didn't do a thing for me. Then I get this new doctor, who as far as I'm concerned was a congenital idiot."

"How long have you had him?," I asked.

"Long enough. I am slowly dying, and he arrives with this other doctor who is supposed to be a genius. 'Heart specialist,' he tells me. Now I know I've got both lungs full of fluid. I don't need a specialist to tell me that, and he doesn't. He examines my chest and says, 'You have powerful lungs.' I think the old bugger was referring to my breast rather than my lungs. 'You will never have a chest problem, you will never get emphysema,' he said. I should have said, 'I already have emphysema. I'm smoking too much. I'm drinking too much. I'm doing everything too much. Haven't you got a pill for all these complaints?'"

"But he didn't?" I asked.

Miss G gave one of her loud cackling laughs, "You can't tell doctors anything. They know everything!"

Not long after that I got a call from Bappie. "Rene, Ava's back across here. She is in St. John's Hospital." Bappie didn't have to tell me to go and see her. She knew I would do that.

In her private room she was sitting up in bed grinning and telling me the story with the usual mixture of Miss G's outrage, horror, hate, alarm, exclamation, exaggeration and loud laughter—even though she gasped a bit with the laughter.

"You know me, Rene. I can't stay in bed. I hate being sick in bed. It makes me sicker. I lost my energy. God, I'm always busting with energy. I explained all this to the doctors, but they couldn't do anything about it except give me more antibiotics. Every day I'd go across to a hotel pool and swim, and do yoga exercises. When I took a deep breath, you know the deep down yoga breath, I'd feel this great stabbing pain—awful like someone stabbing you in the chest. Then it became really bad, and I got frightened, and I called Spolie Mills. You remember the Mills?"

I sure did. They were old friends of Ava's. Spolie was great.

"I said, 'Spolie, I've got to go back to the States. I've got to. Can you help me? Can you help me pack?' She was over by taxi in fifteen minutes. She helped me pack, helped me catch my plane. I had already called Bappie and my doctor to tell them I was coming."

"For a time, I felt okay, then suddenly I got this fiery feeling back in my chest and it was worse. The stewardess took one look at me and knew something was wrong. She took my temperature. As you know Rene, my normal temperature is always two under normal, like my blood pressure, but now it was 103. We are about halfway between London and Los Angeles. I thought, I'm never going to make it that far. So they stretched me out on two seats, and gave me oxygen, and a sleeping pill or something, because I slept. In L.A. International Airport, there was Bappie waiting for me. God knows how I got down those plane steps and across the tarmac. No way am I going with Bappie back to her house in Rincona Drive. She pushed me into a taxi and we raced to St. John's."

"Have they found out what it was?" I asked.

"My dear doctor rushed across and found my temperature was 105 and called a chest specialist. He took one look at my chest x-rays and said, 'This woman has double-pneumonia, and she's had it for a hell of a long time. Her lungs are a mess.'"

"What are they giving you now?" I asked.

"Usual stuff, more antibiotics. I don't think they know what I've got. They have given me every test known to mankind–even tested me for AIDS. Seems to me I'll just have to live with it and get over it."

And she did. I visited her regularly, and she was always the old outrageous Miss G. But she wasn't well. She said, "Rene, my temperature keeps going up and down. Darling, I don't know how high. Sometimes my brain feels as if it's boiling and, of course, I'm not supposed to smoke or drink. Got any booze with you?" She said that with a wicked grin.

Next time I went to see her, she had another story. "The other day it took two nurses to help me to the loo, and I was gasping for breath, so I thought I'd better give up smoking. I remember I asked John Huston once when and how did you do it. He was then living with a can of oxygen. He showed his teeth at me and said, 'When you have to darling, when you have to.' I asked this nice doctor who makes his rounds here the same question. He has given up smoking, and I know his need is as great as mine. 'Well,' he says, 'if you don't inhale,' and I nearly have a seizure laughing, because he knows as well as I do that a real smoker inhales automatically."

Miss G never gave up smoking.

Then it happened. I remember the minute, I remember the hour, and I remember the day the phone rang. It was Bappie. "Rene," she said. "Ava's had a stroke."

37 LAST OF THE LAUGHTER

She was wearing a dressing gown and sitting in a chair. Her face was puffy from cortisone treatments, and the left side of her mouth was pulled down. When she smiled at me, the smile was a little twisted, and it took a big effort for me not to show that my heart sank. It really sank, and I thought, "Dear God, all that beauty, all that beauty?"

Out of Miss G's twisted mouth came the straight, no bull, no asking-for-pity voice, no tears, no recriminations, but explanations coming in a flood tide. She was going to tell me all about it whether I wanted to hear or not. She made it sound so normal.

She explained, "I'm sitting in this chair after dinner. The nurse and I had been watching this old funny Lou Costello movie. Full of laughs. I felt nothing, only this little tingling in my palm, no headache, no falling about, nothing, just sitting here in this room. I suppose the nurse knew something was wrong, because she said, 'Well, it's about time we got you to bed. You've had a long day.' I don't remember what I replied. I guess I was obedient and climbed into bed, and she must have called the doctor, because in fifteen minutes Bill Smith was there smiling down at me and doing little tests. 'Now close your eyes and point your left hand and finger at your nose,' he said, and my hand was wavering and doing all sorts of funny things, and I was laughing and he was laughing because it seemed so like the hokey Lou Costello movie we'd been watching. So I went to sleep happy as a clam. Next morning I woke up and I was paralyzed. The left side all gone. I had no feeling there at all."

"You didn't feel frightened or anything?" I asked.

"No, mentally and emotionally, I wasn't at all frightened. I don't know what protects stroke patients, but I wasn't at all. I know I'm strong, but when I tried to walk, I suddenly realized that this left leg wouldn't move and neither would this left hand and arm. There was no sort of fear or hysteria. The brain must play funny tricks on you, because in one way it protects you probably from going crazy. Being the active person that I've always been, if I had realized that I was paralyzed, fully paralyzed, I guess I might have jumped out of the window if I could have gotten there.

She took a deep breath and went on, "They said it will come back. You've got to work on it. You've got to exercise. You have got to feel it coming back." She looked at me and gave me another of the twisted smiles. "Well, you know how I like exercise."

"Miss G," I said. "It was the same with my legs after my car accident. I thought I'd never walk, but you can see that I did."

Every time I came back to see her after that she had made some improvement. Soon she could move her left leg again and start to walk by herself, though it was a slightly stumbling walk. Her face and mouth recovered almost completely, but from now on it was always slightly puffed from the cortisone she needed to take.

Now she wanted to go home. California had never been home to her. She liked London, and she liked the English countryside because the vistas were smaller and it reminded her of North Carolina. She had lived in England twenty years and made many friends—good friends. She loved Carmen, her small ferocious Colombian maid, even though there was always a small war simmering between them about who was the boss of the household.

She loved her neighborhood with the friendly pub just around the corner. She loved Betty, her cool, pretty and intelligent secretary who worked with her for years and kept her life in order. And she particularly loved Morgan, her handsome, bouncy, brown and white Welsh Corgi who knew he owned the neighborhood and from Miss G's balcony barked his head off at any low-class dog who dared to come under his vision. Carmen also loved him with deep devotion.

Miss G was constantly on the phone giving me news of her condition, and she had bad days and good days. One of her more memorable conversations concerned her exercise program. The phone rang and I picked it up. Miss G said, "Rene, I've broken my back."

I took a deep breath. "Miss G, how did you break your back?"

"I fell off my trampoline and broke my back."

"Miss G, what were you doing on a trampoline?"

"My therapist put me on the trampoline. It is all her fault."

"Miss G, are you sure you've broken your back?"

"Well, it feels as if I've broken my back."

Miss G had not broken her celebrated back. She had forgotten to hold onto the mantelpiece to do her gentle jumping. It was one of her bad days. Other terrors were real.

"Rene, the other night I was trying to get into my nightie, a simple procedure. My arm is no good, so I stick that one in first. Then I was captive inside my own nightie. Getting claustrophobic inside a black hole. I couldn't get out and it was terror. I was screaming with frustration. Fortunately, Carmen heard me and came to the rescue and calmed me down. By God, it is frightening."

In the summer of 1989 Miss G said, "Rene, you know I'm doing my autobiography with this guy who is helping. Can you come across for a few weeks? He's recording all the questions and I've told him you can remember everything far better than I can."

It was a lovely English summer. When I arrived Morgan barked from his balcony—his "office," Miss G called it—his place at the top of the first flight of stairs, outside the door. Carmen eyed everyone with intense suspicion, including me. Miss G was up and down. It was impossible to comfort her, because she was so intuitive and so damned honest, that she knew you were being unrealistic. She had to face the facts, the plain hard truth.

"I'm constantly tired," she said. "Or I'm in pain or just uncomfortable. I've been through, and am going through, terrible emotional and physical trauma. Rene, remember how I ran, swam, and raced around, and I can't do any of that, and it's hard to face. It's replaced by anger and frustration that I've never experienced before. You can't dress yourself properly; you can't eat properly; you can't even cut up your meat; you can't stand up at a party with a drink in one hand and operate with the other.

"You can't go out with your friends and do anything on equal terms. You have to ask people to help you up stairs. You have no desire to dress pretty or even properly. You can't run and throw balls for Morgan, and he wonders why not. Other people have to do it. I can't even cook, which I love to do. The looks have all gone too, but that doesn't matter because I never valued them very highly."

I thought sadly, "Frank Sinatra did, and millions of movie-goers did too."

Miss G continued, "The thing that's keeping me alive is this autobiography, so let's start remembering." So we started our sessions.

"Rene," she questioned, "you got any deep, deep regrets?"

I thought and said, "I don't think so. Have you?"

"Onassis and Churchill," she said. "I've regretted missing the opportunity all my life. A real big ache."

"Tell me," I said.

"Two of the great heroes of my life were Roosevelt and Churchill. I met President Roosevelt on his birthday at the White House in wartime. He invited a crowd of Hollywood stars to look around and watch him give his radio "fireside chat." I got there because I was married to Mickey Rooney. I'll never forget how President Roosevelt polished his glasses and started off in that wonderful theatrical voice. It was so thrilling. I was mesmerized, absolutely mesmerized.

President Roosevelt had been part of my life since I was a little girl reading the political bits out of the newspaper to my Daddy, who was dying of pneumonia in a lousy little room in Newport News, Virginia. Only a few years later, the same President Roosevelt had wished Mickey and me well in the future, and now he was talking to all of America in front of me. It moved me to tears." Her voice broke and the tears came again.

I gave her time and said gently, "And Churchill?"

Miss G thought about it. "It was probably one of those times when I was scuttling around Europe and you were back in the States. I had gone off to Monte Carlo to spend a few days with Grace Kelly. You know I went to her wedding, because we were eternal friends after those months of filming *Mogambo,* when she fell in love with Clark Gable, and Frank was pining away waiting for his role in *From Here to Eternity*.

She continued, "I was staying at Grace's house—sorry, *palace*—with Prince Rainer, the family, the whole lot. So Grace and I had a few drinks and exchanged a few memories, like we are doing now, and Grace said, 'Why don't we go down to the harbor for a change?'"

"And quick off the mark after my few drinks, I said, 'Grace, what do you mean? A couple of middle-aged dolls picking up sailors?' Grace screamed. I screamed. We embroidered on the theme and finished collapsing with tears in our eyes. Then Grace took a deep breath and said, 'Ava, I mean go down to the harbor and meet Aristotle Onassis on his yacht.'"

"Well, I wasn't sure that after-dinner drinks with Greek billionaires was my forte, and I said so."

"'The point is,' continued cunning little Grace, picking her words as if she was making little stitches in the conversation, 'His guest is Winston Churchill. Would you like to meet him? I think he usually stays up pretty late polishing off a few brandies.'"

"I said, 'Winston Churchill? Oh my God, Winston Churchill!' I was crazy about Winston Churchill. The same way I was crazy about President Roosevelt. Churchill and Roosevelt had saved my world, and let nobody doubt that, and I was deeply grateful to them for that."

"So off we go in Grace's chauffeur-driven car down to the harbor. We arrived at the yacht and went aboard. Rene, it wasn't a boat, it was a mansion. The walls were stuffed with Renoirs, Gauguins, Cezannes, Monets, God knows how many great masterpieces he had attached to the walls or bulkhead or whatever they call them. I particularly remember the Picassos and Dalis. I didn't care for them very much, but as it wasn't my yacht, I couldn't complain."

"They'd all finished dinner and were sitting around the table drinking and smoking, and everybody seemed to like the idea of two ancient ex-movie stars joining the party. Churchill was, to put it mildly, perhaps a teeny-weeny bit tipsy, but as we were too that made us level. We sat across the dinner table, me looking at Churchill through a haze of my cigarette smoke, and he looking at me through a haze of his cigar smoke. I don't know what the hell we talked about, but it certainly wasn't the Battle of Britain. I mean what does a foolish little girl from North Carolina have to tell Sir Winston Churchill, except 'I love you,' which, since Lady Churchill was also sitting at the table, wouldn't have gone down as smoothly as the special Onassis oozo that was sliding between my lips."

"That was the first point raised by Churchill. He peered across and said, 'What is that you're drinking?' When I told him he said, 'Well perhaps I had better try some of that.'"

"Anyway he took a great fancy to me, and as I already had a great fancy for him we spent the next three or four hours, or it could have been longer, chatting about Christ knows what, and it was one of the most wonderful times of my life. We arrived back at the palace a little dizzy, but very happy. Then I went back to Spain."

"The phone rang soon afterwards, and it was Onassis on the line. 'Ava,' he said, 'We're going to go on a voyage, a tour through the East Indian islands, stopping where we please, and then finally heading across to the East Coast of the States and up to New York. It's going to take six weeks. Aboard there is going to be only Sir Winston, Lady Churchill and Winston's private secretary. Nobody else. Sir Winston has asked personally if you would care to go with us.'"

There was a long pause from Miss G, and I could tell that even distanced by the years she was troubled and upset by the memory. I urged her on. "So what did you do?"

She replied, "I made a fool of myself. If I'm not a fool, tell me. I don't mind for a second that I didn't get all those jewels from Howard Hughes, or make some of those super movies they offered me, but to say what I did in turning down a special invitation from Winston Churchill? 'No, I couldn't go at the moment. I had things coming up.' You know the usual sort of rubbish."

"Was it the thought of Onassis?" I asked.

"Yes, but that was ridiculous. I was shy and frightened. I didn't want six weeks with Onassis on that yacht. I was sure the man wasn't going to rape me, but I thought it might be a tricky situation."

"Miss G, you were probably right."

"No, I wasn't Rene. Listen darling, I am a very strong lady, and I could have fought off that man because it is very easy to say no, and anyway I'm not sure that he cared a damn about me."

"But you were taking no chances?"

Miss G raised her voice. "No, it was not that at all. You know as well as I do Rene, that when you say 'no' most men will back off. All decent mean will and most indecent men will. If they are crazy or rapists, that's a different matter. So there was no reason at all why I shouldn't have gone. I wasn't doing a film. I wasn't in love. There was no reason on earth why I shouldn't have gone and had that wonderful experience. I had three chances Rene, three chances. When they got to the Canary Islands, Onassis rang again, and said, 'Ava, the invitation is still open. I'll send my private plane to Spain to pick you up, so that you can join us here.'"

"And I said no again. He called one more time. Again he said he would send the private plane, so that I could join them for the last bit of the islands and then go on to New York."

Miss G stopped and drew in a deep breath. I could see she was angry with herself. I helped her out.

"Miss G, we've all got regrets."

"I know Rene, but there are regrets and then regrets. Winston Churchill was one of the great men of our time, and I was a stupid little girl who had nothing to do except sit around Madrid and go out to flamenco every night. I couldn't bother to take six weeks off to spend it in the company of one of the most fantastic men of this century. I've had great times with intelligent men like Adlai Stevenson, Robert Graves, Ernest Hemingway, long letters between myself and Henry Miller, but why did I duck out of this one?"

She was very upset. I tried to change the subject, lighten the atmosphere. I said, "Well, I know one date you ducked out of in the neatest possible way."

She cocked her head. "When, with who?"

"*The Return of the Pink Panther,*" I reminded her. "The guy who rang us up saying you must come to Paris. 'We are doing three episodes of *The Pink Panther* with Peter Ustinov. Let's discuss it,' he said. He sent us the tickets, met us at Orly airport, drove us in, gave us a great dinner, and took us to that marvelous hotel. He went up in the elevator with us to our rooms and said, 'We have this suite here for Miss Gardner and myself. The maid can have the smaller room along the corridor.'"

Miss G gave one of her great yells of laughter, and said, "And I gave him one long cold look and said 'I think Rene and I will share the suite, and you will take the small room down the corridor.' The impertinence!"

I ended the story. "There was the note pushed under the door the next morning. He was afraid, due to various differences, he felt he would not be able to work with Miss Gardner."

Miss G said, "I don't think there was ever any plan to do three episodes at all. I bet Peter Ustinov knew nothing about it."

So we went on browsing through our memories. Miss G said, "You know Rene, I never knew until recently that Ingrid Bergman used to live in Cheyne Gardens. What is that, only about half a mile from Ennismore Gardens? We never met. She would have laughed if she knew how I forged her signature."

I had heard the story. Her good friend, actor Charles Gray, lived just across the road from her. He had friends in North Wales near Snowdonia where Ingrid Bergman's *Inn of the Sixth Happiness* had been shot. Miss G and Charles traveled by train to spend a weekend with them in their cottage. After midnight they were awakened by a loud banging on the door. The houseman went down to attend to it. He found a distraught young man outside. He had plainly just left the pub. The pub had plainly stayed open after hours.

He knew that Ingrid Bergman was staying there. He had missed getting her autograph when she made the film. He must have it now. Would he please ask Miss Bergman if she could come down and sign for him now?

"Jesus," said Miss G. "Everybody knew he had got his actress wrong, but no one was going to try and explain that to him at that time in the morning. So I sailed down the stairs, and he saw me and pleaded, 'Miss Bergman, please, may I have your autograph?' I gave him a great smile and signed his paper "Ingrid Bergman," and he sailed off happily into the night."

Miss G looked pensive. "He must have one of the most original autographs in history, Ingrid Bergman's forged by Ava Gardner."

It was during the last week of that summer reunion that Miss G and I made our last journey together. In the past we had traveled far, and we had traveled fast. We had traveled drunk, and we had traveled sober. And we had fun. Oh, how we had fun.

This was a shorter journey: a couple of hundred yards up Ennismore Gardens, then across the main road, pausing at the traffic island in the middle, then into Hyde Park with its wide expanse of grass and lovely trees stretching before us, and the gleam of the Serpentine Lake in the distance. The reason for the expedition? Morgan needed his run.

We would both get about, but slowly. Miss G with her bad left leg, me with my two wonky ones. Morgan on his lead, his four short trotters ready to race, was anxious to tow us under buses. So we rolled a bit, occasionally bumping into each other like two drunks rolling home from the pub.

We let Morgan off his lead, and he was happy. We went on chatting about old times. And before we knew what happened, we realized that we had walked too far, and we still had to get home. But we could achieve that in easy stages.

Then Miss G said, "Rene, I'm tired. Let's sit down on that bench over there."

I said, "I agree."

Then she said, "I'm too tired to get to the bench. Let's sit on the grass for a few minutes, and then make it to the bench. That was a big mistake! Morgan was not very pleased. That was playtime, down time, ball-throwing time. We ignored him. Then we started to get up, and we couldn't. We just couldn't move our various bits in synchronization to stand up.

I said, "Well, I suppose we could scream for help." Miss G laughed and said, "Let's hope it won't come to that. Why don't we squiggle around onto our knees and crawl across to the bench?" I agreed, and we started our crawl across the grass.

Morgan was bewildered. What were we doing imitating him? He started to circle us, yapping his head off, and Miss G yelled, "Shut up! You'll attract everybody's attention!" We reached the bench, hauled ourselves onto it, and collapsed in great gales of near hysterical laughter. We laughed until the tears poured down our faces. We laughed until it hurt. We laughed until we damn near wet our britches.

Miss G gasped, "Rene, did you ever think it would come to this?"

I sputtered, "No...never, never, never......"

It was about five months after I returned to the States, on January 25, 1990, when Carmen, ever watchful of her mistress, thought she heard a sound sometime after midnight. She knew that Miss G with her bad arm had difficulty in turning over sometimes. She went into the bedroom and began to put her arm around her to make her more comfortable.

Then she heard Miss G sigh and then relax. And Carmen knew she had died.

Carmen wept. Thousands of miles away, I wept too.

The End

ABOUT THE AUTHOR

Mearene Elizabeth Jordan was born in 1922 in St. Louis, Missouri. Her parents, James Mack and Onnie Brooks Jordan, were both Decatur, Mississippi, natives who left the Deep South in search of better opportunities. Rene attended Dunbar School and Washington Tech in St. Louis.

As was the custom, she left home at 16 and went to Chicago, where she found a job in a sewing factory, then as a nurse (nanny) for a Jewish family. Her job description included singing a certain song about a train to coax the baby to eat. At the sound of "Whoooo!" the little fellow opened his mouth, and she got a spoonful of lamb chop in quickly. However, he would spit it out, so Rene started simply eating it herself. After all, there was a depression going on, and she was hungry. By the time her day off rolled around, the baby had such a ravenous appetite he ate well for his parents. They were so delighted they gave her a $5 raise.

Soon after the bombing of Pearl Harbor in 1941, she followed a couple of sewing factory friends to Los Angeles where wartime work was plentiful. Their boss in Chicago, Mr. Huney, was nice enough to help them line up jobs there and give them references. Rene worked in a sewing factory in LA until 1946 when she began her fascinating journey in the employ of screen legend Ava Gardner.

During a "sabbatical" from Ava and Madrid in the late 1950s, she took a beauty course in hopes of one day opening her own business. This she finally did in about 1975 as Gardner's film career began to wind down. Her beauty shop was in the Oak Park section of Sacramento, California, where a sister lived. She and Ava soon began missing each other, so she would leave her shop and customers in the hands of a trusted beauty operator and spend summers either in London or traveling around with "Miss G." One particularly memorable visit was to North Carolina, where they stayed with Ava's sister Elsie Mae Creech, who ran a little country store next to her home near Smithfield.

During Rene's last visit in London in 1989, Ava's stroke had limited her activities, but she was still full of life. Rene noticed how damp and drafty her expensive, exclusive apartment was, even when the heat was running, so she lined the doors and windows with aluminum foil to keep her beloved Miss G from catching pneumonia. Unfortunately, foil was no match for decades of smoking, combined with London's cold, damp air, and this turned out to be Rene's final pow-wow with her famous best friend.

At age 90, Rene has given up the beauty shop. She still resides in Sacramento, where she enjoys a much simpler life. Rarely a day goes by, however, that she doesn't remember and reflect on her amazing life with Miss G.

3727409R00140

Made in the USA
San Bernardino, CA
17 August 2013